The SAGE Key Concepts series provides students with accessible and authoritative knowledge of the essential topics in a variety of disciplines. Cross-referenced throughout, the format encourages critical evaluation through understanding. Written by experienced and respected academics, the books are indispensable study aids and guides to comprehension.

BY STEPHEN WAGG
WITH
CARLTON BRICK, BELINDA WHEATON
AND JAYNE CAUDWELL

Key Concepts in
Sports Studies

Los Angeles | London | New Delhi
Singapore | Washington DC

First published 2009

Apart from any fair dealing for the purposes of research or
private study, or criticism or review, as permitted under the
Copyright, Designs and Patents Act, 1988, this publication
may be reproduced, stored or transmitted in any form, or by
any means, only with the prior permission in writing of the
publishers, or in the case of reprographic reproduction, in
accordance with the terms of licences issued by the Copyright
Licensing Agency. Enquiries concerning reproduction outside
those terms should be sent to the publishers.

SAGE Publications Ltd
1 Oliver's Yard
55 City Road
London EC1Y 1SP

SAGE Publications Inc.
2455 Teller Road
Thousand Oaks, California 91320

SAGE Publications India Pvt Ltd
B 1/I 1 Mohan Cooperative Industrial Area
Mathura Road, New Delhi 110 044

SAGE Publications Asia-Pacific Pte Ltd
33 Pekin Street #02-01
Far East Square
Singapore 048763

Library of Congress Control Number: 2008937557

British Library Cataloguing in Publication data

A catalogue record for this book is available from the
British Library

ISBN 978-0-7619-4964-0
ISBN 978-0-7619-4965-7 (pbk)

Typeset by C&M Digitals (P) Ltd, Chennai, India
Printed in India at Replika Press Pvt Ltd
Printed on paper from sustainable resources

contents

Introduction

The principal purpose of this book is to provide an informed and readable guide to a range of debates about sport as a social phenomenon. To that end, the book has been organised around the concepts that seemed to the contributors to have been most central to these debates.

The writers of the book have each been teaching about the social aspects of sport for some years. This has entailed the use of a number of academic disciplines – chiefly history, politics, philosophy and sociology. The various sections in the book draw intermittently on each of these disciplines, but especially on sociology. Sociology, by its very nature, is about the relatedness of related things and it is inevitable therefore – and quite proper – that from time to time matters discussed in one section are examined likewise in several others.

There are a number of examples of this which may usefully be flagged up here: 'rational recreation' – an early Victorian philosophy of leisure – is discussed in relation to **Rationalisation** and again in the section on **The Civilising Process**; the work of the French sociologist Pierre Bourdieu is dealt with principally in the section on **Habitus**, although, since much of Bourdieu's work is about class, it could have appeared with equal validity in the section on **Social Class**; and, similarly, there are references to the sports policy of the Soviet Union in several sections – those on **Alienation** and **Olympism**, for instance. Likewise, there will be mentions of the work of influential philosophers such as Karl Marx and Michel Foucault in various chapters and the same goes for popular themes, such as Macdonaldisation, and sports brands, such as Nike.

The sections have been arranged in alphabetical order but they should not necessarily be read in this order: for example, it is almost certain that most readers will need to read the chapter on **Methods** before tackling the section on **Ethnography**.

Furthermore, the debates and controversies that the book deals with should not be thought to be confined to the individual sections. Once again some useful cross-referencing can be done: for example, criticisms of the concept of **Globalisation** will be found in the entry on **State, Nation and Nationalism** (and vice versa); Foucault's notion of power has critical implications for the notion of **Hegemony**; the argument in favour of the biographical in the section on **The Sociological Imagination** might provide a good basis for debating the anti-individualist arguments in the section on **Discourse and Post-Structuralism**, and so on.

Finally, it must be stressed that the book attempts to deal dispassionately with matters which the reader: (a) might feel very strongly about (like the use of drugs in sport); or (b) might not have seen as subjects for critical reflection (like the body). Thus there will be arguments presented here that will strike some readers – undergraduates, perhaps – as unusual or controversial. Historically, though, it has been in the nature of sociology as an intellectual enterprise to try to analyse how things *are* and to keep this analysis free from judgements of how they *ought* to be. So, for instance, while many textbooks on sport will straightforwardly assume 'doping' to be a bad thing, in this book it is assessed simply as a social phenomenon (something that people do) and as something that is argued over. Similarly, the section on **The Body/Embodiment** deals in what we might call 'relativist' notions of healthy bodies. Many or most of us take for granted what constitutes a healthy body, but things are changing in this respect and people now argue from a variety of political positions that there is no one 'correct' body – it's all relative. Here again sociology is merely fulfilling part of its historic mission – to take up the vital questions raised in the wider society and to give them critical reflection: in this case, new political ideas and arguments have helped give rise to the sub-discipline known as the Sociology of the Body.

Responsibilities for the contents of this book have been apportioned as follows.

The sections on Alienation; Amateurism; Culture; Doping/Drugs; Gender; Hegemony; History; Ideology; Imperialism/The Post-Colonial; Olympism; Politics/Policy/Power; Race and Ethinicity; Rationalisation; Social Class; State, Nation and Nationalism; The Civilising Process; and The Sociological Imagination were written by Stephen Wagg, who also edited the book.

Carlton Brick wrote on Capitalism; Commodification/Commodity Fetishism; Consumption; Discourse and Post-Structuralism; Ethics; Fandom; Globalisation; Marxism; Methods; Postmodernism/Postmodernity; and Semiotics.

The sections on Ethnography; Extreme Sport; Habitus; Identity and Difference; and the Body/Embodiment were composed by Belinda Wheaton and those on Feminism and Sexuality by Jayne Caudwell.

Paul Norcross helped a good deal in the framing of the book and kindly provided suggestions and material for the section on Ideology.

Many thanks to Pete Bramham, Anne Flintoff, Karl Spracklen and an anonymous referee for reading, and helping to improve, parts of the book. Thanks also to Paul Darby for timely assistance and to Chris Rojek for encouraging us to write the book in the first place and for waiting so long for us to do so.

Stephen Wagg
Leeds Metropolitan University

The Authors

Stephen Wagg is a Professor in the Carnegie Faculty of Sport and Education at Leeds Metropolitan University.

Carlton Brick is a Lecturer in the School of Sciences at the University of the West of Scotland in Paisley.

Belinda Wheaton is a Senior Research Fellow in the Chelsea School, University of Brighton.

Jayne Caudwell is a Senior Lecturer in the Chelsea School, University of Brighton.

the authors

The word 'alienation' has a general usage and it usually refers to a state of detachment – of 'feeling out of things'. In sociology, and in the history of social thought, it has a more specific meaning. This derives from the work of Karl Marx on life under capitalism and, in particular, from his *Economic and Philosophical Manuscripts of 1844* (Marx, 1959). Marx interprets the term in four related ways and these are set out in the *Dictionary of Sociology* as follows: (a) workers become estranged from the products of their own labour, which are owned and disposed of by someone else; (b) work itself becomes an alien activity with no intrinsic satisfaction. People work in order to live, rather than to express themselves, and their labour becomes a commodity; (c) the worker is thus deprived of the opportunity to become fully human and; (d) human beings are alienated from each other. They are individuals in competition, their relationships having been shaped by the market (Abercrombie et al., 2000: 11–12).

'Alienation' as a concept had a wide currency in European philosophy in the nineteenth century, but, following the Russian Revolution of 1917 the opportunity arose to address human alienation through political practice. In the early 1920s groups of intellectuals in Russia campaigned to transform Russian culture and to place it in the service of the proletariat (the working class) and of Soviet communism. Prominent among these was the Proletarian Cultural and Enlightenment Organizations or *Proletkult* who, along with the Hygienists, who were campaigners for physical and mental health, called for an end to competitive sport. As historian Robert Edelman notes: 'They preferred instead what they called "production gymnastics, excursions, and pageants". At times they invented specifically proletarian games, two of which were "Rescue from the Imperialists" and "Smuggling Revolutionary Literature across the Frontier"' (Edelman, 1993: 34). These groups and their ideas had some influence in early Soviet Russia, but, by the late 1920s with the communist party now under the authoritarian leadership of Josef Stalin, the Soviet Union drifted back towards 'bourgeois practices'. In 1952, a year before Stalin's death, they competed in their first Olympic Games (see Parks, 2007: 27–44).

Nevertheless, during the 1930s, the Soviet Union helped to sponsor a workers' sport movement in Europe whose explicit aim was to preserve sport for the healthy recreation of the masses and to keep it safe from the incursions of competitiveness, commercialism and nationalism. Indeed, alternative 'Workers' Olympics', dedicated to internationalism, worker solidarity and peace, were staged in Frankfurt in 1925, Vienna in 1931 and Antwerp in 1937. One tournament, scheduled for Barcelona in 1936, was prevented from taking place by the Spanish Civil War and another, planned for Helsinki in 1943, was cancelled because of World War Two (Riordan, 1984: 98–112). Some communist countries, however, still sought to prevent sport becoming marketised or unduly competitive. In the mid 1970s, for example, China under Mao Zedong attempted to maintain a policy of 'Friendship first, competition second' (see Hoberman, 1984: 222).

Two things are clear, though, when we consider the concept of alienation in relation to contemporary sport. One is that, historically, this is an issue in both philosophy and politics on which sections of the left and the right could make common cause: it is after all, a fundament both of Victorian gentlemanly amateurism and of internationalist worker sport that sport must not be practised with intensity and should instead promote the refreshment and 're-creation' of the individual. The other is that much sport in the early twenty-first century has assumed a form that approximates closely to the condition of alienation, as set out by Marx in the 1840s. This, for some leading writers in the area, evokes a singular irony because it was the Soviet Union, a proclaimed Marxist state, which in the 1930s led the way in applying scientific, achievement-oriented rationality to sport. Most countries today have, or aspire to have, academies for their most gifted athletes and train them toward elite performance. These academies, while still disparaged in the West, were pioneered in the USSR. The wedding of sport, science and commercialism has accelerated since World War Two (Beamish and Ritchie, 2006). As John Hoberman remarks acidly in the mid-1980s, sport has become 'the one international culture which is developing in accordance with a Communist model' (1986: 11).

The political and intellectual response to this development has been diverse. In the mid-1970s the French Marxist writer Jean-Marie Brohm (1987) published *Sport: A Prison of Measured Time* – arguably the plainest and least nuanced exposition of sport as an alienated activity in modern, industrialised societies in the second half of the twentieth century. Brohm argued:

The competitive sportsman is a *new type of worker* who sells his labour power – that is to say his ability to produce a spectacle that draws the crowds – to an employer. The exchange value of his labour power, governed by the law of supply and demand on the market, is determined by the labour time socially necessary for its production. Amateurism ceased to exist a long time ago. All top level sportsmen are professional performers in the muscle show. They are also very often advertising 'sandwich board' men. (1987: 176).

Brohm made no distinction between capitalist and communist societies in this regard. Of the German Democratic Republic he wrote:

A look at the sports system brings to mind a sports factory or a sports barracks: sport has become an essential productive force. Such a penetration of competitive sport into all spheres of society has turned E. Germany into a vast sports laboratory or sports enterprise – some would go as far as to say a sports prison' (1987: 79–80).

But the leading writer on the matter of sport and alienation, while perceptibly angry at what he sees as the perversions of modern elite sport, has nevertheless written consistently out of the belief that something in the way of fair play and honest sporting endeavour could be salvaged from the wreckage. John Hoberman is an American academic, trained originally in Scandinavian languages. His work has combined prodigious scholarship on the history both of sport and science with an often emotive vocabulary, withering in its condemnation of cheating sportspeople and vacillating bureaucrats. The title of Hoberman's principal work in this area – *Mortal Engines: The Science of Performance and the Dehumanization of Sport* (1992) is largely self-explanatory and ties the author, if not to the Marxian notion of alienation, at least to the nineteenth-century humanist philosophy from which it was developed. The book is a detailed historical account of the ways in which scientific intervention has disfigured sport across a range of countries and social systems. Early on in *Mortal Engines* Hoberman acknowledges the difficulty in countering the 'relativizing strategy' which styles 'doping' as simply one performance enhancement among many. 'Why, then', he asks, 'should one technique be banned while others are allowed? A rebuttal must show why some techniques violate the essence of sport while others do not' (1992: 26–7). Hoberman, of course, has his own rebuttals – he argues, for example, that steroids are different because 'they affect the human endocrinological system, which is the physiological basis of gender and sexual functioning' (1992: 27), but the very existence of this philosophical grey area is, for him, evidence of 'scientific ambition out of control' and a 'bioethical crisis of high-performance sport today' (1992: 28).

Six years later, with this perceived crisis apparently deepening, Hoberman reflected angrily on the Tour de France cycle race of 1998, from which the Festina team had been expelled for illegal drug use. In an article ironically appearing on *Meso-Rx*, a website for bodybuilders and other steroid users, Hoberman denounced the event as 'a pharmacy on wheels'. 'The Tour debacle', he wrote, 'has finally made it acceptable to say in public and without provocation what many have known for a long time, namely, that long-distance cycling has been the most consistently drug-soaked sport of the twentieth century' (Møller and Nauright, 2002). This recognition, though, and the riders' general response – peeved rather than contrite – only increased Hoberman's anger with the sponsors and administrators who had tacitly accepted the situation. The expulsions, he gloomily reflected, had come as the result of an

> unprecedented crackdown presided over by a Communist (female) health minister in the cabinet of the socialist prime minister Lionel Jospin...They were dumbfounded precisely because everyone involved, including the press, had been playing the game for so long in the interest of doing business as usual. And why does it matter that the health minister [Marie-Georges Buffet, leader of the French Communist Party] is a Communist? Because the only politicians in Europe who want to deploy the long arm of the law against doping, whether in France, Italy or Germany, are leftists or Greens who do not share the sportive nationalism of their conservative countrymen – the patriots who have always been willing to look the other way in the interest of keeping up with foreigners who just might be using drugs. (Hoberman, 1998)

National sporting elites and the financial backers on whom they depended could, it was implied, no longer be relied upon to preserve even a vestige of post-Victorian fair play: quoting a *New York Times* article on the affair from October of 1998 Hoberman reflected ruefully 'Festina actually reported "that the scandal had a positive effect on sales of its watches and that it would pay the team's $5 million expenses again next year"' (1998).

The following year at a conference on doping in North Carolina, Hoberman expressed his indignation that, following the Festina scandal, leading administrators had called for milder penalties for dopers and for sportspeople to be treated as workers, with their own labour laws. He lent his full support to proposals for an international anti-doping body, which materialised later that year in the form of the World Anti-Doping Agency (WADA) (1999). In 2005, Hoberman published *Testosterone Dreams*, a book in which he gives perhaps greater acknowledgement than hitherto to the medicalisation of everyday life and the ways in which 'People can feel obligated to dope themselves for military, professional or sexual purposes' (2005: 4). Thus sport takes its place alongside the pursuit of greater industrial productivity, military efficiency, extended youth and physical attractiveness as matters which have become the province of medical doctors, scrupulous and otherwise.

John Hoberman's work can be read as expressing a passionate belief that modern sport could, in some way and to some degree, be re-humanised and thus saved from its corrupt and over-scientised self. All that is needed, it is implied, are better safeguards to root out the cheats and indulgent officials. Hoberman seems frequently to draw a line in the sand, only to have it washed away by the next tide of pharmacological transgressions. In their *Fastest, Highest, Strongest*, Rob Beamish and Ian Ritchie, other leading writers in the field, take a more dispassionate view of elite sport. They note how at the headquarters of the sports firm Nike, in Portland, Oregon, in the early twenty-first century there took place 'the latest development in the total integration of commercial marketing interests, vast private sector resources, patriotism, cutting-edge science and technology and world-class, high-performance sport' (Beamish and Ritchie, 2006: 105): Nike assembled some promising runners and maintained them in an hermetically sealed environment, every physical aspect of which had been scientifically controlled to procure optimal performance (Beamish and Ritchie, 2006: 105). Were they alive today, nineteenth-century thinkers such as Marx might have thought that, in advanced capitalist sport, alienation was complete. However, Beamish and Ritchie cannot accept concepts such as 'the essence of sport' or 'true sport' – concepts which, as we saw, power the work of writers such as Hoberman. Their dismissal of these notions comes out of two, linked convictions: first, that myths surround such purportedly carefree, amateur sporting achievements of the late nineteenth and early to mid-twentieth centuries, such as the founding of the modern Olympics or the running of the first sub-four minute mile in 1954 and, second, that sport can, ultimately, only be what human beings say that it is – it has no 'essense' or 'authenticity' beyond that (Beamish and Ritchie, 2006: 112–15; see also Bale, 2004).

Some philosophers and sociologists are prepared to go further and embrace the technological innovations and to dismiss the notion that there might be a 'natural body' or a state of mind that was intrinsically human. The humanist philosophy of the nineteenth century is thus rejected in favour of 'posthumanism' and 'transhumanism'. As a result, in academic commentary on sport, terms such as 'cyborg athlete' and 'genetically modified athlete' are gaining currency. Andy Miah, for example, writes:

> sport is already posthuman. Athletes have already metamorphosed into super-humans, blurred suitably by the softening presentation of modern television. Athletes are ambassadors of transhumanism, placed at the cutting edge of human boundaries of capability. The athlete's body is in a state of flux, continually transcending itself, and thus, perpetuating transhuman ideas about the biophysics of humanity. For this reason, elite sport is a useful case from which one can justify the acceptance of transhumanism. (2003)

The culture of advanced capitalist societies affords little space for the idea of alienation; these societies are governed increasingly by the politics of identity, in which, it is asserted, people can become what they wish to become. Many people are therefore likely to warm to the idea of a mutating sporting body, seeking, and seeking to exceed, its known limits. For others of a Marxian persuasion, outside of skimming a Frisbee round the park on a Sunday afternoon or playing beach cricket with their families, un-alienated sport will be increasingly difficult to find.

REFERENCES

Abercrombie, Nicholas, Hill, Stephen and Turner, Bryan S. (2000) *Dictionary of Sociology*. London: Penguin.

Bale, John (2006) *Roger Bannister and the Four Minute Mile*. London: Routledge 2004.

Beamish, Rob and Ritchie, Ian (2006) *Fastest, Highest, Strongest: A Critique of High-Performance Sport*. London: Routledge.

Brohm, Jean-Marie (1987) *Sport: A Prison of Measured Time*. London: Ink Links.

Edelman, Robert (1993) *Serious Fun: A History of Spectator Sports in the U.S.S.R.* New York: Oxford University Press.

Hoberman, John (1984) *Sport and Political Ideology*. London: Heinemann.

Hoberman, John (1986) *The Olympic Crisis: Sport, Politics and the New Moral Order*. New Rochelle, NY: A.D. Caratzas.

Hoberman, John (1992) *Mortal Engines: The Science of Performance and the Dehumanization of Sport*. New York: The Free Press.

alienation

9

Hoberman, John (1998) 'A Pharmacy on Wheels: The Tour De France Doping Scandal' http://www.thinkmuscle.com/ARTICLES/hoberman/tour.htm (accessed: 20 April 2007).

Hoberman, John (1999) 'Learning from the Past: The Need for Independent Doping Control' paper presented at the Duke Conference on Doping, Durham, North Carolina, 7 May, http://www.law.duke.edu/sportcenter/hoberman.pdf (accessed: 20 April 2007).

Hoberman, John (2005) *Testosterone Dreams: Rejuvenation, Aphrodisia, Doping*. Berkeley: University of California Press.

Marx, Karl (1959) *Economic and Philosophical Manuscripts of 1844*. Moscow: Progress Publishers.

Miah, Andy (2003) '"Be Very Afraid": Cyborg Athletes, Transhuman Ideals and Posthumanity', *Journal of Evolution and Technology*, 13 October, http://jetpress.org/volume13/miah.htm (accessed: 20 April 2007).

Parks, Jenifer (2007) 'Verbal Gymnastics: Sports, Bureaucracy and the Soviet Union's Entrance into the Olympic Games', in Stephen Wagg and David L. Andrews (eds) *East Plays West: Sport and the Cold War*. London: Routledge. pp. 27–44.

Riordan, Jim (1984) 'The Workers' Olympics', in Alan Tomlinson and Garry Whannel (eds) *Five Ring Circus: Money, Power and Politics at the Olympic Games*. London: Pluto Press. pp. 98–112.

FURTHER READING

Beamish, Rob and Ritchie, Ian (2006) *Fastest, Highest, Strongest: A Critique of High-Performance Sport*. London: Routledge.

Brohm, Jean-Marie (1978) *Sport: A Prison of Measured Time*. London: Ink Links.

Hoberman, John (1992) *Mortal Engines: The Science of Performance and the Dehumanization of Sport*. New York: The Free Press.

Miah, Andy (2004) *Genetically Modified Athletes: Biomedical Ethics, Gene Doping and Sport*. London: Routledge.

Amateurism

The word 'amateur' is French in origin and derives from the Latin word for 'love' – the same root that gave us the English word 'amorous'. It was therefore used originally to describe someone who pursued an activity solely for the love of it. Amateurism is generally seen as an English phenomenon (Allison, 2001: 10).

Few people today would understand the word 'amateurism' as primarily denoting love. In the modern world it usually signifies incompetence. Which of us would wish to be identified as one of 'a bunch of amateurs'? Chances are we would far rather be recognised as 'professional' in our approach, professional being for much of the history of modern sport the widely despised antonym of 'amateur'. These days, in sport as in the wider society, there can seldom be enough 'professionalism'.

The history of amateurism in sport is the history of claims about the respective behaviour of different groups of sportspeople and few of these claims stand up to much scrutiny now, if, indeed, they ever did. Amateurism was increasingly recognised as some kind of organised hypocrisy within the administration of sport, as indicated by the increased currency given to the term 'shamateur'. This may make the subject of amateurism difficult to discuss dispassionately. However, a means to sensible discussion is provided by the writer Lincoln Allison (2001: 20–4), who suggests that there are three, often intertwining, ways of defining amateurism:

(a) Social Definitions. In practice, when amateur hegemony in the stewardship of sport was at its height, amateurs were often defined simply in social terms. This was typified by the so-called 'mechanics clauses' adopted in British sports such as rowing and athletics in the late nineteenth century. Here an amateur was said, in effect, to be someone who was not a manual worker – labourers, mechanics, artisans and, in the case of the Amateur Rowing Association, people 'engaged in any menial task' being specifically excluded. Prohibitions such as this led the rowing historian Christopher Dodd to observe: 'Rowing people, in common with other sportsmen, were very good at determining what an amateur was not. But deciding what an amateur is has eluded them' (Dodd, 1989: 281).

(b) Ethical Definitions. Here the amateur was defined by the values that s/he held and, it was assumed, expressed in the sporting arena. In this context, the word approached its true meaning, since: it defined a person who played sport for pleasure; was comparatively careless of the outcome of sport encounters; played fairly; accepted both the decisions of officials and the results of contests with a good grace; and gained no extrinsic reward (usually wages or compensation for loss of earnings) for playing. It goes without saying that people who played sport with this philosophy could not, or should not, logically have been confined to one particular social group.

(c) Bureaucratic or Financial Definitions. These arose when governing bodies wished to use either of the first two kinds of definition as a basis for excluding and/or controlling groups within a particular sport. Both exclusion and control were widespread. In 1895, for example, the Northern Union (the forerunner of Rugby League in the north of England) disengaged from the Rugby Football Union over the issue of 'broken time payments', which the latter body refused to condone. These payments were also a matter of contention in the Olympic movement during the first half of the twentieth century. In 1882 the Amateur Athletic Association actually set up a fund to finance prosecutions of athletes falsely claiming to be amateurs according to the AAA definition; some were subsequently found guilty of fraud and sentenced to six months' hard labour (Crump, 1989: 51).

The most cursory examination of the history of amateurism as a concept suggests that it has often worked as a metaphor for the British upper classes and as an ideological rendering of their actions, objectives and self image. It was rooted in the cult of games which developed in the British public schools in the mid- to late nineteenth century. During this time athletic pursuits, and the body itself, acquired a newly exalted status. Part of the ethos that surrounded these games was that the people who played them played fairly. The amateur ideology was subsequently often deployed in a way that suggested that players from outside this social world – the working class and foreigners, for instance – could not be relied upon to play as fairly as the public school 'gentleman'. The invocation of amateurism thus became a means of defining the Other in sport.

The sporting metaphor and the notion that the British had a special facility for playing fairly strongly characterised the British Empire. The rivalry between the British and Russian empires, for example, was frequently referred to as 'The Great Game' and colonial (and postcolonial) sportspeople (Pakistani cricketers, for instance) were often styled as cheats. At the same time in British colonial territories – in Australia, the East Coast of America and elsewhere – anglophile elites emerged that dedicated themselves to upholding the mythical values of fair play. Bill Woodfull who captained Australia in the 'Bodyline' cricket series of 1932–3 is reputed during one Test Match to have said 'There's only one side out there playing cricket – and it's not England'. These historic (and highly questionable) notions still have a strong resonance in state politics. For example, on a visit to Africa in January of 2005, the then British Chancellor of the Exchequer Gordon Brown said:

The days of Britain having to apologise for its colonial history are over. We should talk, and rightly so, about British values that are enduring, because they stand for some of the greatest ideas in history – tolerance, liberty, civic duty – that grew in Britain and influenced the rest of the world. Our strong traditions of fair play, of openness, of internationalism, these are great British values. (*The Guardian*, 1 March 2005: 24)

'Fair play', as the historian Richard Holt (1989) has suggested, was the watchword of the upper-middle-class gentleman amateurs and there's little doubt that many of these men lived and played according to the amateur ideal. The football club Corinthian Casuals, for example, founded in 1882 by ex-public schoolboys and taking their name from a city state in Ancient Greece, were pledged never to train or to compete for trophies. After the penalty kick was introduced into association football in 1891, they withdrew their goalkeeper on conceding one: the very idea of trying to save the kick, and thus profit from a foul, was anathema to the gentleman footballer.

The point, though, is not that 'true' amateurism never existed – that it was wholly 'ideological' – but that it could not be confined to a specific social group: 'gentlemen'. History suggests that 'amateurism' was a response to the rise of 'professionalism'. Certainly the latter term came into popular usage later, 'professionalism' being in currency in the 1850s and 'amateurism' not until the 1880s. The popular suppositions that seemed to define the amateur – that he was careless of the result of the game, that he played fairly, that he disdained material reward and so on – were all incompatible with the evidence. England's most famous cricketer Dr W.G. Grace, for instance, played as an amateur but is generally held to have played hard, with scant regard for fairness, and to have pocketed £9,000 (a very large sum at the time) from a benefit awarded to him by his county Gloucestershire in 1895 (Rae, 1999: 396). Similarly, members of the Amateur Rowing Association, arguably the most exclusive of all Britain's sporting bodies, had no qualm either about rowing for trophies or about training for races (Wagg, 2006). Conversely, a number of professionals – the cricketer Sir Jack Hobbs, the tennis player Rod Laver, the footballers Bobby Charlton and Gary Lineker, and legions more – have been acknowledged as chivalrous, self-deprecating players – fair in the amateur mode. Amateurism has to be seen therefore as a means through which to exclude and/or to control working-class sportspeople. Indeed, as noted earlier, some sports governing bodies voted to ban 'artisans, mechanics and labourers' from membership. In British rowing the phrase 'or is engaged in any form of menial duty' was added. Amateur hegemony grew often in relation to the success of working-class and professional players (not always the same thing) in various sports: rugby players in the North of England, for example, and watermen, many of whose families had worked a river for generations and who dominated the early boat races.

Behind the growing militancy of the gentleman amateur lay the ongoing political and social wrangle between the entrenched landed classes, finance capitalists and Southern-based professionals and the rising Northern and Midlands-based industrial middle class, with their ethos of openness, competition and free trade. As Allison puts it, 'there were two conflicting tendencies in the society of the time, one which saw the commercial possibilities of urban markets and the other which abhorred those possibilities' (Allison, 2001: 18). A number of reforms, notably those giving the vote to male men of property in 1832 and to the skilled male working class in 1867 are indicative of this social change. In the realm of sport the Southern, gentlemanly elite and its class allies around the country wished to conduct matters on their own terms and to keep notions of competition and markets at bay. Traditional hierarchy sought to rebut (qualified) equality of opportunity.

Neither of these major social class groupings, however, was especially sympathetic to professionalism or to the growing working-class power of which it was a symbol. What emerged are two ways of dealing with professionalism and/or working-class sportspeople.

One amounted essentially to exclusion and the maintaining of separate spheres. The Amateur Rowing Association, based on elite clubs and stretches of river, excluded lower middle-class and working-class rowers from prestigious regattas, such as the one held annually at Henley. A separate rowing organisation – the National Amateur Rowing Association – was founded in 1890 and catered to the merely amateur, as opposed to gentleman amateur, oarsman. Similarly Northern rugby players were effectively expelled from the Rugby Football Union in 1895 for receiving 'broken time payments'. Likewise amateur footballers seceded from the FA in 1907, returning only in 1914.

The second strategy was founded on the notion of getting professionalism into the open, making it easier to control. In cricket, for example, amateurs and professionals played together, but, until the 1960s and 1970s, this was in circumstances of secure amateur hegemony, both on and off the field. A similar political strategy informed moves to form the

Football League in 1888: Northern administrators thought a better way of containing professionalism was to make it legitimate.

The late nineteenth century is widely seen as the 'golden age' of the amateur sportsman. In the twentieth century the term became progressively discredited and the word 'shamateurism' was widely preferred. One by one, bodies of sport governance abandoned the distinction between amateurs and professionals, beginning with English cricket in 1962 (Smith and Porter, 2000). In 1980 the International Olympic Committee, for so long a bastion of amateurism, and latterly 'shamateurism', effectively endorsed professionalism when its president, Juan Antonio Samaranch, declined to offer a definition of amateurism, delegating this responsibility to national Olympic committees.

The term survives now in common parlance only as a denotation of incompetence.

REFERENCES

Allison, Lincoln(2001) *Amateurism in Sport*. London: Frank Cass.

Dodd, Christopher (1989) 'Rowing' in Tony Mason (ed.) *Sport in Britain: A Social History*. Cambridge. Cambridge University Press. pp. 276–307.

Crump, Jeremy (1989) 'Athletics' in Tony Mason (ed.) *Sport in Britain: A Social History*. Cambridge. Cambridge University Press. pp. 44–77.

Holt, Richard (1989) *Sport and the British*. Oxford: The Clarendon Press.

Rae, Simon (1999) *W.G. Grace*. London: Faber & Faber.

Wagg, Stephen (2006) 'Base Mechanic Arms?', *Sport in History*, December, 26(3): 520–39.

Smith, Adrian and Porter, Dilwyn (eds) (2000) *Amateurs and Professionals in Post-War British Sport*. London: Frank Cass.

FURTHER READING

Allison, Lincoln (2001) *Amateurism in Sport*. London: Frank Cass.

Porter, Dilwyn and Wagg, Stephen (eds) (2006) *Sport in History,Special Edition on Amateurism*, December.

Smith, Adrian and Porter, Dilwyn (eds) (2000) *Amateurs and Professionals in Post-War British Sport*. London: Frank Cass.

amateurism

Capitalism

(for Anti-Capitalism see Globalisation; Marxism)

CAPITALISM AND THE ORIGINS OF MODERN SPORT

Capitalism is the name given to the historically specific form of economic production and social organisation, which begins to dominate the societies of Western Europe during the early eighteenth century. By late nineteenth century capitalism is widely recognised as the globally dominant economic and social system. The key features of capitalistic societies are: a division of labour and a system of wage-labour; the establishment of private property; and commodity production. Commodities are goods that are made and exchanged for profit rather than for immediate use or to meet the needs of the producers. The writings of the political economists Adam Smith (1723–1790), and Karl Marx (1818–1883) have been highly influential in shaping how we have come to understand the origins and socio-economic structure of capitalist societies. Early forms of capitalism emerged in England during the sixteenth century, as the feudal social order was slowly undermined and replaced by a new merchant class. Adam Smith is credited with laying the foundations of liberal laissez-faire economics, and in his book *An Enquiry into the Nature and Causes of the Wealth of Nations* (1776) he offers one of the first critical theories of capitalism as a system – although during Smith's time the term capitalism was not itself used. Smith referred to this new form of economic production as the 'system of natural liberty'. Central to Smith's thought is the belief in the power of the market (and what he described as its 'invisible hand') to correct economic crisis without the need for state or other forms of conscious organised intervention. Karl Marx on the other hand, suggests, in a deliberate critique of Smith, that capitalistic economic production is shaped by the emergence of a two class grouping – the bourgeoisie or capitalist class who, according to Marx own the means of production, and the wage-labour or working class (the proletariat) who are required to sell their labour power to the capitalist. It is, Marx suggests, in the interests of both these classes to consciously intervene in capitalist production. The capitalist class, through the state, will strive to maintain and reproduce the conditions necessary for capitalist accumulation – the exploitation of the working class. The working class must organise themselves to resist and ultimately dismantle the capitalist social order, replacing it with communism (see **Marxism**). Capitalist production is organised on the principle of producing value in the form of profit, rather than producing things to use. This new form of production is called 'commodity production' whereby commodities are produced and exchanged (via the market) for a value that is in excess of the cost or investment made in the initial production of the commodity.

Commodity production encourages the increasingly specialised division of labour through the mechanisation and technological development of production. Feudal forms of governance and social structure (religion, the crown, hereditary hierarchies …) are replaced by increasingly secular and democratic institutions, such as parliament, the nation state and the rule of law. However it was not until the late eighteenth and early nineteenth centuries that capitalism established its classical form with the wholesale industrialisation of commodity production, whereby early forms of capitalistic production, agrarian and mercantile in form, were replaced by mass production methods of manufacture within a factory system shaped by an increasingly specialised division of labour. This is the classic form of capitalism and is generally referred to as 'Industrial Capitalism'. The increasing mechanisation of production within industrial capitalism results in the deskilling of labour and the formal routinisation of work.

Social scientists consider sport as a central expression of capitalistic economic and social relations. Historically, modern sport emerges as a codified, structured social institution just at a time when European capitalism undergoes rapid economic and industrial development during the eighteenth and nineteenth centuries. The transformation of the economic and productive base is mirrored at the level of social relations and culture. It is in this context that sport emerges as a significant area of social and economic activity. Capitalist social relations transforms previously ad hoc and disparate pastimes and games into rationalised activities that are subject to structured bureaucratic, institutional control which in turn become codified sport, as standardised rules and regulations are developed. Mason (1980) suggests that with reference to

English football the process of codification takes place between 1845 and 1862, when the leading public schools consigned the rules of their various codes and games to print (cited in Horne et al., 1999: 40). These codified sets of rules become subject to and enforced by governing bodies at regional, national and then international levels. Formed in 1863 the Football Association, then a Southern based organisation, established itself as football's leading authority in the late 1870s. Football's world governing body, FIFA, was formed in 1904; however, it was not until 1946 that the English FA finally joined (UEFA, the European governing body was not formed until 1954). Similarly, the Amateur Athletic Club (AAC) was formed in 1886. The AAC was later to become the Amateur Athletics Association (or 'three As'), the governing body of athletics in Britain. The International Olympic Committee (IOC) was formed in 1894 with the first modern Olympic games held in 1896. Formed in 1787 the Marylebone Cricket Club (MCC) became the leading influence in developing cricket within the new industrial society, and was to establish itself as the games governing body (Horne et al., 1999).

As society was dramatically remade by capitalism, so were sports. From being primarily aristocratic pursuits in their modern origins, sports very quickly came to reflect the mass nature of industrial society. The institutionalisation of games in the late nineteenth century made them more 'work like' (Haley, 1978). This had both economic and social consequences. Many of the most famous sporting clubs and teams have their origins in the factory and industrial system of the nineteenth century, as many factory owners and industrialists recognised the benefits of using sport, such as football, to boost the profile of their companies. As sport became more 'work like' so it became an occupation and a career. Talking of the development of professional football in England (the Football League, a body representing the interests of the first professional clubs was founded in 1888 with 12 members), Tischler (1981) suggests that it reflected the nature and tensions of the labour relations that existed at the time. The emergence of professional sportsmen was bound up in the new industrial culture as working-class players, who had little or no leisure time, demanded financial recompense for the time and effort they were giving free to play in works teams. During this period sporting activity becomes subject to the economic rationales of the market. Not only does it become, like work, an area of financial recompense, but sport also begins to take on, outwardly at least, the vestiges of a commercial activity, as opportunities are spotted to make money from the new emerging sports. With the establishment of professionalism, the paying spectator quickly follows, as club owners seek to recoup the financial outlay made through now having to pay wages to their players. Between the years 1890 and 1914 spectator sport became a significant part of British national culture. However, these processes were not without tensions and points of conflict, themselves reflecting the social and economic inequalities of class and power within capitalist society. There was pronounced opposition to, and resentment of, the early expressions of commercialisation and professionalisation which accompanied increasing working-class participation in sport, on the part of the new middle-class elite. This elite considered themselves to be not only the administrative and institutional leaders of modern sport, but also its moral guardians. Modern sport has its origins in the elite schooling system that emerged during the eighteenth and nineteenth centuries. The public school system was considered the central institution whereby the new capitalist class was to educate and train a new generation of leaders, administrators, politicians, generals and social architects, equipped with the skills and ideologies to govern the new social and economic order embodied in capitalism. As a result, sport was readily inscribed with the same ideology. This ideology has been described as one of athleticism, or Muscular Christian. Hargreaves (1986) notes that the 'athleticist' ideology that shaped sport's origins also reflected and permeated the country's political and economic cultures and has had a long lasting influence upon the nature and social character of the development of sport in Britain.

Within prominent sections of the new capitalist middle class, sport had particular social uses. An ideology of 'rational recreation' was readily co-opted as a means to alleviate the perceived social problems associated with mass urbanisation and industrialisation. Sport was to provide a means by which the new capitalist class sought to 'civilise' and morally educate the new but poor working classes. Holt (1989: 139) has noted the conscious promotion of sport within poor urban communities, whereby, through the playing of sport, new forms and structures of discipline are inculcated into the poor. As has been noted, "'religious, humanitarian and educational bodies" became concerned as the century progressed, that the labouring classes should be provided with "as many accepting and improving activities as possible"' (Golby and Purdue 1984: 92, cited in Horne et al., 1999: 17). Although this overtly class-based prejudice has its origins in elitist Victorian social thought, the idea that sport plays a social function in offering structure, discipline, character and self esteem to particular under privileged or excluded sections of society still pervades the modern political imagination.

POSTMODERN CAPITALISM

With the apparent decline in industrial manufacturing within Western capitalist economies, the increasingly global nature of the division of labour, and the emergence of service and information based industries during the late twentieth century, many sociologists and other commentators have suggested that capitalism has entered a new stage of development. There are three principal characterisations of this new phase. They are 'post-industrial capitalism'; 'dis-organised capitalism'; and 'late capitalism'.

In his book the *Coming of Post-Industrial Society*, Daniel Bell (1973) suggests that the core features that define post-industrial capitalism are: the growing predominance of the tertiary (services) sector over the primary (agriculture and mining) and secondary (manufacturing) sectors. There is an increasing emphasis upon the role of knowledge-based and educational sectors, and, finally, a noticeable decrease in polarised industrial class conflict, as capitalism's organisational structures become less hierarchical. Within post-industrial capitalism social development is essentially driven by technological change rather than by industrial production.

Dis-organised capitalism is a term coined to describe the fragmentation of social, economic and political institutions (such as class and the state) within Western democracies. It is suggested that capitalist structures are now defined by their seemingly disorganised nature rather than by their rational organisation. The tendency towards globalisation and the transition to postmodern forms of social organisation disrupt and ultimately transgress the traditional systems, networks and boundaries that have characterised the previous period of capitalist development (modernity) (see Lash and Urry, 1987).

As a concept 'late-capitalism' was first used in Europe towards the end of the 1930s. Developed by a group of Marxist social scientists in Germany (known collectively as 'The Frankfurt School') to describe a stage in capitalist development which they considered to be characterised by profound economic and social crisis, the distinct features of 'late-capitalism' during this period were: a tendential web of bureaucratic control and the increasing interrelationship of government and big business – a development they termed 'state capitalism'. In this respect the Frankfurt School considered the development of Nazism in

Germany and the New Deal in the USA during the 1930s, as being related systems of government, since they were both representative of forms of state capitalism and a response on the part of the capitalist class to the profound global economic and social crisis that characterised this period of history. However, by the 1970s, as a term, 'late capitalism' (or 'late-stage capitalism') had all but thrown off its negative connotations of capitalist crisis. The concept was being increasingly associated with the development of post-war capitalism, and more specifically of financial capital, which had undergone a dramatic revival and had given rise to a period of protracted economic boom.

Within the literature of contemporary sociology the term 'late-capitalism' is perhaps most associated with the writings of American Marxist, Fredric Jameson (1934–), particularly his highly influential text *Postmodernism: Or, the Cultural Logic of Late Capitalism* (1991). As Jameson sees it, the development of 'late capitalism' is synonymous with the development of postmodernism in the 1950s. In his work this term is used to trace and describe the trends and developments (social, cultural, political, economic and ideological) that occur during the 1950s and 1970s. According to Jameson these developments give rise to fully fledged postmodern capitalist social relations. In Jameson's theoretical framework the term 'late capitalism' is not used merely to suggest or describe a simple linear period or epoch of capitalist development, but rather to demarcate a profound transformation whereby the totality of social experience is not only distinct but is incomparable with previous periods of capitalist development.

The sports sociologist David L. Andrews has been highly influenced by Jameson's work on 'late capitalism'. Andrews (2004: 3) suggests that whilst in early periods of capitalist development, sport may have maintained a certain sense of autonomy from the explicit profit orientated motivations of the market, within late capitalism sport is now an integral ideological and economic expression of global capitalism. Indeed Andrews suggests that the now commonplace notion of a 'sports industry' is misleading. The production and consumption of sports related goods and services span a variety of industrial sectors, such as manufacturing, sports wear and apparel, travel, biomedicine, building and construction and so on – reflecting the postmodern nature of late capitalist production. As such, the identification of a separate distinct sphere of economic activity as the 'sports industry' has, as Andrews suggests, become increasingly difficult. However, it is the sphere of commercial mass media which clearly illustrates the late capitalist nature of sport.

Sports media, Andrews suggests, play a central role in the wider cultural reshaping of late capitalist culture and society. Such is the extent of the embedded nature of sports media within late capitalism, it is suggested that sport has replaced work, religion and community as the 'glue of collective consciousness in latter twentieth century America' (Goldman and Papson, 1998: 66, cited in Andrews 2004: 3). The core shift from industrial to late capitalism has occurred at the level of production. Mass industrial production has been replaced by mass cultural production. Value within late capitalist postmodern economies is produced within the cultural and symbolic realm, rather than the traditional realm of industrial production. Within this new late capitalist reconfiguration of value creation, sport is both a symbolic value, and a creator of symbolic value (see **Postmodernism/Postmodernity**).

REFERENCES

Andrews, D.L. (2004) 'Sport in the Late Capitalist Moment', in T. Slack (ed.) *The Commercialisation of Sport*. London: Routledge. pp. 3–28.

Bell, D. (1973) *The Coming of Post-Industrial Society: A Venture in Social Forecasting*. New York: Basic Books.

Golby, J.M. and Purdue, A.W. (1984) *The Civilisation of the Crowd: Popular Culture in England 1750–1900*. London: Batsford Academic and Educational.

Goldman, R. and Papson, S. (1998) *Nike Culture*. London: Sage.

Haley, B. (1978) *The Healthy Body and Victorian Culture*. New Haven: Harvard University Press.

Hargreaves, J. (1986) *Sport, Power and Culture: A Social and Historical Analysis of Popular Sports in Britain*. Cambridge: Polity Press.

Holt, R. (1989) *Sport and the British: A Modern History*. Oxford: Oxford University Press.

Horne, J., Tomlinson, A. and Whannel, G. (1999) *Understanding Sport: An Introduction to the Sociological and Cultural Analysis of Sport*. London: E & FN Spon.

Jameson, F. (1991) *Postmodernism: Or, the Cultural Logic of Late Capitalism*. London: Verso.

Lash, S. and Urry, J. (1987) *The End of Organised Capitalism*. Cambridge: Polity Press.

Mason, T. (1980) *Association Football and English Society 1863–1915*. Brighton: Harvester.

Tischler, S. (1981) *Footballers and Businessmen. The Origins of Professional Soccer in England*. New York: Holmes & Meier.

Commodification/
Commodity Fetishism

During the last decade of the twentieth century and the first decade of the twenty-first, the sociological and cultural analysis of sport has identified commodification as one of the key dynamics shaping sporting culture. The term is closely associated with the intensification of commercial interests (itself a notable dynamic in the development of modern professional sports since the late nineteenth century) within elite sports, that accompanied the development of satellite and pay-per-view broadcasting platforms, and the closer association of sports with market values, in the late 1980s and 1990s (Horne et al., 1999: 268). As a concept, commodification has been closely associated with the writings and theories of Karl Marx (1818–1883), the founder of communism, particularly his theoretical development of 'commodity fetishism', and as such has acquired a particularly radical leftist connotation. However Marx never actually developed commodification as an analytical concept – the term only appears in common usage during the mid 1970s (in part reflecting the tendency towards more culturally orientated explanations of capitalism and the post-war consumer society). Whilst the concepts of commodification and commodity fetishism seem similar, they are different in their theoretical implications and in the processes they are used to explain.

Commodification has been identified as a key aspect of global economic organisation (Williams, 2002: 526) and is generally used to describe the process by which aspects of life that are not necessarily economic in nature, such as human relationships and services, become subject to market principles (Abercrombie, 1996). The commodification thesis suggests that capitalist market values dominate not only economic life but all aspects of modern capitalist social relations – public, private, and personal. As such, aspects of social and cultural life that are not by their nature commercial or economic become tradable and viewed as potential sources of profit. Within a sporting context Walsh and Giulianotti (2001, 2007) have referred to this process as 'hyper-commodification', which has resulted in an explosion in the market value of sports, and an intensification of the commodification of 'secondary, non-play aspects' of sport, such as club merchandising, televisions contracts, sponsorship and the off-field earnings and activities of players. Williams (2002) suggests that, within much of the social science literature, commodification is considered a negative process, undermining traditional forms of social organisation and culture. This is certainly the case when looking at the social science of sport.

It is suggested that the commodification of sport is detrimental on a number of different levels. Whannel (1994) suggests that sporting performance is undermined by the introduction of market values. As the market becomes more dominant, value creation begins to take precedence. As a result, sporting performance is transformed into a 'spectacle' – physical performance becomes subservient to the construction of sport as a media event. During the FIFA 2006 World Cup, in an effort to appease television broadcasters, the roof of the Commerzbank Arena stadium in Frankfurt was closed for the game between Korea and Tonga, so as to reduce the shadow cast across the pitch, which it had been suggested was spoiling television pictures. This was despite temperatures in excess of 30 degrees. This is a clear example of the impact of commodification, as sporting performance undergoes profound 'spectacularisation' within which the well-being and ability of the athletes to perform is deemed secondary to the ability to globally broadcast images to paying consumers watching on their television screens.

Kidd (1981) suggests that processes of commodifiction have had profound impacts upon the ideological organisation and construction of national identities and notions of nationhood. Drawing upon the experiences of the Canadian National Hockey League (NHL), Kidd suggests that the problem of the increasing 'Americanisation' of the sport, and its subsequent inability to promote a Canadian national identity, is neither the result of 'US expansion nor national betrayal, but in the dynamics of capital' (cited in Jarvie and Maguire 1994: 248). According to Kidd (1981: 713) it has been the intensification of the commodification of the sport that has served 'to accelerate the disintegration of beliefs and practices that had once supported and nurtured autonomous Canadian institutions' (cited in Jarvie and Maguire, 1994: 248).

Walsh and Giulianotti (2001: 53) suggest that the 'hyper-commodification' that has taken place in English football since the 1990s has undermined both the 'competitive structures and *ethos* of the sport' (original emphasis). This has resulted in a structure whereby both the financial and competitive dominance and success of a few clubs is preserved over the interests of the sport as a whole. Furthermore, they contend that it has fractured the cultural relationship between the sport and its traditional community – the localised inner-city working-class fan base. A consequence of the commodification of sport 'involves the supplanting of more democratic structures of community-tied ownership [of sporting institutions] by distinctly impersonal, corporate frameworks of power' (Walsh and Giulianotti, 2001: 56). This process, the authors contend, results in the *'exclusion of traditional soccer fans from resources and activities to which they once had access'* (Walsh and Giulianotti, 2001: 63, original emphasis). As a result of commodification, traditional fans are excluded in favour of new consumers more familiar with the machinations of the global consumer market. Since as far back as the 1960s it has been noted that the increasing penetration of market principles has fed into the processes of transformation of the social relationships embedded in sport. As Critcher (1979) has noted, the post-war transformation of British football has openly incorporated the language of the market, wherein the relationship between club and supporter becomes one akin to that between producer and consumer. Increasingly it is suggested that the football supporters' emotional investment in a football club is now subject to high degrees of commodification. The explosion of merchandising, replica shirts, pay-per-view and subscription television, are just a few examples of how the relationship between supporter and club, a relationship that is already by its very nature a commercial one, has, it is argued, become subject to and dominated by commercial interests.

The commodification thesis seems an apposite description and reflection of the processes that dominate contemporary sport. There can be little doubt of the dramatic changes that have occurred to the structures, economics and organisation of contemporary sporting institutions, and how these sports are played, mediated and consumed. However, one should not accept it without question. Williams (2002) has suggested that a central problem with the commodification thesis is that 'hardly any evidence is ever provided to show the extent of commodification or how more of social life is mediated through the market' (2002: 528). Much of the discussion of commodification within the social science of sport is restricted to the role and function of media and the visual image, and the narrow often unsubstantiated counter position between the 'traditional' localised supporter, and the globalised 'new consumer' (Brick, 2001; Jones, 2003).

Notably, recent discussions of the commercialisation of sport have tended to emphasise the psychological or 'emotional' aspects of commodification as a process (Walsh and Giulianotti, 2001, 2007). Following Anderson (1993), Walsh and Giulianotti (2001: 55) have suggested that rather than a material process, commodification is an 'attitude that views objects and practices as potential commodities'.

Commodification is perceived as a system of meanings, a way of seeing the world, rather than a materially grounded process.

The theory of commodity fetishism, however, stresses the material and social nature of the relationships embodied within commodity and market relations. For Marx the distinguishing feature of a capitalist economy is that it is a commodity economy, based on the production of goods for the purpose of exchange. Moreover, within capitalism commodities are produced primarily for their economic exchange value rather than for their use value. Marx (1983) considered the commodity as the root or 'cell' of bourgeois capitalist society, expressing not only economic relations but the fundamental social relationships that shaped the totality of life within capitalist societies. Marx developed this analysis through his theory of commodity fetishism. Contemporaneously, commodity fetishism has been popularly appropriated to describe the apparently market-led materialism of global consumer society, and the 'obsessive' drive of the modern consumer to accumulate 'things'. However, as noted above, for Marx it describes a much more fundamental relationship within capitalist society – that of the private appropriation of that which has been produced by and for society. Via the standpoint of dialectical materialism, Marx outlines how, under the capitalistic production of commodities, active social relationships between humans manifest themselves and appear as their direct opposite – the anti-social relationship between passive things. For something to be exchanged it is assumed that there is a property within the thing that can be measured against that which we are exchanging it with or for – a shared common property. For Marx the common equivalence of the exchange value of commodities is in fact premised upon their being the products of human labour, in its abstract form. Under capitalism human labour power is transformed into, and sold as, a commodity. The worker sells his labour to the capitalist for wages. As with other commodities, this exchange appears as the exchange of equivalents – so many hours work exchanged for an equivalent monetary amount in the form of a wage. However, as Marx points out, the exchange of the commodity of labour power is an unequal one, which favours the capitalist. Nevertheless, he suggests that, in the relations of production (the 'human relations of domination and servitude' – Jakubowski, 1990: 88) this exchange assumes the appearance of equality. That is, the relationships of exchange between commodities appear as the autonomous exchange of things that are by their 'nature' equivalent in value. It is this aspect of the relationship that Marx terms as 'fetishism': the social relationship between humans which assumes the form of a relation between things

(Marx, 1983). For Marx, capitalism mystifies the nature of social relations, in that the social and human nature of the act of production only appears as such at the point when the products of labour are exchanged as commodities in the market, and appropriated privately. 'Commodity fetishism' argues that what are the actual social relations between persons within capitalism, appear only as the relations between things.

Žižek (1989: 24) underlines the importance of this theory as a means of understanding the contemporary moment, noting the act of 'misrecognition' that the theory of commodity fetishism exposes – that active social relationships between humans appear as the passive relationships between things in commodity form. Žižek suggests that this 'misrecognition' does not simply take place within the 'relations between things' but also within the 'relations between men', in that the passive relationship between things assumes the appearance of the active relationship between humans. Within capitalistic forms of production (of meaning as well as of exchange value), the social relationships between humans not only appear as though they are relationships between things in commodity form, they are increasingly interpreted and understood as relationships between things in commodity form (Brick 2004: 102). Brick (2004) utilises this model of commodity fetishism in an analysis of the function of sporting merchandise within the political economy of contemporary sport, suggesting that, for example, the consumption of replica shirts (within soccer fan culture) is often 'misrecognised' as a symbol of a supporters' loyalty, whereas within what might be termed 'traditional' or 'authentic' fan cultures, the wearing of a replica shirt is often met with suspicion and derision, in that it is interpreted as a commodified act.

REFERENCES

Abercrombie, N. (1996) 'Cultural Values and Commodification: The Case of the Publishing Industry', in A. Godley and O.M. Westall (eds) *Business History and Business Culture*. Manchester: Manchester University Press. pp. 99–115.

Anderson, E. (1993) *Value in Ethics and Economics*. Cambridge, MA: Harvard University Press.

Brick, C. (2001) 'Anti-consumption or "New" Consumption? Commodification, Identity and "New Football"', in J. Horne (ed.) *Leisure Cultures, Consumption and Commodification*. Eastbourne: Leisure Studies Association. pp. 3–15.

Brick, C. (2004) 'Misers, Merchandise and Manchester United: The Peculiar Paradox of the Political Economy of Consumption', in D.L. Andrews (ed.) *Manchester United: A Thematic Study*. London: Routledge. pp. 101–11.

Critcher, C. (1979) 'Football Since the War', in J. Clarke, C. Critcher and R. Johnson (eds) *Working Class Culture: Studies in History and Theory*. London: Hutchinson. pp. 161–84.

Horne, J., Tomlinson, A. and Whannel, G. (1999) *Understanding Sport: An Introduction to the Sociological and Cultural Analysis of Sport*. London: E & FN Spon.

Jakubowski, F. (1990) *Ideology and Superstructure in Historical Materialism*. London: Pluto Press.

Jarvie, G. and Maguire, J. (1994) *Sport and Leisure in Social Thought*. London: Routledge.

Jones, C. (2003) 'The Traditional Football Fan: An Ethical Critique of a Selective Construction', *The Journal of the Philosophy of Sport*, 30(1): 37–50.

Kidd, B. (1981) 'Sport, Dependency, and the Canadian State', in M. Hart and S. Birrell (eds) *Sport in the Sociocultural Process*. Iowa: Brown. pp. 707–21.

Marx, K. (1983) *Capital: A Critique of Political Economy, Vol. 1*. London: Lawrence and Wishart.

Walsh, A. and Giulianotti, R. (2001) 'This Sporting Mammon: A Narrative Critique of the Commodification of Sport', *Journal of the Philosophy of Sport*, 28(1): 53–77.

Walsh, A. and Giulianotti, R. (2007) *Ethics, Money and Sport*. London: Routledge.

Whannel, G. (1994) 'Sport and Popular Culture: The Temporary Triumph of Process over Product', *Inovations*, 6: 341–50.

Williams, C.C. (2002) 'A Critical Evaluation of the Commodification Thesis', *Sociology Review*, 50(4): 525–42.

Žižek, S. (1989) *The Sublime Object of Ideology*. London: Verso.

Consumption

(see also Capitalism; Postmodernism)

Closely associated with the development of forms of consumer capitalism (the consumer society), the issue of consumption became an important area of sociological analysis during the 1960s (Burns, 1966). However, it is in the last decades of the twentieth century that consumption becomes a dominant ideological, political and sociological paradigm. Increasingly, social scientists, politicians and policy makers have begun to look at and understand consumption as the prime sphere or realm where, as individuals and as groups, we form identities and understand the society that we live in. This has in part been a consequence of the increasing influence of postmodern theory.

Postmodern theorists have suggested that, certainly since the Second World War, Western capitalism has shifted its central organisational locus away from production, towards consumption. Their general contention is that classical social theory, developed in the nineteenth century, is principally concerned with the character of early industrial capitalism, and the subsequent primacy given to production and the relations of production as the dynamics that shape and confer meaning upon society, no longer provide the necessary analytic nuance to understand the development of late capitalism (see **Capitalism; Postmodernism**). It is instead in the sphere of consumption that the sociologist can find the necessary insight into the contemporary nature of social division, inequality and conflict in capitalist societies. It is now through forms of consumption, as consumers rather than as producers, that social actors construct and authenticate their self-identity.

Postmodern theory emphasises that as subjects, we 'function as active agents in the construction of our identities, rather than responding automatically to the dynamics that act upon us' (Bradley, 1996: 212). As social actors, it is suggested, we now construct our identities from an ever increasing and changing palette of consumption patterns, choices and options around which we (de)construct and (in)authenticate our lifestyles (a term which itself emphasises the ways in which social structure is now influenced by the issue of consumption). As Burns suggested back in 1966, lifestyle has been a pronounced feature of the development of post-war capitalism:

> The general thesis suggested by the sociological study of consumer behaviour is that consumption is the expressive aspect of style of life, and that style of life has developed a much greater significance as a mode of organizing individual behaviour and leisure, careers and, therefore as a form of social structure. (Burns, 1966: 322, cited in Horne, 2001: v).

Burns' emphasis upon the role of lifestyle suggests that (post)modern consumption is about much more than simply the things that we buy and consume. Buying commodities is of course a central feature of a society premised upon the production of goods for profit, but the idea of a consumer society is representative of a major shift in how society functions and views itself. Fundamentally it is argued that the rise of lifestyle orientated consumption embodies the transformation from modernity to postmodernity. As Bocock (1993) suggests:

consumption

it implies a move away from productive work roles being central to people's lives, to their sense of identity, of who they are. In place of work roles it is roles in various kinds of family formations … in leisure time pursuits, in consumption in general, which have come to be seen as being more and more significant for people. (Bocock, 1993: 40)

Underlying this shift Zygmunt Bauman (1988) has suggested that a new consumer orientated ethic has replaced the traditional work ethic as the bedrock dynamic of capitalist societies. This is not to suggest that work has become less important – indeed the vast majority of us cannot survive without wage labour. Furthermore, capitalism itself as a social system is entirely dependent upon the wage labour–capital relationship. However, what Bauman does illustrate is the radical transformation at the level of social thought whereby consumption has replaced production as the paradigm by which society is understood, related to and functions. Bodies concerned with work and production (for instance, trade unions) have long been prominent among the collectivist institutions (other examples include church, education system, welfare state) by which the state has governed, and otherwise related to, the wider society. However, the movement from modernism to postmodernism has undermined these relationships. New institutional forms and arrangements are required, and increasingly these new forms are informed by the 'consumer ethic'. Political parties are now more likely to appeal to the electorate through individual rather than collective issues. Increasingly these issues are orientated around consumption and consumer behaviour. For example, the global issue of climate change is inextricably linked in public discourse to consumption. Our individual behaviour as consumers, and our lifestyles, have, it is suggested, a pronounced impact upon the environment.

The issue of consumption has become increasingly central to understanding the machinations of contemporary sport and leisure. As noted above, consumption, it is widely thought, has become the prime sphere via which we now form our identities, and topics related to consumption have become significant areas of research and theoretical development within the social and cultural study of sport in recent years (Horne, 2006). Issues of authenticity, group identity, inclusion/exclusion, gender and race are notable themes that are explored through the relationship between sport and consumption. These issues are particularly prevalent in sociological research on new and alternative sports, such as windsurfing, snowboarding and extreme sport (see e.g. Rinehart and Sydnor, 2003). Considered as being postmodern in nature, these sports are usually associated with forms of conspicuous consumption (Veblen, 2001, originally published 1899). Through his study of nine-teenth-century bourgeois American society, the American political economist Thorstein Veblen (1857–1929) notes the emergence of a new 'leisure class'. The significant feature of this new class, Veblen argues, is its utilisation of consumption as a primary source of status and privilege. For this section of American bourgeois society, wealth is expressed as a form of social power through their consumption of leisure. Although Veblen's use is specific to a particular section of nineteenth-century American society, the term 'conspicuous consumption' is now broadly applied to individuals, groups and patterns of consumerism, whereby consumption is predicated upon expressing aesthetic desire rather than material need, and since the 1960s the term has been associated with the general increase in consumerism and the emerging consumer society. 'Conspicuous consumption', in this sense, refers to the style in which participants consume sport as lifestyle and culture.

However, it would be wrong to simply associate the consumption of style and identity with 'postmodern' sport. Sports such as football (soccer) have a long sociological tradition in providing ample evi-dence and illustration of the emergence of style based consumer cultures (see e.g. Robins, 1984; Taylor, 1971). Writing of the devel-opment of British football after the Second World War, Chas Critcher (1979) notes the emerging patterns of consumerism that begin to dominate the relationship between the football supporter and the football club. Critcher suggests that the traditional relation-ship between the supporter and football club, 'an informal set of rec-iprocal duties and obligations' (Critcher, 1979: 170), is replaced by consumer orientated relationships motivated by market choice and best value, rather than loyalty. These developments flagged up by Critcher in 1979 have become key issues in modern sport as com-modification, commercialisation and consumerism have become increasingly prevalent (Crawford, 2004; Edwards, 2000; Horne, 2006). The cultures of soccer fandom that have emerged in late twentieth-century capitalism have wholeheartedly adopted patterns of stylised conspicuous consumption (see e.g. Brick 2001, 2004; Giulianotti, 1999, 2002), whereby the conscious orientation towards the consumption of soccer culture – where and how you consume, and with whom – have become central markers in the demarcation and development of notions of authenticity and inauthenticity.

REFERENCES

Bauman, Z. (1988) *Freedom*. Milton Keynes: Open University Press.

Bocock , R. (1993) *Consumption*. London: Routledge.

Bradley, H. (1996) *Fractured Identities*. Cambridge: Polity.

Brick, C. (2001) 'Anti-consumption or "New" Consumption? Commodification, Identity and "New" Football', in J. Horne (ed.) *Leisure Cultures, Consumption and Commodification*. Eastbourne: Leisure Studies Association. pp. 3–15.

Brick, C. (2004) 'Misers, Merchandise and Manchester United: The Peculiar Paradox of the Political Economy of Consumption', in D.L. Andrews (ed.) *Manchester United: A Thematic Study*. London: Routledge. pp. 101–12.

Burns, T. (1966) 'The Study of Consumer Behaviour: A Sociological View', *Archives Européennes de Sociologie*, VII: 313–29.

Crawford, G. (2004) *Consuming Sport: Fans, Sport and Culture*. Abingdon: Routledge.

Critcher, C. (1979) 'Football Since the War', in J. Clarke, C. Critcher and R. Johnson (eds) *Working Class Culture: Studies in History and Theory*. London: Hutchinson. pp. 161–84.

Edwards, T. (2000) *Contradictions of Consumption: Concepts, Practices and the Politics of Consumer Society*. Buckingham: Open University Press.

Giulianotti, R. (1999) *Football: Sociology of the Global Game*. Cambridge: Polity.

Giulianotti, R. (2002) 'Supporters, Fans, Followers and *Flaneurs*: A Taxonomy of Spectator Identities in World Football', *Journal of Sport and Social Issues*, 26(1): 25–46.

Horne, J. (ed.) (2001) *Leisure Cultures, Consumption and Commodification*. Eastbourne: Leisure Studies Association.

Horne, J. (2006) *Sport in Consumer Culture*. Basingstoke: Palgrave Macmillan.

Rinehart, R.E. and Sydnor, S. (2003) *To The Extreme: Alternative Sports Inside and Out*. Albany: SUNY.

Robins, D. (1984) *We Hate Humans*. Harmondsworth: Penguin.

Taylor, I. (1971) '"Football Mad": A Speculative Sociology of Soccer Hooliganism', in E. Dunning (ed.) *The Sociology of Sport*. London: Cass. pp. 352–77.

Veblen, T. (2001) *The Theory of the Leisure Class*. New York: The Modern Library. Originally published 1899.

Culture

This word is a deceptively flexible one, with a diversity of different meanings in the social sciences. The Penguin *Dictionary of Sociology* (Abercrombie et al., 2000: 83) identifies six discrete interpretations of the term, four of which can serve as a framework for relating the concept to sport.

First, 'culture' can be seen to refer to every aspect of human behaviour that is not derived from biology – that is, in other words, *learned.* The standard contention of sociologists (and others) is, of course, that most human behaviour is rooted in culture and not in biology and, to a significant degree, they may be thought to have won this argument. That's to say, whereas in the nineteenth and early twentieth centuries, a majority of scientists believed that human behaviour was largely biological in origin, today only a small and marginalised minority holds this view. This, as we have seen elsewhere in this book, is due in large part to the historic campaigns against sexism (the feminist movement) and racism. Sport has been an important arena for these struggles and for the clinching of some of these arguments. Sport, for example, has historically been a theatre in which women could refute biological theories and, to an extent, gain control over their own bodies (Hargreaves, 1992). Similarly, sport has been a means to combating racism. For instance, the campaign for a black captain of the West Indies cricket team ran in tandem with the nationalist independence movement in the Caribbean, both being manifestations of the same emancipatory impulse (Beckles, 1998: 74–8). To be sure, as we have also seen, battles continue to be fought over the biology/culture (or nature/nurture) divide in relation to sport – particularly, as discussed elsewhere in this book, over the purported genetic advantages of black athletes.

Secondly, culture has often been taken to refer to 'civilisation', excellence and high art. The distinction between 'high' and 'mass' or 'popular' culture was strong in Western societies until the 1960s and its vital importance was stressed in British intellectual life by, among others, the Cambridge English lecturer and cultural critic F.R. Leavis (see e.g. Dean, n.d.). At a time when such high culture could be readily identified (classical music, ballet, opera, the plays of Shakespeare and the novels of D.H. Lawrence, the paintings of Picasso, and so on) sport was, in general, excluded, although there were exceptions. Cricket, for instance, had cultural credibility among the British intelligentsia, and two of its most famous chroniclers – Neville Cardus (1889–1975) and John Arlott (1914–1991) – worked in the arts, Cardus as a music critic and Arlott as a poetry producer for the BBC. Nowadays, it is widely accepted that the culture of human societies has become globalised and 'postmodern', and one of the acknowledged fundaments of postmodern culture is the collapse of any distinction between 'high' and 'low' culture. In writing about postmodern culture this is frequently referred to as 'de-differentiation' (see e.g. Featherstone, 1993). One consequence of this is that sport has become pervasive in national cultures and a recurrent feature of public discourse – with politicians, for example, ever anxious to proclaim their loyalty to a football or a baseball team. Thus the terms 'sportisation' (see e.g. Maguire, 1999) and 'footballisation' have become current among sociologists and cultural commentators.

Thirdly, especially in the functionalist theory (see e.g. Parsons, 1951) which dominated American sociology in the 1950s, culture was seen as a kind of binding agent which held social structures together. This notion is inherent in the idea of 'national sports' and as been explored from a functionalist perspective by writers such as Janet Lever (1995) in relation to Brazilian football.

Fourthly, in Marxist theory, culture is contrasted with the material or economic. It is the realm of ideas, beliefs and practices. Plainly, in contemporary societies, Marxists would see sport as belonging in both these sectors, since it is both a social world in which identities and values are made and affirmed as well as being an important part of the global economy. Indeed, the revenue of the world's top sport governing bodies – FIFA and the IOC – now comfortably exceeds that of a number of the world's poorer countries: in 1992 the then President of FIFA, João Havelange declared himself 'the democratically elected head of one of the most powerful states on earth – football' (Wagg, 1995: 180).

The use of the term 'culture' in the study of sport can be extended into other important areas. One entails the idea of 'cultural capital' – a concept devised by the French sociologist Pierre Bourdieu (1930–2002). In his most famous work *Distinction* (1984; see also Tomlinson, 2004: 161–72), Bourdieu proposes a number of different types of capital – *economic* (the ownership of wealth), *social* (access to social networks), *symbolic* (reputation or social honour) and *cultural* (qualifications – usually educational – and forms of socially useful knowledge). It is not difficult to see how sport could be an important source of cultural capital and, as such, could provide access to the other three forms of capital. Top sportspeople today can make a great deal of economic capital and, given the collapse of the distinction between high and low/popular culture this will likely bring with it both social and symbolic capital. This is not guaranteed: in Britain, for instance, wealthy footballers can be derided for their taste in houses or marriage partners – the theme of the ITV drama *Footballers' Wives* (2002–6). Alternatively, particular forms of cultural capital – the ability to play polo, for instance, allied to a string of ponies or a respectable golf handicap – could be particularly profitable in the acquisition of symbolic capital. As long ago as the late 1950s the American sociologist C. Wright Mills was complaining that in the United States 'a man who can knock a small white ball into a series of holes with more skill and efficiency than anyone else thereby gains social access to the President of the United States' (1956: 74). There is also the vexed question of *cultural imperialism*. The debate over cultural imperialism is, at the same time, a debate about globalisation and popular culture and it has various dimensions. In essence, the argument for cultural imperialism is as follows: Western nations – chiefly Britain and the United States – have successfully exported their cultural forms to the other countries of the world – in particular, those of the 'developing world' – and have thereby helped to obliterate indigenous cultures: this is the issue that the eminent sociologist Stuart Hall (1997) calls 'the West and the Rest'. The history of sport seems to lend powerful support to this argument: after all, all countries of the world now engage in sports – be it association football, tennis, athletics, golf, horse racing, etc. – that originated in Britain, while the distribution of other sports such as cricket and rugby football is clearly contoured by the old British Empire. (One broad strand of the cultural imperialism thesis – that the world is increasingly subject to 'Americanisation' is less applicable to sport, since the United States tends to embrace as national sports games such as gridiron football, baseball and basketball, none of which is widely played internationally. The argument for Americanisation, therefore, seems more viable is relation to the international currency of TV programmes, films, popular music and 'junk' food, such as burgers.) While it is true that modern sports of British origin have tended to gain a global dominance and, although polo and snooker originated in India, very few forms of sport have flowed in the opposite direction, the argument over cultural imperialism has, predictably, become more complex.

One of the biggest difficulties is that, in an increasingly globalised world – one, in other words, in which national boundaries are of decreasing significance – discrete national cultures are, inevitably, harder to define. There are other problems, many of them identified by the American academic Allen Guttmann. In his book *Games and Empires* (1994), Guttmann argues, with Edward Said, that 'The history of all cultures is the history of cultural borrowing'. Moreover, he points out that modern sports help to bind together otherwise divided societies (Sugden and Bairner, 2000). Similarly, apologists for empire will proffer what might be called the *Life of Brian* or 'What have the Romans ever done for us?' argument – namely that empires bring benefits which colonial peoples, once independent, would not wish to discard. So with sport: it may have been brought by invaders, but former colonies would not want to abandon it on that ground. In any event, these sports were not imposed quite in the way that other aspects of colonial rule were imposed. On the contrary, colonial populations invariably embraced these sports in the hope, among other things, of beating the colonial masters at their own game – as with cricket in the British Empire. Here Trevor Burton has argued for a 'creolisation' of the game, whereby cricket was made by black West Indians 'to embody the counter-values of aggression, reputation and individualism that govern street culture' (Burton, 2003: 25). Guttmann, therefore, rejects the notion of cultural imperialism and prefers to talk of *cultural hegemony* and of *ludic diffusion*, the latter term meaning simply 'the spread of games'.

Another important and related area of debate concerns 'McDonaldisation' – a term coined by the American sociologist George Ritzer (2004) to refer to a perceived process by which more and more sectors of social and economic life around the world come to be organised on the same principles as McDonalds, the global fast food chain. These principles were set down by Frederick Taylor (1915), an American writer on 'scientific management' in the early 1900s, and they represent a standardisation and rationalisation of procedures, designed to maximise productivity. Has there been a McDonaldisation of sport? Here, once again, there is no simple reply. Certainly, we have seen a growing marketisation and commodification of sport (one only has to think of the Olympics) but, as the sociologist John Horne observes, 'efforts to use successful sports clubs to make money may come up against stiff opposition if they conflict with the social and cultural values associated with the teams' – an argument that may be illustrated by the recent takeovers by wealthy business people of several Premiership football clubs (Horne, 2006: 14). On the other hand, a good deal of standardisation seems to be taking place in global sport: players, coaches and athletes move from country to country and it is arguable that they are coming to form a global technocracy, founded on rationality and intolerant of local or national differences. We have entered the era, for example, of the 'laptop coach', using science to procure maximal outcomes.

REFERENCES

Abercrombie, Nicholas, Hill, Stephen and Turner, Bryan S. (2000) *Dictionary of Sociology*. London: Penguin.

Beckles, Hilary McD. (1998) *The Development of West Indies Cricket, Vol.1: The Age of Nationalism*. London: Pluto Press.

Bourdieu, Pierre (1984) *Distinction: A Social Critique of the Judgment of Taste*. London: Routledge and Kegan Paul.

Burton, Trevor D.E. (2003) 'Cricket, Carnival and Street Culture in the Caribbean' in Grant Jarvie (ed.) *Sport, Racism and Ethnicity*. London: Falmer Press. pp. 5–22.

Dean, Paul (n.d.) 'The Last Critic? The Importance of F.R. Leavis', http://newcriterion. com/archive/14/jan96/dean.htm

Featherstone, Mike (1993) *Consumer Culture and Postmodernism*. London: Sage.

Guttmann, Allen (1994) Games and Empires. New York: Columbia University Press.

Hall, Stuart (1997) 'The West and the Rest: Discourse and Power', in Stuart Hall and Bram Gieben (eds) *Formations of Modernity*. Cambridge: Polity Press, with the Open University Press. pp. 275–332.

Hargreaves, Jennifer (1992) *Sporting Females*. London: Routledge.

Horne, John (2006) *Sport in Consumer Culture*. Basingstoke: Palgrave Macmillan.

Lever, Janet (1995) *Soccer Madness: Brazil's Passion for the World's Most Popular Sport*. Long Grove, IL: Waveland Press.

Maguire, Joseph (1999) *Global Sport: Identities, Societies, Civilisations*. Cambridge: Polity Press.

Mills, C. Wright (1956) *The Power Elite*. New York: Oxford University Press.

Parsons, Talcott (1951) *The Social System*. London: Routledge and Kegan Paul.

Ritzer, George (2004) *The McDonaldization of Society*. London: Pine Forge Press.

Sugden, John and Bairner, Alan (eds) (2000) *Sport in Divided Societies*. Aachen: Meyer and Meyer.

Taylor, Frederick (1915) *The Principles of Scientific Management*. New York: Harper and Brothers.

Tomlinson, Alan (2004) 'Pierre Bourdieu and the Sociological Study of Sport: Habitus, Capital and Field' in Richard Giulianotti (ed.) *Sport and Modern Social Theorists*. Basingstoke: Palgrave Macmillan. pp. 161–72.

Wagg, Stephen (1995) 'The Business of America: Reflections on World Cup '94', in Stephen Wagg (ed.) *Giving the Game Away: Football, Politics and Culture on Five Continents*. London: Leicester University Press. pp. 179–99.

FURTHER READING

Bairner, Alan (2001) *Sport, Nationalism and Globalization: European and North American Perspectives*. Albany: State University of New York Press.

Guttmann, Allen (1994) *Games and Empires*. New York: Columbia University Press.

Tomlinson, John (1991) *Cultural Imperialism*. London: Pinter.

culture

37

Discourse and
Post-Structuralism

(see also Postmodernism; Semiotics)

DISCOURSE

In its most literal sense discourse is a form of communication that runs back and forth. Within social analysis, discourse, or discourse analysis, is the study of the processes of communication and the construction of meanings. The analysis of discourse has become a prominent, multi-methodological approach within the contemporary social sciences (Howarth, 2000), and has its roots in a number of theoretical traditions, most notably structuralist (Barthes, 1973; Levi-Strauss 1968, 1977; Saussure, 1974) and post-structuralist (see e.g. Derrida, 1982; Foucault, 1982) reactions to positivistic perceptions of the social world. The study of discourse focuses primarily upon the role of, and relations between, language, social structures and forms of social action and agency. However, given its theoretical diversity there is no single definitional approach to discourse. For example, in semantics, discourses are generally considered as linguistic units such as conversations, arguments or speeches. Other approaches do not confine discourse to spoken or written forms of language, but extend it to non-verbal forms of communication, and as we shall see in relation to post-structuralist approaches to discourse, the analysis of institutionalized frameworks which confer boundaries upon what can and can not be said. In this sense discourse theorists are particularly interested in the socially constructed nature of truth and the discursive formations that make up our perceptions of objective reality.

Some approaches foreground the role of linguistics and semiotics in shaping the world and how we perceive it. For instance Tonkis defines discourse as 'the study of language and texts as forms of *discourses* which help to create and reproduce systems of social meaning' (1998: 245, original emphasis). However, for other approaches, notably those framed within post-structuralist points of reference, discourse is not simply a linguistic exercise, and not just concerned with how linguistic rules influence the construction and structured meanings of particular statements. Foucualt suggests that:

> The question asked by linguistic analysis, concerning a discursive act, is always: According to what rules has this statement been constituted and consequently. According to what rules could similar statements be constructed? The description of discourse asks a different question: How is it that this statement appeared, rather than some other in its place? (1998: 307)

As Foucault proposes above, post-structuralist approaches to discourse focus upon the problematic question of what rules allow particular statements or meanings to appear in the first place, either de-legitimating or preventing others from appearing in their place. In this sense, discourse is as much about what has not been said, as it is about what has been.

POST-STRUCTURALISM

Post-structuralism is the name given to a key set of intellectual developments and reactions within France during the 1960s, and is often referred to as 'continental philosophy'. Key theorists of post-structuralist theory include Jacques Derrida (1930–2004) and Michel Foucault (1926–1984) (however it should be noted that the term post-structuralist is often applied by others to their work and is not necessarily adopted by the theorists themselves). In short, post-structuralism represents a reaction to the structuralist claim that the constituent elements of a 'sign' – the 'signifier' and the 'signified' – are independent of each other (see **Semiotics**). Within the reconfiguration and re-conceptualisation of the relationship between the signified and signifier, post-structuralism rejects knowledge claims to absolute truth, considering meaning and the central concept of the 'self' or self contained subject as a fiction, constructed through 'subjectifying symbolic systems' of produced meaning or truths (Andrews, 2002: 113).

In his authoritative overview of the emergence of post-structuralist influences within the sociology of sport, David Andrews notes Sturrock's important observation that, 'post-structuralism is not "post" in the sense of having killed structuralism off, it is "post" only in the sense of coming after and of seeking to extend structuralism in its right-ful direction' (Sturrock, 1986: 158, cited in Andrews, 2002: 113).

The post-structuralist claim that 'There is nothing outside of the text' (Derrida, 1976: 158) or the Foucaldian version that there is nothing out-side discourse is predicated and expands upon the emphasis Ferdinand de Saussure (1857–1913) places upon the role of discourse in the develop-ment of his structural theory of semiotics (see **Semiotics**). Post-structuralism represents a development upon structuralist approaches to discourse in that, as already noted above, it begins with the premise that there is no stable relationship between the signified and the signifier (i.e. no rooted foundation or structure of meaning). Instead the relationship is always fluid and constantly shifting, as meaning is itself always shifting and unstable. It is in this respect that post-structuralism according to Andrews (2002: 108), should not be overly identified with the development of post-modernist social theory (see **Postmodernism**). Although post-structuralist thought and theorists have been readily identified as important influences within the rise of postmodern thought, Andrews suggests 'The focus of post-structuralism would thus appear to oscillate between modern, late modern and indeed postmodern conjunctures' (Andrews, 2002: 108). Post-structuralism then does not seek to construct itself as a theoretical alternative to modernist conceptions of social reality, as postmodernism does, rather post-structuralism's subject is the very construction of the notion of the modern itself, in its modernist, late and postmodernist con-ceptualizations. The means by which it does this is through discourse.

DIFFÉRENCE AND DISCOURSE

Saussure's linguistic theory introduces the concept of difference as a key factor within the relationship between signifier and signified. However Jacques Derrida considered Saussure's development of this relationship to be incomplete and, as such, flawed. In response to Saussure, Derrida (1982) reconceptualises difference as *différence* – a conflation of the Latin verb *differe*, and its two associated meanings; *to differ*, that is not to be identical; and *to defer*, 'to temporize, to take recourse … a detour that suspends the accomplishment' (Derrida, 1982: 8, cited in Andrews, 2002: 114). Through the emphasis upon *différence*, Derrida underlines the post-structuralist premise that 'meaning' is not explicit in the act of signification, in that the sign can only be represented through what it is not. In this sense our understanding of 'meaning' (or truth) has always to include non-meaning, that is what it is not, its substantive otherness. Because of the unstable nature of the unity of the *signifier* and *signified* (the sign) this *différence*, ensures that the ability of the objective reality (or meaning) of the sign to reveal itself fully is always deferred. As such, meaning, if present at all, appears only as a fleeting fragment or trace.

POST-STRUCTURALIST SPORT

Post-structuralism, despite being a 'constant feature of contemporary intellectual life' (Andrews, 2002: 106) has only recently begun to exert influence within the social and cultural study of sport. Andrews suggests that there has been on the whole a 'perplexing mixture of defensive dismissal and haughty disdain by large sections of the sociology of sport community' (Andrews, 2002: 107), which has in part tended to cling to the 'institutional and ideological' formations of modernity, of which sport was such an obvious product (Andrews, 2002: 107).

However, Andrews (2002) continues, due to the seemingly terminal nature of modernity's contemporary crisis, and a heightened awareness, within the sociology of sport, amongst a new generation of researchers, of the limits of established theoretical paradigms, post-structural approaches have attained a position whereby they offer a substantive challenge to the established schools of thought within the discipline (Andrews, 2002: 107).

From the outset post-structuralism challenges sport's implicit relationship to modernity, which as Andrews suggests involves the development of readings of sport which both subvert and go beyond 'the oppressive, symbolically violent and exclusionary vices of its modern incarnations' (Andrews, 2002: 116). Here Andrews is pointing to what he considers the essence of post-structuralist thought in relation to sport, which problematises the embedded nature of sport within the project of modernity. As such he suggests the goal of post-structuralist analysis is in fact 'Post-Sport', in that the interrogation of the experience and structures of modern sport lead to the inescapable conclusion that 'the uncritical belief in the possibility of progress as expressed through the sporting cannot be upheld with the plausibility or conviction it once possessed' (Andrews, 2002: 116). Post-structuralist analyses thus 'make "accessible to sight" the "not seen" (Derrida, 1976: 163) aspects of contemporary sport culture, and thereby illuminate the contradictions, corruptions and coercions that fester beneath the common-sense fetishising of sport within the late modern era' (Andrews, 2002: 116).

As a consequence post-structuralist influenced research has been largely successful in the reorientation of focus of sports analysis to areas such as the body, sexuality, identity, consumerism and the construction and deployment of systems of knowledge as technologies of discipline and control (Andrews, 2002: 229). The theorist, who has had most influence in shaping the sociology of sport's post-structuralist turn, has without doubt been Michel Foucault. Despite an initial under-representation of Foucauldian discourse within the sociology of sport compared to other areas of academic and intellectual social investigation (Andrews, 1993; Rail and Harvey, 1995), there is now a substantial body of work by scholars within the sociology of sport, who have utilised Foucault's approach to discourse (see e.g. Bridel and Rail, 2007; Helstein, 2007; Johns and Johns, 2000; Markula, 2004; Pringle, 2005; Shogan, 2002). Undoubtedly Foucault's influence is most evident in the study of the sporting body (see Andrews, 1993; Rail and Harvey, 1995). Andrews (2004: 121) suggests that Foucault's focus upon the body makes his work most readily applicable to the analysis of sport. Foucault emphasises the constructed nature of the human body, which is not simply a biological or physical fact, but the result of the technologies of power, discipline and knowledge that are formed through discourse. Given its implicit emphasis upon the physical, and the biological, sport provides a key expression of the discursive nature of power symptomatic of late modern social relations and culture.

REFERENCES

Andrews, D.L. (1993) 'Desperately Seeking Michel: Foucault's Genealogy, the Body, and Critical Sport Sociology', *Sociology of Sport Journal*, 10(2): 148–67.

Andrews, D.L. (2002) 'Posting Up: French Post-Structuralism and the Critical Analysis of Contemporary Sporting Culture', in J. Coakley and E. Dunning (eds) *Handbook of Sports Studies*. London: Sage. pp. 106–37.

Barthes, R. (1973) *Mythologies*. London: Paladin.

Bridel, W. and Rail, G. (2007) 'Sport, Sexuality, and the Production of (Resistant) Bodies: De-/Re-Constructing the Meanings of Gay Male Marathon Corporeality', *Sociology of Sport Journal*, 24(2): 127–44.

Derrida, J. (1976) *Of Grammatology*. Baltimore, MD: Johns Hopkins University Press.

Derrida, J. (1982) *Margins of Philosophy*. Chicago: University of Chicago.

Foucault, M. (1982) 'The Subject of Power', in H.L. Dreyfus and P. Rabinow (eds) *Michel Foucault: Beyond Structuralism and Hermeneutics*. Brighton: Harvester Press. pp. 208–26.

Foucualt, M. (1998) 'On the Archaeology of the Sciences: Response to the Epistemology Circle', in F.D Faubion (ed.) *Michel Foucault: Aesthetics. Essential Works of Foucault 1954–1984, Vol 2*. London: Penguin. pp. 297–333.

Helstein, M.T. (2007) 'Seeing Your Sporting Body: Identity, Subjectivity, and Misrecognition', *Sociology of Sport Journal*, 24(1): 78–103.

Howarth, D. (2000) *Discourse*. Buckingham: Open University.

Johns, D.P. and Johns, J.S. (2000) 'Surveillance, Subjectivism and Technologies of Power: An Analysis of the Discursive Practice of High-Performance Sport', *International Review for the Sociology of Sport*, 35(2): 219–34.

Levi-Strauss, C. (1968) *Structural Anthropology. Vol 1*. Harmondsworth: Penguin.

Levi-Strauss, C. (1977) *Structural Anthroplogy. Vol 2*. Harmondsworth: Penguin.

Markula, P. (2004) '"Turning into One's Self": Foucault's Technologies of the Self and Mindful Fitness', *Sociology of Sport Journal*, 21(3): 302–21.

Pringle, R. (2005) 'Masculinities, Sport and Power: A Critical Comparison of Gramscian and Foucauldian Inspired Theoretical Tools', *Journal of Sport and Social Issues*, 29(3): 256–78.

Rail, G. and Harvey, J. (1995) 'Body at Work: Michel Foucault and the Sociology of Sport', *Sociology of Sport Journal*, 12(2): 164–79.

Saussure, F. de (1974) *Course in General Linguistics*. London: Fontana.

Shogan, D. (2002) 'Characterizing Constraints of Leisure: A Foucaltian Analysis of Leisure Constraints', *Leisure Studies*, 21: 27–38.

Sturrock, J. (1986) *Structuralism*. London: Fontana.

Tonkis, F. (1998) 'Analysing Discourse', in C. Seale (ed.) *Researching Society and Culture*. London: Sage. pp. 245–60.

Doping/Drugs

In sport, as in the wider world, these terms carry a specific meaning which is both pejorative and misleading. People who are said to 'take drugs' or, worse still, to 'deal drugs' are invariably thought to be an affront to decent society. Sociologists who have investigated the 'drug culture' are thought, for the sake of their research, to have walked, however briefly, on the wild side. But modern societies *are*, in effect, drug cultures. Most of us visit the doctor and, when we do, we can expect to be prescribed drugs. Huge trans-national companies exist to deal drugs. This is respectable, however, because it is done for medical purposes – to eradicate illness, injury and discomfort and to ease pain. Some drugs are permissible, and some are not. A medical case can be made for cannabis, for example, although it is illegal in most contemporary societies. But drugs, per se, are not an issue. Sports culture reflects this. Athletes of the modern age take a great many substances into their bodies in pursuit of excellence and success. Sociologists such as Ivan Waddington now speak of the 'medicalisation of sport' and Waddington cites the observation of Sir Arthur Porritt, President of the Royal College of Surgeons and a former Olympic sprinter, in the early 1960s that 'those who take part in sport and play games are essentially *patients*' (Waddington, 2000: 123–4, emphasis added). But, as in the wider society, sport authorities proscribe some of the substances that may be administered to these 'patients' and permit others.

A report on drugs in sport by the British Medical Association in 2002 quotes the IOC definition of doping[1] as follows:

> the use of an expedient (substance or method) which is potentially harmful to athletes' health and capable of enhancing their performance, or the presence in the athlete's body of a prohibited substance or evidence of use thereof, or evidence of the use of a prohibited method. (BMA, 2002: 2)

A cursory glance at this definition shows: (a) that it applies not only to drugs, but to 'methods'; (b) that it is based partly on the notion of enhancing performance; (c) that it rests also on the criterion of potential harm; and (d) that, in the main, it states 'doping' simply to be practices which are banned. Indeed, the BMA go on to suggest that a

> universally accepted definition of a 'performance-enhancing' drug remains elusive. The term may be potentially misleading or restrictive in scope. Sports people may use drugs for a number of reasons other than for performance enhancement, including for legitimate therapeutic use, performance continuation or recreational/social use. Those who fail drug tests may not have intended to cheat. Hence, the IOC list of banned substances and methods includes prohibited substances and methods that may be taken or used by the athletes to enhance, maintain or restore performance. (BMA, 2002: 2)

That is to say, the distinction between practices defined as doping and practices defined as permissible in the day-to-day business of being an athlete is quite arbitrary and, thus, difficult to make. Moreover, official discourse about doping assumes that there is such a thing as a 'natural' body and not, as sociologists are inclined to argue now, that the body is an 'open text', constantly being reconstituted by fitness regimes, training programmes and the like.

The BMA report, like much of the literature on doping/drugs in sport, concentrates on the efficiency and possible improvement of anti-doping procedures. This constitutes one of the main emphases in the literature, the other being to 'set out the facts', be it in the realm of the 'hard science' of doping (see e.g. Mottram, 2005), of the legalities of the matter (see e.g. O'Leary, 2001) or its politics (Wilson and Derse, 2001). Sociologists, in continuing to question the concept of doping itself, have contributed considerably to literature and debates in the latter category. Questioning of the concept, in turn, draws on the history, in particular, of the Olympic movement but also of stimulants in sport more generally. These historical accounts seem agreed, regardless of their provenance, that the consumption of substances by athletes in the hope of a consequent improvement in their performance goes back to ancient times – certainly to ancient Greek games (see e.g. BMA, 2002: 5–6; Waddington, 2000: 98–9). We can say, then, that the taking of 'performance-enhancing drugs' is older than modern sport and, in effect, as old as sport itself. For the greater part of that time, these ingestions have not been seen as a problem – social, political or legal.

The emergence of 'drugs in sport' as an issue in these terms did not occur until after the Second World War when it began to be discussed among physicians who were attached to sporting bodies and teams. It seems to have surfaced in the Olympic movement – undoubtedly its main theatre – around 1960. Certainly, in their chronology of the drugs issue in the Olympic movement, the American academics Jan Todd and Terry Todd begin with the session of the International Olympic Committee in San Francisco that year, when the use of 'pep pills' was debated (Todd and Todd, 2001). The same year Danish cyclist Knud Jensen fell off his cycle during a road race in the Rome Olympics and died of a fractured skull. He was found to have used a blood stimulant. This was the first death in the Olympics since the tournament of 1912 in Stockholm and, as the Todds and other writers have shown, official concern about doping grew in IOC circles through the 1960s. Random testing took place for the first time in an Olympic tournament at Mexico City in 1968. Since that time other sports organisations have followed suit, testing has in general become more rigorous and the dominant discourse on the topic of doping has been on whether it is killing this sport or that and whether testing procedures can be strengthened. But sociologists are more concerned to ask why these tests were introduced in the first place.

Formally speaking, drawing both on the principal literature and on the above definition rendered by the IOC, tests were instituted for two reasons: to protect athletes and to ensure fair competition (Black, 1996, quoted in Waddington, 2000: 97). But, given that the activity today styled as 'doping' is, as we've seen, as old as modern sport itself, why the sudden upsurge of concern in the 1960s to protect athletes and ideals of competition? This question is given added impetus by recent arguments that Jensen's death was not doping-related, while accepting that it did act as a catalyst for the strengthening of anti-doping policy (Møller, 2005).

A number of factors provoked sport's purported, and comparatively recent, 'war on drugs'.

First, there had been a shift in the scientific assumptions upon which the training of athletes was carried out. Until the 1950s, as Rob Beamish and Ian Ritchie (2005a) point out, the key assumption here was one of 'fixed human capacities'. This meant that, when athletes used stimulants, it was assumed that they were making the maximum use of their capacities. From the 1950s, it was increasingly thought that such stimulants could *enlarge these capacities themselves*. Moreover, as the same two writers have observed, changes in scientific thinking fed changes in political ideology and propaganda. Leading politicians and spokespeople in the West believed that Hitler's Third Reich had used steroids to bolster the physique and aggressiveness of German troops during the Second World War. Once this war was over, and the Cold War between the United States and the Soviet Union had begun (circa 1950), these fears were transposed onto communists (Beamish and Ritchie, 2005b). A special anxiety centred on the muscular appearance of East European female athletes in the early Cold War Olympiads (the USSR participated for the first time at Helsinki in 1952) and another powerful impulse for drug testing at Olympic tournaments is likely to have come from the United States Olympic Committee, mindful of the national prestige at stake. The anxiety here can only have been heightened by the fact that the Rome Olympiad of 1960 was the first to be televised in the United States.

There was also an important gender dimension to this new political wrangle over sport and drugs. The American lesbian writer Patricia Nell Warren has written:

Unencumbered by 'decadent Western' notions that femininity meant being as beautiful, sexy and soft as a movie star, a Soviet woman could glory in her physical strength, her muscles, her sweat and manual skills, in a way that many American women were reluctant to do. The average American, however, lived in a system where religious beliefs that 'women are weaker', that 'women shouldn't do men's work' still had their own powerful influence. (Warren, n.d.)

In Warren's view these cultural anxieties powered the belief that East European governments were using drugs effectively to transform women into men. Thus, from 1968 onward, Olympic testing for drugs often now entailed testing for gender. This testing took various forms, but invariably involved examining an athlete's chromosomal make-up. Thirteen women 'failed' the test between 1972 and 1984. These tests were finally abandoned in 1999, prior to the Sydney Olympics. Warren's arguments were part of a vigorous critique triggered by dope-testing, in which writers argued that the testing not only affirmed narrow Western notions of femininity, but expressed a wider politics of the body: it enforced a shallow and misleadingly dichotomous model of the human body (insisting that it had to be straightforwardly 'male' or 'female') and it stigmatised lesbians. Rebecca Ann Lock, for example, wrote in 2003 that the politics of doping were such as to affirm what the American philosopher Judith Butler has called the 'heterosexual matrix' – a set of widely assumed links between sex, gender, sexuality and desire. Lock suggests that female athletes suspected of taking banned substances usually attracted the same range of stigmatising labels as lesbians and other women who don't conform to the ideals of heterosexual femininity. In a telling example, Lock points out that when the American athlete Florence Griffith Joyner ('Flo Jo') was suspected of taking drugs, her previously admired femininity was denied: 'In 1984 in Los Angeles', said one critic, 'Florence was an extremely feminine person. Today she looks and runs more like a man than a woman. She must be doing something not normal to break these records' (Joachim Cruz, quoted in Lock, 2003: 405). Conversely, at her death in 1998, obituaries seem to see Joyner's glamour as mitigation of her widely suspected drug offences (Lock, 2003: 407).

Powerful academic voices still speak out against doping. Most notable among sociological writers is the American cultural critic John Hoberman, whose book *Mortal Engines* (1992) is a critique not just of drugs in sport, but of elite modern sport itself. However, it seems likely that, sometime in the twenty-first century, the political and philosophical case for anti-doping may collapse. One reason for this is that athletes are increasingly inclined to refuse the protection that anti-doping is supposed to offer them. Dr Vivienne Nathanson, Head of Ethics at the British Medical Association said in 2004:

> There are some very frightening bits of research which show that if you talk to people aspiring to be elite athletes and you say to them 'If we could give you a drug which would guarantee that you'd win a gold medal at the Olympics but you'd be dead within five years, would you do it?', the majority would say 'yes'. (Interview with Kenan Malik, *Analysis*: *Tainted Gold*, BBC Radio 4, 4 January)

Moreover, sociologists are increasingly of the view that there is no such thing as a 'natural' human body and that drugs are simply one of a long series of technological interventions in the matter of sport performance. British sociologist, Ellis Cashmore argues:

> If, for example, we turn the clock back and look at the time when spikes were introduced, for example, there was a hue and cry over it. People said hang on, you can't run in spikes, that's giving you an unfair advantage over the competitors who run in flats. (Interview with Kenan Malik, *Analysis*: *Tainted Gold*, 4 January 2004; see also Cashmore, 2000: *189–218*)

Thirdly, if major tournaments are increasingly perceived and consumed as a *spectacle* – and the assumption must be that they are – then public opinion may be decreasingly concerned with how that spectacle was contrived (see e.g. Møller, 2004).

NOTE

1. The BMA are quoting the IOC Medical Commission's *Olympic Movement Anti-doping Code* of 1999.

REFERENCES

Beamish, Rob and Ritchie, Ian (2005a) 'From Fixed Capacities to Performance Enhancement: The Paradigm Shift in the Science of "Training" and the Use of Performance-Enhancing Substances', *Sport in History*, 25(3): 412–33.

Beamish, Rob and Ritchie, Ian (2005b) 'The Spectre of Steroids: Nazi Propaganda. Cold War Anxiety and Patriarchal Paternalism', *International Journal of the History of Sport*, 22(5): 777–95.

Black, Terry (1996) 'Does the Ban on Drugs in Sport Improve Societal Welfare?', *International Review of the Sociology of Sport*, 31(4): 367–84.

British Medical Association (BMA) (2002) *Drugs in Sport: The Pressure to Perform*. London: BMJ Books.

Cashmore, Ellis (2000) *Making Sense of Sports*. London: Routledge.

Hoberman, John (1992) *Mortal Engines: The Science of Performance and the Dehumanization of Sport*. New York: The Free Press.

Lock, Rebecca Ann (2003) 'The Doping Ban: Compulsory Heterosexuality and Lesbophobia', *International Review of the Sociology of Sport*, 38(4): 397–411.

Møller, Verner (2004) 'Doping and the Olympic Games from an Aesthetic Perspective', in John Bale and Mette Krogh Christensen (eds) *Post-Olympism? Questioning Sport in the Twenty First Century*. Oxford: Berg. pp. 201–10.

Møller, Verner (2005) 'Knud Enemark Jensen's Death During the 1960 Rome Olympics: A Search for Truth?', *Sport in History*, 25(3): 452–71.

Mottram, David R. (ed.) (2005) *Drugs in Sport* (4th edn). London: Routledge.

O'Leary, John (ed.) (2001) *Drugs and Doping in Sport: Socio-Legal Perspectives*. London: Cavendish Publishing.

Todd, Jan and Todd, Terry (2001) 'Significant Events in the History of Drug Testing in the Olympic Movement: 1960–1999' in Wayne Wilson and Edward Derse (eds) *Doping in Elite Sport: The Politics of Drugs in the Olympic Movement*. Champaign, IL: Human Kinetics. pp. 65–128.

Waddington, Ivan (2000) *Sport, Health and Drugs: A Critical Sociological Perspective*. London: Routledge.

Warren, Patricia Nell (n.d.) 'The Rise and Fall of Gender Testing', http://lesbi.gay.md/eng/story.php?sid=13 (accessed: 26 March 2007).

Wilson, Wayne and Derse, Edward (eds) (2001) *Doping in Elite Sport: The Politics of Drugs in the Olympic Movement*. Champaign, IL: Human Kinetics.

FURTHER READING

Hoberman, John (1992) *Mortal Engines: The Science of Performance and the Dehumanization of Sport*. New York: The Free Press.

Sport in History (2005) Special Issue on Drug Use in Sport, 25(3) December.

Waddington, Ivan (2000) *Sport, Health and Drugs: A Critical Sociological Perspective*. London: Routledge.

doping/drugs

Ethics

The application and study of ethics to sporting contexts has been one of the most prolific areas of intellectual activity in recent years. The growing importance and influence of commercial interests and the changing importance of sport within wider society have obliged both academics and administrators to address fundamental issues about the values associated with, and expressed by, sporting practices and practitioners. Key issues here include: values; fairness and fair play; equality; exploitation; violence, injury and risk; doping and drugs; and human rights (see e.g. Loland et al., 2006; McFee, 2004; Miah, 2004).

Although often used interchangeably with the term *morality* in modern everyday usage, *ethics* refers to the ways in which morals (universal codes or principles of right conduct) are understood and studied. According to McNamee and Parry (1998: xvii) there are four basic questions which need to be asked when conceptualising sport as ethical. They are:

- Is a common morality for sport possible?
- Is a common morality for sport desirable?
- Is sport an inherently moral practice which contributes to moral education?
- Can moral rules or principles provide the complete context of sport ethics?

Morgan (2002: 208) suggests that there are 'two pressing and highly controversial questions' that shape the contemporary ethical study of sport. First, how do, and how should, athletes and practitioners treat one another? Further, in the case of animal based sports, how are they treated? And should they be treated as sentient beings. The second question raises the matter of the individual and collective behaviour of athletes and practitioners, and how they 'comport themselves in the pursuit of athletic excellence'. Each question Morgan notes raises a set of issues. The first question speaks directly to issues that are familiar in contemporary sport, such as sportsmanship, competition, cheating, gender and sexuality, 'race' and ethnicity. The second question is notable for its raising of the issue of how athletes and sport relate to and appropriate new technologies, particularly those that are presumed to enhance performance (such as, but not exclusively, the use of drugs and blood doping), and the moral questions such developments raise.

SPORT, RULES AND QUESTIONS OF FAIRNESS

Sport is a rule-bound practice. Sport is also a goal-orientated activity, and in the pursuit of these goals the rules of sport are frequently 'broken' or contravened. In order to pursue the ethical nature of sport as a cultural activity, this section will explore some of the central issues, questions and problems raised by the breaking of sports rules.

According to Steenbergen and Tamboer (1998: 37), sport is understood through a set of concepts and notions, such as sportsmanship, fair play, goals, means and cheating. These concepts, they conclude, can only be understood in relation to the specific rules of a given sport. In this sense sport is an *autotelic* activity (that is it has a purpose that is defined by the activity itself, and not outside itself). However, whilst sport remains autonomous, it is unquestionably connected to a wider system of values, norms and morals that shapes the cultural and social environment within which the sport is situated.

For Warren Fraleigh (1998: xvii) the growth of interest in sports ethics is unquestionably premised upon the recent 'degeneration of moral standards as noted in the actions of athletes, coaches and other agents of sports practices'. There has been much focus upon the relationship between sport's recent commercialisation and its increasingly commodified nature, and sport's recent 'moral degradation'. Morgan (1994) suggests an explicit link between the moral nature of sport and its economic nature. The institutionalization of market norms, has, Morgan suggests, resulted in a situation whereby sportsmen and women 'have no compelling reason to value or engage in competitive challenges save for extrinsic rewards or money' (cited in Cashmore, 2002: 65). Cheating becomes an instrumental tool to achieve sporting ends, encouraged by sports cooption of market logic. As sports practices are considered on a par with business and economic transactions, so the 'logic of the market' creates a 'win at all costs' attitude within sport. For Morgan (1994) this situation gives rise to an ethical paradox, whereby, for example, performance enhancing drugs are banned by the institutions and governing bodies of sport, but yet are legitimised and encouraged by the increasing emphasis placed upon competitive success.

ethics

51

Morgan (1994) clearly views the capitalist market as a corrupting influence upon sport. However, as Loland (1998: 79) illustrates, the defining concept by which sporting morality is traditionally described (Steenbergen and Tamboer, 1998: 39) – 'fair play' – has its historical roots in the emergence of new economic relationships and interests that form around the transition from a feudal to a capitalist market system. Predicated upon a wider social obligation 'to follow the rules', the notion of 'fair play' both corresponds with and conforms to the interests of the politically and economically dominant social class – the bourgeoisie (Loland, 1998: 79). Indeed, the demand for greater sporting impartiality and fairer outcomes increased as betting upon sporting events became much more popular (Elias, 1986: 139), during the nineteenth and early twentieth centuries.

The concept of sporting 'fair play' is understood through the normative framework of the rules of the sport or game in question – the formal or written rules and the unwritten rules or 'ethos' that function as an informal regulative framework (d'Agostino, 1981; Eassom, 1998: 83). These frameworks are also defined through their constitutive and regulative natures. Constitutive rules are those upon which the existence of a sport or game is logically dependent (and reflect the formal character of the game's laws). The constitutive aspect of the rules is distinct from the existence of regulative rules (which in part reflect the informal rules) which modify already existing practice or behavior between and amongst the athletes and practitioners of the game (Steenbergen and Tamboer, 1998: 39). As such, 'fair play' has a dual nature – it is constituted through the formal, constitutive framework, and it is also constituted through the informal regulative nature of rules. These two aspects of 'fair play' are often in conflict with each other, raising further ethical problems and paradoxes on how we morally regulate and evaluate competitive sports. For example, in soccer it is stipulated in the formal, constitutive rules of the sport that a player who is fouled and sustains an injury requiring treatment as a consequence must then leave the field of play. The player can only return to the field once play restarts and he/she has been instructed to do so by the referee. Due to circumstances that are largely not of their own making one team is penalised by the fact that they are required to (temporarily) reduce the number of players they have on the field of play. The opposing team – who committed the foul, however, are allowed to keep the full complement of players on the field of play (unless of course the foul committed has been deemed serious enough to send the offending player from the field of play). In this respect are the constitutive, formal rules of sport 'fair' or 'ethical'? In attempting to answer this question, d'Agostino (1981, cited in Steenbergen and Tamboer, 1989: 40) argues that moral judgements in sport cannot be derived from the formal rules that govern a particular sport, but are constituted within the informal, unwritten regulative frameworks that shape the specific 'ethos' and the conduct between the participants themselves. It is to this issue, and the controversial question of cheating in sport as a form of morally acceptable behaviour, that I now turn.

'THE HAND OF GOD', OR WHY CHEATING IS ETHICAL

22 June 1986, Mexico City, World Cup Quarter-Final, Argentina versus England. Fifty-one minutes into a game poised at 0–0, the Argentinean striker Diego Maradona, chases a seemingly futile high looping ball into the English penalty area. Given the Argentinean's diminutive stature (5ft 5 inches – 165 cm), the England goalkeeper, Peter Shilton (6ft – 183 cm) is clear favourite to win the ball. However, despite the apparent mismatch in heights Maradona seems to get to the ball first, forcing it into the back of the English goal. Very quickly it becomes clear that Maradona has used his hand (an act he later accredited to God) to put his side in front. Despite concerted protestations from the England players the referee (who has not seen the initial handball) allows the goal to stand. Argentina go on to win the game 2–1.

Maradona's 'Hand of God' goal has become the archetypal example of cheating. Cheating is one of the most used concepts in describing and judging forms of behaviour or ways in which sports and games are prevented from achieving a 'mutually acceptable' or transparent conclusion (Reddiford, 1998: 227). Cheating is nominally understood as an act of deception, or a contravention of the constitutive formal rules of a game, employed in an attempt to gain an unfair advantage. However, it is important to note that not all acts of deception are cheating. As Reddiford (1998: 229) notes, 'The rules of tennis make possible the playing of disguised drop shots, and the rules of cricket are neutral on the bowling of the "googly"'. Furthermore, to break the formalised rules of a game is not enough to categorise sporting behaviour as cheating. For example Reddiford (1998: 231) notes that particular sporting 'activities may be condemned, but not proscribed by the laws' of the game. For example, the taunting or 'sledging' of an opponent (as, for example, in cricket) is often considered a form of 'unsporting behaviour' but is not censored by the formal rules of sport. Other acts, Reddiford (1998: 231) continues, are penalised by the formal rules of the sport but are not condemned outright, such as, for example, the delivery of a no-ball in cricket. We might also consider here the ethical dilemma posed by the cricket captain who instructs his bowler to deliver the ball under arm in order to prevent the opposing batsman scoring the boundary required to win a game. To bowl under arm is not against the formal rules of the game, but it is deemed as unsporting, particularly by the participants themselves, as it contravenes the informal expectations of how a cricketer should conduct themselves within the context of a game. (When Australian cricket captain Greg Chappell ordered his brother to do this in a one day International against New Zealand at Melbourne Cricket Ground in 1981, New Zealand Prime Minister Robert Muldoon remarked: 'It was an act of cowardice and I consider it appropriate that the Australian team were wearing yellow'. Malcolm Fraser, Prime Minister of Australia said the action was 'contrary to the traditions of the game'. The New Zealand players walked away in disgust and respected cricket commentator Richie Benaud pronounced the incident 'disgraceful'.) We are again faced with the question of which normative framework (the constitutive or regulative) is used to ethically evaluate particular forms of play as either 'fair' or 'unfair' and are returned to the tension between the informal and formal rules of a given sport.

Returning to the issue of Maradona's 'Hand of God' goal and the ethical question as to whether Maradona should have acknowledged the goal was 'illegitimate' or not, Steenbergen and Tamboer (1998) draw a distinction between the formal and informal rules, suggesting that two ethical positions can be adopted. In terms of the formal rules of 'fair play', Maradona might ask the question:

> why should I tell the referee? There is no constitutive rule in soccer which says that a player should correct the referee. On the other hand, with regard to informal fair play, he [Maradona] could have given the following answer: Yes I should have told the referee that it was not a legitimate goal. Although it is not imposed by a constitutive rule, the spirit or purpose of the soccer game is to find out which is the best side, not to measure the eyesight of the referee and linesman (Steenbergen and Tamboer, 1998: 40).

The different ethical judgements given above reflect the way in which a particular sport is characterised or valued, and the normative framework (formal constitutive rules or informal regulative rules) upon which the judgement is made. Thus, in terms of the formal rules of fair play, Maradona's refusal to acknowledge his goal as illegitimate is ethically justifiable in that there is no constitutive rule that demands he should inform the referee as to his wrong doing. In terms of the informal rules of fair play Maradona's goal is ethically unsound in that it contravene the unwritten 'spirit' or 'ethos' of the game, and, as such, following d'Agostino's (1981) insight that moral judgements can only be made upon assessing the informal regulative nature of the sports rules, then we can morally censure Maradona, and condemn his behaviour as unethical. However, using the same distinctions between the formal and informal notions of fair play, Claudiou Tamburrini (2000) argues that Maradona's handball is fundamentally an ethical act.

Tamburrini rejects the widespread premise that 'cheating' is the result of the growing culture of win by whatever means necessary, fuelled by growing commercialisation. Rather, Tamburrini suggests that far from than cheating, Maradona acted rightly, and that furthermore, violations of the codes of good sportsmanship should be encouraged as they enhance the quality of the game (Tamburrini, 2000: 10). His argument is based upon the notion that within sport fairness is a relational concept, and decisions of what constitutes an unfair advantage or not depends upon the context in which a game is played. Tamburrini argues that Maradona's handball does not run counter to the way the game is played in a modern context. In this respect, within the context of a game of soccer, handball, deliberate or otherwise, is not an exceptional act; rather it is a very common violation of the formal rules of the game. He suggests: 'If everyone does it – or if everyone would do it, given a suitable occasion – the cheater simply acts as if she/he (reasonably) expects others to act in similar circumstances. No contractual breach can be derived from that' (Tamburrini, 2000: 20). Tamburrini places emphasis upon the informal regulative ethos, or the way in which players treat and compete with each other, within a commonly accepted rule set, independent of the formal constitutive set of rules. Within the informal rules, Tamburrini suggests, there is an expectation that participants will violate the formal rule sets in order to gain advantage. He continues that there is no unfair advantage to be gained by cheating, 'provided it is (somehow) considered as part of the game by regular practitioners and everyone has that opinion' (Tamburrini, 2000: 21). In this sense then, within the context of the informal rule set or 'ethos of the game' Maradona's hand ball represents neither a contractual break, nor does it yield an unfair advantage. In this respect Maradona's 'illegitimate' goal, is both legitimate and morally correct.

On the second substantive point, that cheating should be actively encouraged, Tamburrini stands on its head the commonplace assumption that the deliberate violation of the formal rules of a game somehow lowers the quality, or impairs the enjoyment, of 'a good game'. However, as

Tamburrini (2000) suggests, there is no a priori assumption, or guarantee that keeping to the rules in any way enhances the quality of a game. In fact the deliberate breaking of rules often acts as a stimulus through which the game and its enjoyment is both enriched and enhanced. Although contrary to the formal written rules of the game, incidents of cheating are ethically right in that they have a positive impact upon the quality of the game and can act as an excitant.

CONCLUSION

The rules of sports and games are necessary for the successful transaction of these activities. In this respect the rule bound nature of sports is largely interpreted as imposing constraints upon behaviour, as limiting the potential excesses of the participants (Eassom, 1998: 58; McFee, 1998: 19). However, sports' rules do not merely regulate or confine the players of games. They have a much more fundamentally liberating or subversive function (Reddiford, 1998: 229). For Searel (1969, cited in Loland 1998: 84) rules are not simply a constraint or bulwark against potentially damaging and excessive behaviour, 'but as it were they create the very possibility of playing such games'. Rules create greater possibilities, which are often (and sometimes can only be) achieved through their violation.

REFERENCES

Cashmore, E. (2002) *Sports Culture: An A-Z Guide*. London: Routledge.

d'Agostino, F. (1981) 'The Ethos of Games', *Journal of the Philosophy of Sport*, VIII: 7–18.

Eassom, S. (1998) 'Games, Rules and Contracts', in M.J. McNamee and S.J. Parry (eds) *Ethics and Sport*. London: Routledge. pp. 57–78.

Elias, N. (1986) 'The Genesis of Sport as a Sociological Problem', in N. Elias and E. Dunning (eds) *Quest for Excitement – Sport and Leisure in The Civilising Process*. Oxford: Blackwell. pp. 126–50.

Fraleigh, W.P. (1998) 'Forward', in M.J. McNamee and S.J. Parry (eds) *Ethics and Sport*. London: Routledge. pp. xvii–xix.

Loland, S. (1998) 'Fair Play: Historical Anachronism or Topical Ideal?', in M.J. McNamee and S.J. Parry (eds) *Ethics and Sport*. London: Routledge. pp. 79–103.

Loland, S., Skirstad, B. and Waddington, I. (eds) (2006) *Pain and Injury in Sport: Social and Ethical Analysis*. London: Routledge.

McFee, G. (2004) *Sport, Rules and Values: Philosophical Investigations into the Nature of Sport*. London: Routledge.

McFee, G. (1998) 'Are There Philosophical Issues in Respect of Sport (Other Than Ethical Ones)?', in M. J. McNamee and S. J. Parry (eds) *Ethics and Sport*. London: Routledge. pp. 3–18.

key concepts in sports studies

McNamee, M.J. and Parry, S.J. (eds) (1998) *Ethics and Sport*. London: Routledge.

Miah, A. (2004) *Genetically Modified Athletes. Biomedical Ethics, Gene Doping and Sport*. London: Routledge.

Morgan, W.J. (1994) *Leftist Theories of Sport*. Urbana and Chicago: University of Illinois Press.

Morgan, W.J. (2002) 'The Philosophy of Sport: A Historical and Conceptual Overview and a Conjecture Regarding its Future', in J. Coakley and E. Dunning (eds) *Handbook of Sports Studies*. London: Sage. pp. 204–12.

Reddiford, G. (1998) 'Cheating and Self-deception in Sport', in M.J. McNamee and S.J. Parry (eds) *Ethics and Sport*. London: Routledge. pp. 225–39.

Searel, J. (1969) *Speech Acts: An Essay on the Philosophy of Language*. Cambridge: Harvard University Press.

Steenbergen, J. and Tamboer, J. (1998) 'Ethics and the Double Character of Sport: An Attempt to Systematize Discussion of the Ethics of Sport', in M.J. McNamee and S.J. Parry (eds) *Ethics and Sport*. London: Routledge. pp. 35–53.

Tamburrini, C.M. (2000) *The 'Hand of God': Essays in the Philosophy of Sports*. Göteborg: Acta Universitatis Gothoburgensis.

Ethnography

ORIGINS

Ethnography is a qualitative research method which originated in the field of anthropology where it was used to study cultures seen as 'exotic' or unfamiliar in 'the West'. The term 'ethnography' is used to describe both the research style and the 'written product of that research activity' (Atkinson, 1990: 3). The 'Chicago School' of urban sociologists – writers such as Howard Becker, Albert Cohen, Robert Park, Ned Polsky and William F. Whyte – who were prominent from the 1940s to the mid-1960s and were committed to symbolic interactionism, have also had a seminal influence on the development of the 'genre' of sociological ethnography (Atkinson, 1990). They helped to fix its focus on the micro community, subculture or sub-world.

The aim of ethnography is to comprehend the totality of the culture, group, social world or subculture being studied. It endeavours to understand how people behave in their 'natural' settings, and to construct the participant's perspective (the emic perspective) and make explicit *their* taken for granted assumptions (Hammersley and Atkinson, 1995). Ethnographic studies involve in-depth and extended study. Although participation observation has been 'taken as the type-case of ethnographic procedures' (Atkinson, 1990: 29), within ethnographic investigation a number of research techniques are employed including document analysis, participant observation and in-depth interviews.

CONTEMPORARY SPORTS ETHNOGRAPHIES

Over the past few decades ethnographic research has become popular in many fields of study, including sports studies. It is not my intention here to detail the development of the field or give an overview of various sporting ethnographies, as some excellent summaries of these aspects already exist (see for example *Sociology of Sport Journal*, Special Issue, 1997). However it is important to recognise that the meaning and practice of ethnography, in sport as in other fields, varies considerably. As Silk (2005) argues, a variety of different 'approaches, schools or sub-types exists' under the 'banner' of ethnography (Silk, 2005: 65) and these are underpinned by different and often opposing theoretical, philosophical, epistemological and ontological assumptions. Thus, the genealogy of contemporary ethnography needs to be understood as a 'constant process of oppositions' (Silk, 2005: 65).

Early work in sport (during the 1970s) in the symbolic interactionist tradition focused on cultural description, reflecting early anthropological work. But writers in this tradition did not place their findings in their broader social and historical contexts (Donnelly, 1985), nor did they explore the wider power relationships involved. In the 1980s and 1990s, sport sociologists adopted more contextualised ethnographic approaches to study different life worlds, subcultures and identity practices and these ranged from football fans to golf, from climbing to skateboarding (see overview in Beal, 2002). Such a contextualising approach attempts not just 'to understand cultural experience in its face to face production and location in time, it also wants to situate that interaction in the social reproduction of relations and society as a whole' (Hollands, 1985: 17). In this context Beal (2002) gives a detailed review of the ways in which symbolic interactionsim and cultural studies have been combined in critical ethnography. Recent subcultural studies of sport, for example, have integrated a critical cultural studies perspective 'with the rigorous documentation of interactions which generate symbolic meanings and identity' (Crosset and Beal, 1997: 82). Ethnographic work on deviance has been another productive line in sporting research, generating numerous studies of the performance of masculinity in football fan cultures (see Giulianotti, 1995; Hughson, 1998), as well as boxing (Sugden, 1996) and criminality among tickets scalpers (Atkinson, 2000). Another interesting strand of work is the use of ethnography to study sports institutions (Sugden and Tomlinson, 1999) and sports media, addressing, for example, their institutionalised practices (e.g. Silk, 2005), the gendered nature of production (e.g. MacNeill, 1996) and the consumption of sports media by audiences (e.g. Wheaton and Beal, 2003).

RESEARCH PARADIGMS AND TRADITIONS

The adoption of a qualitative research 'method' like ethnography is based upon philosophical, ideological and epistemological assumptions about the social world, and methodology's place within it (Bryman, 1984). To understand the differences between qualitative and quantitative methods as competing models of social research, it is necessary to examine the opposing philosophical positions on the nature of knowledge that underpin them, namely 'positivism' and 'naturalism' (Hammersley and Atkinson, 1995: 3). The theoretical paradigm underpinning most contemporary ethnographic work comes from interpretivism (see Donnelly, 2000; Gratton and Jones, 2004), a theoretical position (or collection of positions) that has developed from naturalism. Naturalist and interpretavists reject positivistic views of science and scientific research, such as the ideal of a detached objective account that depicts or mirrors social reality and social facts (Foley, 1992), and in which the researcher is an invisible observer, with no influence on the research process. Instead they argue that 'social phenomena are distinct in character from natural phenomena' (Hammersley and Atkinson, 1995: 6); that behaviour must be understood in context as social reality is grounded in the experiences of the people concerned. They therefore stress the necessity for studies of 'real' social situations rather than the construction of artificial ones via the use of experimental designs or survey studies.

The differences between naturalism and positivism can also be examined at an epistemological level. Epistemology refers to the study of how knowledge about the social world is acquired, and how we understand the nature of 'reality' (Stanley and Wise, 1993). A given epistemological framework specifies not only what 'knowledge is and how to recognise it, but who are the 'knowers' (Stanley and Wise, 1993: 188). Epistemological assumptions about the nature of social reality, and thus what is accepted as knowledge, are conflicting for the paradigms of naturalism and positivism; they entail antithetic views of what social reality is, and thus of methods of 'objective' study. However some commentators argue that this view of positivism and naturalism as two distinct paradigms is overstated and that the bond between epistemology and method is therefore exaggerated (Hammersley and Atkinson, 1995). It is argued that that both approaches are distinctive, and appropriate for different types of research questions; that is, the nature of the question dictates the nature of the research method. Moreover, they highlight that there are other important ethical, political and ideological implications that will also help determine the research strategy.

VALIDITY AND GENERALISABILITY

The primary strength of ethnography is that it is able to capture the complex meanings of everyday human activities. As a strategy it can accommodate changes in ideas and research direction more easily than quantitative methods can; theory and theorising is often inherent throughout (Hammersley and Atkinson, 1995). The internal validity of observational methods is high, that is it verifies 'the truth of the claim made' (Hammersley, 1992: 78), especially in situations where the researcher can participate and get close to the data. Thus, the participant observation data are 'the key-stone of the claim to authenticity' (Hobbs and May, 1993: ix).

The criticism most often made of ethnography is the difficulty in 'objectively' assessing validity and reliability. Ethnographic data are usually ideographic, that is involving micro-level case studies. 'The gains offered by ethnographic research are brought at the expense of certain weaknesses, notably in its ability to generalise to larger populations and to identify causal relationships' (Hammersley, 1992: 125). Yet while seminal ethnographic subcultural studies, such as the work of Willis (1977) on working-class lads, have been criticised for lacking generalisability beyond the group under study, these studies are valuable 'commentaries on society as a whole' (Woods, 1986: 36). Despite their micro-sociological focus, the underlying social process described often transcends time and place. That is, theoretical inferences and debates as well as empirical or inductive generalisations are important (Hammersley, 1992), a concern reflected in the 'Grounded

Theory'(Glaser and Strauss, 1967) approach, a prominent framework for the analysis of ethnographic data in which concepts are generated that can form the building blocks of theory (Glaser and Strauss, 1967).

Furthermore, there is considerable debate, and disagreement, over what constitutes good interpretation in ethnography, even if validity is an appropriate term (Denzin and Lincoln, 1994; Hammersley, 1992). Some argue validity reflects 'a concern for acceptance within a positivist concept of research vigour' (Kincheloe and McLaren, 1994: 151), and that notions other than 'validity' and 'representativeness' are important in validating ethnographic data. Hammersley suggests that we should assess the research's *relevance* as well as its validity (1992: 88). Some critical postmodern ethnographers believe that the character of qualitative research is such that there can be no criteria for judging it, a position which 'doubts all criteria and privileges none' (Denzin and Lincoln, 1994: 480), a debate I return to later in this discussion.

ENTERING THE FIELD: DOING PARTICIPANT OBSERVATION

Doing ethnographic research, particularly participant observation, raises a number of practical and methodological issues. Initially there are the problems of gaining access and negotiating with gate keepers; then there are decisions about which field roles to adopt. Some roles may involve risk, or role conflicts may develop during the course of the research. Ethnographers usually face a number of ethical questions and dilemmas, which can surface throughout the research process, from obtaining funding to publishing results. While ethical issues are prevalent in most research projects, the specific idiosyncrasies of ethnography give ethical issues a 'distinctive accent' (Hammersley and Atkinson, 1995), especially issues surrounding informed consent, deception (see Homan and Bulmer, 1982) and the breach of privacy, which are particularly significant in cases involving covert methods or some deception. Palmer (2000), for example, posed as a journalist in her study of the La Société du Tour de France as this was the only strategy available for gaining access to this social world.

There are a number of detailed and frank explorations of the methodological, practical and ethical issues and dilemmas faced by sport ethnographers (see e.g. Sugden, 2004). Here I will focus on some of the issues raised doing insider research.

Hammersley and Atkinson (1995) outline four different ethnographic roles, ranging from the complete observer to complete participant, discussing

ethnography

their advantages and disadvantages (Hammersley and Atkinson, 1995). Researchers, however, chose a role based on a number of pragmatic as well as theoretical factors. In her research on the windsurfing culture in England, Wheaton (2002) adopted a 'complete participant' role (Hammersley and Atkinson, 1995) which involves 'total immersion' in the subculture; the researcher cannot just pass as a group member, s/he must become one (Hammersley and Atkinson, 1995). She adopted a covert insider role based on her established place within the group, the existing network of relationships, and her familiarity with the main setting under observation (Wheaton, 1995). Insider familiarity helps achieve knowledge of a situation, which might take an outsider longer to gain, especially in specialist subcultures, like sport, where specialist knowledge and language are required (Donnelly, 1985). It also minimises the effect of the researcher on the environment s/he is studying (Hammersley and Atkinson, 1995). Wheaton (1995) claimed that despite the moral and ethical dilemmas, the 'complete participant' role was the only possible observation option for gaining full access, that her intrusion on the privacy of her subjects was minimal, and they were not exposed to any risks.

Within the study of sport and leisure subcultures there has been a widespread recognition of the value of this 'insider' approach, whether by an existing association with the subculture studied, or a field role adopted during the research (see Giulianotti, 1995; Redhead, 1993; Wheaton, 2002). This support has also stemmed from the critiques of earlier subcultural research such as Hebdige's (1979) seminal study of youth subcultures, in which his non-participatory role has been widely denounced. It is argued that non-participant observers often misunderstand, or ignore, what the sport culture means to its participants – they do not explain the subjective experiences of everyday life. In the context of participatory sport cultures, such as surfing, some go so far as to argue that participation in the activity is a prerequisite to understanding the sport's meaning and aesthetic. Sands uses the term 'experiential ethnography' to illustrate how researchers become complete participants, including learning the lived bodily experiences, feelings, emotions and sensations (Sands, 2002). Wheaton (2002) likewise outlines how being a proficient and active windsurfer was vital for a *female* field worker gaining access to a *male-dominated* subculture.

Hammersley and Atkinson (1995), however, warn that the complete participant researcher becomes so involved in the group's social practices, that they 'must behave in expected ways', which can be counterproductive to data collection. Furthermore, the researcher must find a balance between personal involvement and detachment to maintain their critical edge. The term 'going native' has been used to describe the researcher who integrates so successfully with the group that s/he over empathises with the members of the culture, defending and romanticising their values, losing their critical detachment (Woods, 1986). This over identification with the group has been discussed by many sporting ethnographers (see Armstrong and Giulianotti, 1997).

In summary, the ethnographer needs to consider how different field roles present different advantages, problems and issues, while recognising that most research projects exploit a variety of different roles in each setting, at different temporal stages of the project, or to investigate different types of data.

CRITICAL ETHNOGRAPHY

Over the past few decades on-going philosophical debates about the nature of knowledge (ontology) and scientific enquiry in the social sciences have contributed to a re-evaluation of many of the basic assumptions about scientific method, epistemology, and, specifically, ethnography. While these so-called 'crises of representation' (Marcus and Fisher, 1986) and of 'legitimation' (Denzin, 1994) are often claimed to be 'postmodern' or post-structuralist developments, their roots (and ideas) are firmly embedded in a number of earlier critiques of method and epistemology, most notably feminist and interactionist critiques of positivism (Morgan, 1992; Stanley and Wise, 1993). The implications of this epistemological 're-evaluation' are numerous, ranging from the rejection of grand narratives, to notions of a one-to-one relationship between reality and textual based accounts of it (Stanley and Wise, 1993: 190). This has implications for how we do ethnographic research, how we write about ethnographic research, the role of the researcher, the claims we make about our research, and the ways we validate ethnography.

The concern with 'reporting ethnography' affects the style in which ethnography is presented, and the procedures used. During the 1960s a new 'genre' of ethnography surfaced that has been referred to as the confessional (Van Maanen, 1988) or autobiographical account (Bryman and Burgess, 1994). In these accounts the role and authority of the ethnographer is problematised (Fontana, 1994), as is the notion that the researcher is outside the research process, an invisible observer, with no influence on it: '[Postmodern] ethnographers seek to deconstruct the dominant position of the ethnographer. This is not done by making the ethnographer 'disappear', but by making him or her 'public'' (Fontana, 1994: 212). The 'confessional' documents how the fieldwork was carried out, no longer seeing the problems encountered in fieldwork as matters to be ignored in an attempt to present a more 'objective' study. Rather they become 'topics of research in themselves' that demonstrate the problems encountered (Fontana, 1994: 208). For example the researcher can write a 'research diary' or 'audit trail' that documents his/her experiences of the research process, and focuses on the procedures of data collection and analysis (Bryman and Burgess, 1994). Here the researcher's experiences of the research setting, context and process are set out, adding a 'dimension of reflexivity to ethnography' (Fontana, 1994: 208) and illustrating the relationship between the author, the object of analysis and the final constructed text.

Another dimension of this discussion revolves around the style of reporting ethnography. Rather than adhering to positivistic rhetorical practices in the narrative that make a text authoritative and persuasive, such as third person reporting (Fontana, 1994), ethnographic accounts tend to be more reflexive accounts, reported in the first person. The narrative situates the field worker in the ethnographic account, recognising who the ethnographer is, and how s/he actually produced the account. The ethnographer's authoritative influence is reduced through emphasising the dialogue between the researcher and the informants (Marcus and Fisher, 1986).

As noted above, another central issue has been to recognise whose voices are heard and whose are marginalised in our representations of sporting cultures and identities. It has become increasingly evident that in most of these sporting ethnographic texts the 'lived experience' that the researchers were detailing, were specifically the realities, identities and experiences of white, Western, middle-class men. As already noted, feminist researchers have had a crucial influence both on debates about the nature of scientific knowledge and on research practices, such as ethnography. Yet despite sport sociology's widespread acknowledgement of the *importance* of feminist theory, and, increasingly, post-colonial and black feminists' critiques of the universalised and essentialised white male Western subject, it has not always led to an *engagement* with its implications for ethnographic practice (Wheaton, 2002). For example, despite reflection on the 'self' as a cultural insider, researchers have often failed to investigate the 'self' as a gendered or racialised subject. Many sporting ethnographies conducted by male researchers fail to acknowledge – or make visible – their own maleness, or whiteness (Free and Hughson, 2003; Wheaton, 2002).

Sporting ethnography offers the possibility to improve the human condition (Beal, 2002) especially in its critique of Western ethnocentric imperialist practices, and in opening up spaces for the voices and experiences of previously marginalised groups (such as own women, gays, lesbians, minorities and those 'others' in non-Western cultures) (Silk, 2005). Silk (following Denzin) suggests that one of the most exciting possibilities for ethnography as a 'civic, participatory and collaborative project' lies in the engagement with 'fictional and storied representations' (2005, 71). These ethnographies blur the boundaries of ethnographic research to include poetry, drama, conversation and so on, and draw heavily on narratives of the self (auto-ethnographies) (Richardson, 2000). Such approaches are still quite limited in sport sociology, but have become popularised particularly by the students of Norman Denzin in North America (see e.g. Bruce, 1998; Denison and Rinehart, 2000; Markula and Denison, 2005). More broadly, auto ethnographies, such as the one developed by Andrew Sparkes in writing about sporting injury and masculinity (Sparkes, 1996) are becoming popular in the context of the 'narrative turn', referred to earlier, in which researchers try to address the textual issues of who get represented, by whom, and the political consequences of those representations (Sparkes, 1997).

A final theoretical issue that needs to be considered in contemporary ethnographic research is the changing meaning and context of culture in an increasingly fragmented and globalised world (see also **Globalisation**). The global flow of people, images and capital leads to the increasing inter-connectedness of places and cultures, challenging the idea that there are fixed and bounded cultures we can study (Gupta and Ferguson, 1997). 'Local' subcultures no longer exists in isolation (Clifford, 1997), and the global/local matrix becomes increasingly important as a framework for understanding identity. 'Multi-sited ethnography' (Marcus, 1998, cited in Saukko, 2003: 176) has emerged which explores how phenomena take shape, across multiple locales, illustrating the global as well as local connections between these sites and 'scapes' (Appadurai, 1996).

Contemporary ethnographic practice continues to be influenced by a number of different theoretical positions, and while most recently postmodernism and post-experimentalism have had a profound impact, there are also strong continuities with past orthodoxies (Silk, 2005). As this section has tried to show, ethnographic research presents a number of difficulties and problems, but, it also raises exciting questions that are some of the most important in the current intellectual debates (Gray, 2003: 23).

ethnography

REFERENCES

Appadurai, A. (1996) *Modernity at Large: Cultural Dimensions of Globalization*. Minneapolis: University of Minnesota Press.

Armstrong, G. and Giulianotti, R. (1997) *Entering the Field: New Perspectives on World Football*. Oxford: Berg.

Atkinson, M. (2000) 'Brother, Can you Spare a Seat? Developing Recipes of Knowledge in the Ticket Scalping Subculture', *Sociology of Sport Journal*, 17: 151–70.

Atkinson, P. (1990) *The Ethnographic Imagination: Textual Constructions of Reality*. London: Routledge.

Beal, B. (2002) 'Symbolic Interactionism and Cultural Studies: Doing Critical Ethnography', in J. Maguire and K. Young (eds) *Theory, sport and society*. Oxford: JAI. pp. 353–74.

Bruce, T. (1998) 'Postmodernism and the Possibilities for Writing "Vital" Sports Texts', in G. Rail (ed.) *Sport and Postmodern Times*. Albany: SUNY.

Bryman, A. (1984) 'The Debate about Quantitative and Qualitative Research', *British Journal of Sociology*, XXXV: 75–92.

Bryman, A. and Burgess, R. (1994) *Analysing Qualitative Data*. London and New york: Routledge.

Clifford, J. (1997) *Routes: Travel and Translation in the Late Twentieth Century*. London: Harvard University Press.

Crosset, T. and Beal, B. (1997) 'The Use of "Subculture" and "Subworld" in Ethnographic Works on Sport: A Discussion of Definitional Distinctions', *Sociology of Sport Journal*, 14: 73–85.

Denison, J. and Rinehart, R. (2000) 'Introduction: Imagining Sociological Narratives', *Sociology of Sport Journal*, 17: 1–5.

Denzin, N. (1994) 'The Art and Politics of Interpretation', in N. Denzin and Y. Lincoln (eds) *Handbook of qualitative research*. Thousand Oaks, CA: Sage. pp. 500–15.

Denzin, N. and Lincoln, Y. (1994) *Handbook of Qualitative Research*. Thousand Oaks, CA: Sage.

Donnelly, P. (1985) 'Sport Subcultures', *Exercise and Sport Sciences Review*, 13: 539–78.

Donnelly, P. (2000) 'Interactionism', in J. Coakley and E. Dunning (eds) *Handbook of Sport Studies*. London: Sage.

Foley, D. (1992) 'Making the Familiar Strange: Writing Critical Sport Narratives', *Sociology of Sport Journal*, 1: 36–47.

Fontana, A. (1994) 'Ethnographic Trends in the Postmodern Era', in D. Dickens and A. Fontana (eds) *Postmodernism and Social Enquiry*. London: UCL Press. pp. 203–23.

Free, M. and Hughson, J. (2003) 'Settling Accounts with Hooligans: Gender Blindness in Football Supporter Subculture Research', *Men and Masculinity*, 6: 136–55.

Giulianotti, R. (1995) 'Participant Observation and Research into Football Hooliganism: Reflections on the Problems of Entree and Everyday Risks', *Sociology of Sport Journal*, 12: 1–20.

Glaser, B. and Strauss, A. (1967) *The Discovery of Grounded Theory: Strategies for Qualitative Reserach*. Chicago: Aldine.

Gratton, C. and Jones, I. (2004) *Research Methods for Sport Studies*. London: Routledge.

Gray, A. (2003) *Research Practice for Cultrual Studies: Ethnographic Methods and Lived Cultures*. London: Sage.

Gupta, A. and Ferguson, J. (eds) (1997) *Culture, Power, Place: Explorations in Critical Anthropology*. Durham NC: Durham University Press.

Hammersley, M. (1992) *What's Wrong with Ethnography: Methodological Explorations*. London: Routledge.

Hammersley, M. and Atkinson, P. (1995) *Ethnography: Principles in Practice*. London and New York: Routledge.

Hebdige, D. (1979) *Subculture, the Meaning of Style*. London and New York: Routledge.

Hobbs, D. and May, T. (1993) *Interpreting the Field*. Oxford: Clarendon Press.

Hollands, R. (1985) 'Working for the Best Ethnography', Centre for Contemporary Cultural Studies, University of Birmingham.

Homan, R. and Bulmer, M. (1982) 'On the Merits of Covert Methods: A Dialogue', in M. Bulmer (ed.) *Social Research Ethics*. London: Macmillan. pp. 217–51.

Hughson, J. (1998) 'Among the Thugs: The "New Ethnographies" of Football Supporting Subcultures', *International Review for Sociology of Sport*, 33: 42–57.

Kincheloe, J. and McLaren, P. (1994) 'Rethinking Critical Theory and Qualitative Research', in D. Denzin and Y. Lincoln. *Handbook of Qualitative Research*, Thousands Oaks, CA: Sage. pp. 138–57.

MacNeill, M. (1996) 'Networks: Producing Olympic Ice Hockey for a National Television Audience', *Sociology of Sport Journal*, 14: 103–4.

Marcus, G.E. and Fisher, M.J. (1986) *Anthropology as Cultural Critique: An Experimental Moment in the Human Sciences*. Chicago: University of Chicago Press.

Markula, P. and Denison, J. (2005) 'Sport and the Personal Narrative', in D.L. Andrews, D.S. Mason and M. Silk (eds) *Qualitative Methods in Sports Studies*. Oxford: Berg. pp. 165–184.

Morgan, D. (1992) *Discovering Men*. London and New York: Routledge.

Palmer, C. (2000) 'Spin Doctors and Sportsbrokers: Researching Elites in Contemporary Sports a Research Note on the Tour de France', *International Review for Sociology of Sport*, 35: 364–77.

Redhead, S. (1993) *Rave Off: Politics and Deviance in Contemporary Youth Culture*. Aldershot: Avebury.

Richardson, L. (2000) 'New Writing Practices in Qualitative Research', *Sociology of Sport Journal*, 17: 5–20.

Sands, R. (2002) *Sporting Ethnography*. Champaign, IL.: Human Kinetics.

Saukko, P. (2003) *Doing Research in Cultural Studies: An Introduction to Classical and New Methodological Approaches*. London: Sage.

Silk, M.L. (2005) 'Sporting Ethnography: Philosophy, Methodology and Reflection', in D.L. Andrews, D.S. Mason and M. Silk (eds) *Qualitative methods in sports studies*. Oxford: Berg. pp. 65–103.

Sparkes, A. (1996) 'The Fatal Flaw: A Narrative of the Fragile Body-self', *Qualitative Inquiry*, 2: 463–94.

Sparkes, A. (1997) 'Ethnographic Fiction and Representing the Absent Other', *Sport, Education and Society*, 2: 25–40.

Stanley, L. and Wise, S. (1993) *Breaking Out Again*. London: Routledge.

Sugden, J. (1996) *Boxing and Society*. Manchester: Manchester University Press.

Sugden, J. (2004) 'Is Investigative Sociology just Investigative Journalism?', in M. McNamee (ed.) *Philosophy and the Sciences of Exercise, Health and Sport*. London: Routledge. pp. 192–206.

Sugden, J. and Tomlinson, A. (1999) 'Digging the Dirt and Staying Clean: Retrieving the Investigative Tradition for a Critical Sociology of Sport', *International Review for the Sociology of Sport*, 34: 385–97.

Van Maanen, J. (1988) *Tales of the Field: On Writing Ethnography*. Chicago: University of Chicago Press.

Wheaton, B. (1995) 'Covert Ethnography and the Ethics of Research: Studying Sport Subcultures', in A. Tomlinson and S. Fleming (eds) *Ethics, Sport and Leisure: Crises and Critiques*. University of Brighton. pp.163–72.

Wheaton, B. (2002) 'Babes on the Beach, Women in the Surf: Researching Gender, Power and Difference in the Windsurfing Culture', in J. Sugden and A. Tomilson (eds) *Power Games: Theory and Method for a Critical Sociology of Sport*. London: Routledge. pp. 240–66.

Wheaton, B. and Beal, B. (2003) '"Keeping it Real": Subcultural media and the Discourses of Authenticity in Alternative Sport', *International Review for the Sociology of Sport*, 38: 155–76.

Willis, P. (1977) Learning to Labour. Aldershot: Gaver Publishing.

Woods, P. (1986) 'Observation', in *Inside Schools*. London: Routledge. pp. 33–51.

FURTHER READING

For an introductory text, see:

Gratton, C. and Jones, I. (2004) *Research Methods for Sport Studies*. London: Routledge.

Sands, R. (2002) *Sporting Ethnography*. Champaign, IL: Human Kinetics.

For more comprehensive essays on sports ethnography, see:

Beal, B. (2002) 'Symbolic Interactionism and Cultural Studies: Doing Critical Ethnography', in J. Maguire and K. Young (eds) *Theory, Sport and Society*. Oxford: JAI. pp. 353–74.

Silk, M.L. (2005) 'Sporting Ethnography: Philosophy, Methodology and Reflection', in David L. Andrews, M.D.S. Silk amd M.L. Silk (eds) *Qualitative Methods in Sports Studies*. Oxford: Berg. pp. 65–103.

Sugden, J. and Tomlinson, A. (1999) 'Digging the Dirt and Staying Clean: Retrieving the Investigative Tradition for a Critical Sociology of Sport', *International Review for the Sociology of Sport*, 34(4): 385–97.

Wheaton, B. (2002) 'Babes on the Beach, Women in the Surf: Researching Gender, Power and Difference in the Windsurfing Culture', in J. Sugden and A. Tomlinson (eds) *Power Games: Theory and Method for a Critical Sociology of Sport*. London: Routledge. pp. 240–66.

For an introduction to doing ethnography see:

Hammersley, M. and Atkinson, P. (1995) *Ethnography: Principles in Practice* (2nd edn). London: Routledge.

Extreme Sport

(alternatively known as lifestyle sport, new sport, whiz sport)

There is now a body of academic literature examining the 'phenomena' of what have been variously termed 'extreme', 'alternative', 'lifestyle', 'whiz', 'panic', 'action' and 'new' sports. These labels encompass a wide range of participatory and made-for-television sporting activities, including residual cultural forms such as surfing and emergent activities such as kite-surfing and BMX biking. While these labels are used synonymously by some commentators, there are differences which signal distinct emphases or expressions of the activities (see Rinehart, 2000). For example, alternative sport includes activities such as residual folk games, that are neither extreme (see Rinehart, 1998, 2000) nor can they be considered lifestyle sports. The term 'extreme sport' has been enthusiastically adopted by the media and advertisers, and is widely associated with North American, Disney owned, sport media channel ESPN's X games (formerly called the eXtreme games) the spiritual home of the 'extreme sport' concept (Kusz, 2004; Rinehart, 1998). This media-driven sporting spectacle features male and female participants competing in a range of summer and winter based 'extreme sports'.

Lifestyle sports are a specific type of alternative sport and include both established activities, like climbing and skateboarding, and newly emergent sports like kite-surfing. Unlike some alternative and extreme sports, lifestyle sports are fundamentally about participation, not spectating, either in live or mediated settings (see Wheaton, 2004). The term *lifestyle* reflects the terminology used by those who participate in these activities, and encapsulates the cultures that surround them. While each lifestyle sport has its own history, identities and development pattern, there are commonalities in their ethos, ideologies and, increasingly, the transnational consumer industries that produce the commodities that underpin their cultures. For example, snowboarding, skateboarding, windsurfing and kite-surfing, have roots in, and are all strongly influenced by surfing. As Bourdieu (1984) observed, many of these sports originated in North America and were then imported to Europe and beyond. With their roots in the counter-cultural social movement of the 1960s and 1970s many have characteristics that are *different* to the rule bound, competitive and masculine cultures of dominant sports. Despite differences in nomenclature, most commentators see such activities as having presented an *alternative* and *potential* challenge to traditional ways of 'seeing' 'doing' and understanding sport (see debate in Rinehart, 2000; Rinehart and Sydnor, 2003; Wheaton, 2004).

The emergence of these sports and their associated lifestyles is related to wider issues around changing contemporary Western society (Wheaton, 2004). Theorists have represented the emergence of these sporting activities and subcultures as a new phase in the development of sports, characterised by some as 'postmodern' (see Rinehart and Sydor, 2003; Wheaton, 2004). In these sports we can see some of the central issues and paradoxes of late-modern capitalist societies, such as the expression of self-identity becoming increasingly self-reflexive, fluid and fragmented, with sport and leisure being increasingly significant sites for identity construction (Wheaton, 2004). In these lifestyle sports, consumers are sold a complete style of life, one that emphasises many of the aspirations of postmodern consumer culture (Wheaton, 2004).

In the twenty-first century lifestyle sports are enjoying a period of unprecedented growth and transformation in many Western industrialised nations. As outlined in Wheaton (2004) and Jarvie (2006) participation in many lifestyle sports continues to grow rapidly, outpacing the expansion of many traditional sports,[1] both among the 'traditional' consumer markets of teenage boys, and, increasingly, among older men, women and girls. For example, in Britain a 'surfing boom' has seen membership of the British Surfing Association increase by 400% in the first five years of the twenty-first century (Barkham, 2006), and in Brazil it is the second most popular sport to football (Jarvie, 2006: 269). Moreover, despite mass media images which represent these activities in terms of youth and masculinity, these sports appeal to significant numbers of female participants. In Britain – mirroring trends in many other countries – surfing participation among women has experienced extensive growth over the past few years (Asthana, 2003, 2004) with some commentators suggesting a 10-fold increase (Barkham, 2006). Women – like men – often continue to surf in their

40s and 50s, reflecting wider trends of an increasingly active aging demographic. Participation for some continues into retirement, evidenced by organisations like the Sea Vets, that cater for the 'silver' (wind) surfers. These participants/consumers range from the 'poseurs', buying into a desirable lifestyle and the occasional participants who experience a range of different alternative and traditional sports, to the 'hard core' committed practitioners who are fully familiar with the lifestyle, argot, fashion and technical skill of their activity. Nevertheless, while some activities are becoming increasingly popular with female participants, and there is evidence of the popularity of these sports outside of the 'global core', the majority of participants are young (or more aptly youthful), affluent, white males from affluent Western industrialised nations.

Wheaton (2004) outlines the key characteristics of lifestyle sports (see also Rinehart and Sydnor, 2003). Participants show high commitment in time and/or money and a style of life that develops around the activity. They have a hedonistic and individualistic ideology that promotes commitment, but often denounces regulation and institutionalisation, and tend to be critical of, or ambivalent to, commercialism and formal 'man-on-man' style competition. They emphasise the aesthetic realm in which one blends with one's environment. Some practitioners refer to their activities as art. The body is used in non-aggressive ways, mostly without bodily contact, yet they embrace and fetishise notions of risk and danger. The locations in which these sports are practised are often new or re-appropriated (urban and/or rural) spaces, without fixed or delineated boundaries. Underpinning these cultural forms are lived cultures that are fundamentally about 'doing it', about taking part. Research on different lifestyle sport cultures (see chapters in Rinehart and Sydor, 2003; Wheaton, 2004) has illustrated that membership, identity and status are influenced by such factors as commitment, attitude, style, gender, class and 'race'. However the 'real' or the 'authentic' tends to be defined around the performance of the activity, around 'doing it'. The *meaning* of participation is articulated around personal expression and gratification, such as the 'thrill of vertigo', and the natural high experienced in an adrenaline rush. As Rinehart (2000) suggests, the posers and 'pretenders' in lifestyle sports are soon revealed.

Wheaton (2004) outlines two themes that are central to the research on lifestyle sport cultures. First, the increasing influence of global capitalism in their development, sporting practices and identities (see also

extreme sport

71

Wheaton, 2005). Despite their counter-cultural heritage, many lifestyle sports now have competitive and commercial dimensions. Surfing, for example, has become a highly institutionalised activity in some countries like Australia and, increasingly, North America, where the sport is well established on a competitive basis and is even part of the school curriculum. This penetration of market forces is particularly evident in the ever expanding array of commodities linked to these activities, such as equipment, clothing and style accessories, video games, DVDs and magazines (Wheaton, 2004). Lifestyle sports have been embraced to sell products ranging from cars to soft drinks to the sought after teenage male consumer audience. Commentators have therefore seen alternative sport, especially in media versions such as ESPN's X-Games, as a 'co-opted' sporting movement, increasingly controlled or dictated by transnational and media conglomerates (see Rinehart, 2000). Nevertheless, commercialisation is not *solely* a co-opting force; lifestyle sports cultures – like many youth cultures – also adapt and change, contesting subcultural meanings, spaces and identities (Wheaton, 2005).

Another aspect of this selling-out debate is found in participants' attitudes to the increasing institutionalisation of lifestyle sports, especially in terms of feelings about formal competitions and other forms of regulation. In some activities there have been (ideological and 'real') battles over their inclusion in traditional 'mainstream' forms of sporting competition such as the Olympic Games (see Rinehart, 2000; Rinehart and Sydnor, 2003; Wheaton, 2005). Whereas in mainstream sport global sporting competitions such as the Olympics Games are considered the pinnacle of sporting achievement, in many lifestyle sports, practitioners have been wary of their incorporation in such institutionalised competitions, seeing it as a form of betraying their alternative values and ideologies. For example, snowboarding's inclusion in the Olympics (it first featured in the Winter Olympics of 1998 in Nagano, Japan) caused much debate in the snowboarding culture and subcultural media, with many elite performers refusing initially to take part, seeing it as an attempt by the FIS (international ski federation) to appropriate snowboarding for its own commercially driven ends.

The second research theme explored in Wheaton (2004) is whether lifestyle sports challenge the gender roles, identities and power relationships in 'traditional' sports (see also Anderson, 1999; Thorpe, 2005). Do these newer non-traditional sports 'offer *different* and potentially more *transformatory* scripts for male and female physicality, than the hegemonic masculinities and femininities characteristic of traditional sports cultures and identities?' (Wheaton, 2004). Chapters in Wheaton (2004) suggest that lifestyle sports present some *opportunities* for more transgressive embodied social identities that differ from masculinities in traditional sports. In some lifestyle sports the boundaries of gender identity are expanded, but in most cases sporting femininities continue to be 'framed by discourses and practices that perpetuate stereotypes of white heterosexual attractiveness, and masculinities based on normative heterosexuality and whiteness, skill and risk, working within, rather than subverting traditional patterns of gendered and bodily domination in sport' (Wheaton, 2004: 19). Kusz (2003, 2004), in analysing media discourses of extreme sport in North America, links them to a revival of 'traditional' American values such as self-reliance, individualism and risk taking, values that are associated with white masculinity and privilege. He therefore interprets the rise of extreme sport as a celebration of white masculinity, part of the white male backlash politics of the 1990s.

While the research on lifestyle sport has proliferated over the past decade, many important issues and questions remain unanswered (see discussion in Ford and Brown, 2005; Jarvie, 2006; Wheaton, 2004). For example, in understanding the experiences of lifestyle sport participants research so far tends to focus on 'core' participants, and particularly white men in the global core. What are the experiences of more marginal participants? How do gender, race, sexuality, age and disability intersect in the process of inclusion and exclusion in these sports and their subcultures? What are the experiences of lifestyle sports among their growing communities in Africa and South America? Are participants, for example, drawn solely from the affluent classes? (Wheaton, 2006). In terms of sport policy, despite the exclusion of many lifestyle sports from national sport policy agendas, such activities might help in the promotion of civic engagement and healthy lifestyles (Kay, 2005; Tomlinson et al., 2005)

One final important issue, as Jarvie (2006: 277) contends, is understanding the relationship between lifestyle sport and forms of collective action such as new social movements like environmentalism. Work on the environmental pressure group, Surfers against Sewage (Wheaton, 2007) illustrates the ways in which lifestyle sports are connected to, and form part of, a broader global wave of new political issues and protest actions that are transforming political culture. Given the appeal of lifestyle sport to marketers, can it manage – on a more sustained level – to move beyond utopian and individualistic issues, and link itself to progressive social change in ways that challenge, or provide an alternative to, global capitalism, ultimately providing a 'new politics of sport in the twenty first century'? (Jarvie, 2006: 279).

NOTE

1. See for example the 15th annual SUPERSTUDY of sport participations conducted by American Sports Data Inc. (ASD) for the Sporting Goods Manufacturers Association (SGMA) 2001, cited in 'Extreme sport', *Sport Business*, 14, August 2001: 17.

REFERENCES

Anderson, K. (1999) 'Snowboarding: The Construction of Gender in an Emerging Sport', *Journal of Sport and Social Issues*, 23(1): 55–79.

Asthana, A. (2003) 'Girls Just Want to Have Fun Too', *The Observer*, 14 September, p. 20.

Asthana, A. (2004) 'Surf's Up for the Beach Girls', *The Observer*, 29 August, p. 17.

Barkham, P. (2006) 'A Bigger Splash, a Lot More Cash', *The Guardian*, 17 July, p. 6–9.

Bourdieu, P. (1984) *Distinction: A Social Critique of the Judgement of Taste*. London: Routledge and Kegan Paul Ltd.

Ford, N. and Brown, D. (2005) *Surfing and Social Theory: Experience, Embodiment and Narrative of the Dream Glide*. London: Routledge.

Jarvie, G. (2006) 'Sport, Lifestyles and Alternative Culture', in *Sport, Culture and Society: An Introduction*. London: Routledge. pp. 267–82.

Kay, J. (2005). 'Extreme Sports and National Sport Policy in Canada', in A. Flintoff, J. Long and K. Hylton (eds) *Youth, Sport and Active Leisure: Theory, Policy and Participation*. Eastbourne: Eastbourne Leisure Studies Association. pp. 47–56.

Kusz, K. (2003) 'BMX, Extreme Sports, and the White Male Backlash', in R. Rinehart and S. Sydor (eds) *To the Extreme: Alternative Sports, Inside and Out*. Albany: State University of New York Press. pp. 145–52.

Kusz, K. (2004) '"Extreme America": The Cultural Politics of Extreme Sports in 1990s America', in B. Wheaton (ed.) *Understanding Lifestyle Sports: Consumption, Identity and Difference*. London: Routledge. pp. 197–214.

Rinehart, R. (1998) 'Inside of the Outside: Pecking Orders within Alternative Sport at the ESPN's 1995 "The eXtreme Games"', *Journal of Sport and Social Issues*, 22(4): 398–414.

Rinehart, R. (2000) 'Emerging Arriving Sport: Alternatives to Formal Sport', in J. Coakley and E. Dunning (eds) *Handbook of Sport Studies*. London: Sage. pp. 504–19.

Rinehart, R. and Sydnor, S. (eds) (2003) *To the Extreme: Alternative Sports, Inside and Out*. Albany: State University of New York Press.

Thorpe, H. (2005) 'Jibbing the Gender Order: Females in the Snowboarding Culture', *Sport in Society*, 8(1): 76–100.

Tomlinson, A., Ravenscroft, N., Wheaton, B. and Gilchrist, P. (2005) *Lifestyle Sport and National Sport Policy: An Agenda for Research*. Report to Sport England, London.

Wheaton, B. (ed.) (2004) *Understanding Lifestyle Sports: Consumption, Identity and Difference*. London: Routledge.

Wheaton, B. (2005) 'Selling Out? The Globalization and Commercialisation of Lifestyle Sports', in L. Allison (ed.) *The Global Politics of Sport*. London: Routledge. pp. 140–61.

Wheaton, B. (2006) 'Re-(en)visioning Action Sport: South Africa Street Kids and Skateboarding', paper presented at North America Sociology of Sport Association. Re-imagining community/re-(en)visioning sport. Vancouver.

Wheaton, B. (2007) 'Identity, Politics, and the Beach: Environmental Activism in Surfers Against Sewage', *Leisure Studies*. 26(3): 279–302.

FURTHER READING

Jarvie, G. (2006) 'Sport, Lifestyles and Alternative Culture', in *Sport, Culture and Society: An Introduction*. London: Routledge. pp. 267–82.

MacNamee, M. (ed.) (2006). *Philosophy, Risk and Adventure Sports*. London: Routledge.

Rinehart, R. and Sydnor, S. (eds) (2003) *To the Extreme: Alternative Sports, Inside and Out*. Albany: State University of New York Press.

Wheaton, B. (ed.) (2004) *Understanding Lifestyle Sports: Consumption, Identity and Difference*. London: Routledge.

Wheaton, B. (2005) 'Selling Out? The Globalization and Commercialisation of Lifestyle Sports', in L. Allison (ed.) *The Global Politics of Sport*. London: Routledge. pp. 140–61.

Young, A., and Dallaire, C. (2008) 'Beware *#! Sk8 at Your Own Risk: The Discourses of Young Female Skateboarders,' in M. Atkinson and K. Young (eds), *Tribal Play: Subcultural Journeys Through Sport* (Volume IV 'Research in the Sociology of Sport'). Bingley: Jai. pp. 235–54.

extreme sport

Fandom

Fandom – the cultural signification and performance of being a fan – has been one of the most dynamic and most contested concepts within recent sociological discussions of sport. Whilst the paying spectator has been an integral element of the economics of sport, tied as it is to the development of professionalism and commercialisation of society during the late nineteenth and early twentieth centuries (Horne et al., 1999), by the outbreak of World War One (1914), having to pay to see sporting events was an established part of the patterns of British leisure and national cultural life (Dobbs, 1973). The notion of fan*dom*, however, is a much more recent development within sports culture.

The *Oxford English Dictionary* dates popular usage of the term to 1903, with many of its associated usages referring to sport. (Despite its secular modernist origins, fandom often resonates with religious or spiritual themes. Cashmore (2002) notes the entomological origins of the term 'fan'. The term is a shortened form of 'fanatic' and the fan has been seen as expressing the excessive, obsessional, devotional and often unreasonable emotions and behaviour of the fundamentalist. Indeed to emphasise the pseudo-religious devotion of the fan, Cashmore notes that the root of the word is derived from the Latin for temple – 'fanum'). Other aspects of popular culture that became associated with early expressions of fandom include science fiction writing and film, and the establishment of celebrity fandom based around the film and music industries. However, it is not until the last decades of the twentieth century that sports fandom becomes a discrete subject of academic discussion in its own right. With the emergence of postmodern (or late-capitalist) social relations, and the growing importance afforded to the role of consumption in late twentieth-century social and cultural life, sports fandom becomes emblematic of important shifts within the relationships between the individual and wider social forms and practices whereby forms of social signification and identity construction become increasingly expressed through performative narratives and styles of consumption.

Jensen (1992: 9) suggests that within popular characterisation and discussion, fandom is frequently 'haunted by images of deviance'. This has certainly been the case in academic and media discussion of fandom within British soccer from the late 1960s to the 1990s, which is characterised by the dominance of studies, and often fraught discussions, of hooliganism and violence. Within the context of British sport, Williams notes that there has recently been a move away from the somewhat 'dry' and often 'solipsistic' accounts of soccer hooliganism (Williams, 2007: 127) to an evaluation of the cultural practice of fandom as a social expression of social identity, belonging, place and community, which encompasses wider and more varied forms of sports and sports fandom, such as in cricket (see Greenfield and Osborn, 1998; Parry and Malcolm, 2004) British ice hockey (Crawford, 2001, 2004) and British basketball (Falcous and Maguire, 2005) and rugby league (Falcous, 1998).

SPORTS FANDOM

In a sporting context, fandom implies more than simply watching. It suggests a much more active and partisan relationship with sport than the perhaps more passively neutral act of spectating or just simply watching. Being a fan implies an unconditional taking of sides. Fandom in part characterises the subcultural organisation of the practices, spaces and places where this 'taking of sides' is afforded (sub)cultural significance and legitimation. It is not enough simply to say one is a fan – membership of a fandom is conferred through processes of (often hierarchical) cultural legitimation, characterisation and authentication. To be a fan – to gain membership of a fandom – is in part a process of cultural contestation, involving particular expressions of, or orientations towards, consumption, both in the physical consumption of the material world and the objects of fandom, and in the more abstract value systems of moral structures that frame the objects of fandom. In her analysis of dance-based youth subcultures that developed around rave in Britain during the 1980s, Sarah Thornton (1995) draws upon the notion of subcultural capital to illustrate how ideas of authenticity and 'otherness' are constructed in order to demarcate particular subcultures and styles from other expressions of cultural identity. In her analysis Thornton draws heavily upon the Pierre Bourdieu's ('The Forms of Capital', 1986; see also 1984) notion of 'cultural-capital' – forms of knowledge, skills or education (emotional and physical, formal and informal) with which individuals and social groups enhance and maintain positions of status and distinction.

In her studies of 'lifestyle' sports participation (particularly in windsurfing subcultures – see e.g. Wheaton, 2004, 2007) Belinda Wheaton makes particular use of Thornton's notion of subcultural capital in examining the ways by which windsurfers construct hierarchies in which particular styles, and an ethos of consumption are either authenticated or de-legitimated. Similar approaches (see e.g. Brick, 2004) have been used in the analysis of soccer fan cultures. Although not explicitly drawing upon the notion of '(sub)cultural-capital', Brick's analysis focuses upon the role of the commodity and the performance of consumption within particular styles of soccer fandom, as a means by which particular styles of fandom are either legitimated, or de-legitimated as 'authentic' or inauthentic expressions of fandom.

THEORY

Richard Giulianotti (2002) draws upon Thornton's (1995) analysis of 'subcultural capital' in his analysis of the impact of commodification and forms of mediatised consumption upon fan culture. Through a discussion of the processes of distinction and status that evolve through the contemporary consumption of British football, Giulianotti concludes that fandom can be characterised by discrete typologies. Central to this discussion are the 'traditional' or 'hot spectator' and the 'cool fan.' The traditional spectator is defined by 'a long-term personal emotional investment in the [football] club' and this is underpinned 'by a conscious commitment to show thick personal solidarity' (Giulianotti, 2002: 33). The relationship between the 'traditional supporter' and the club is akin to those with close family and friends. In this sense the 'traditional supporter' is culturally contracted to their club, a contract which expresses itself as 'a lived experience, rooted in a grounded identity' (Giulianotti, 2002: 33). The 'traditional' or 'hot' supporter is counterposed to the (often both spatially and emotionally) distant postmodern 'cool' or 'post-fan' (Giulianotti, 1999; Redhead, 1997). Whilst expressing a knowledge of and intimacy with the club, the relationship is both more distant and cool. The 'cool' fan's identification is not as culturally 'deep' as that of the 'traditional' fan, in that it is 'inordinately unidirectional in its affections' (Giulianotti, 2002: 36), driven by the 'hyper commodified' (Walsh and Giulianotti, 2001) and mediatised forms of consumption. The reference points of the 'cool' fan's identity are embedded in the symbols and signs of the sporting star system and contemporary celebrity culture (Giulianotti, 2002: 37; see also Williams, 2006).

The conceptualisation of fan identities as a series of typologies or taxonomies – each constituent type characterised by an orientation towards either a traditional (modernist) pattern of consumption, or the postmodern consumer society – forms the dominant academic discourse on sports fan culture (Williams, 2007). According to John Williams, fan culture is currently shaped by globalised flows within which 'modernist spectator allegiances are rapidly morphing into new and more complex forms of "late-modern" sporting affiliation' (Williams, 2007: 128). Within the context of global transformation, Williams suggests, academic study of sports fandom is largely premised upon the production of 'ideal-type taxonomical sets' which counterpose the 'traditional' with the 'new'. The 'traditional' fan, characterised by patterns of match attendance and a 'residual' of 'traditional' 'working classness' – premised upon the ties of family and place (see e.g. Crabbe and Brown, 2004; Giulianotti, 2002) – stands in opposition to the 'new consumer' fan (Williams, 2007).

The exhaustion of the hooligan debate – a debate which by the late 1980s had become politically unsustainable (Giulianotti, 1994; Taylor, 1991) – corresponds with an economic and cultural restructuring of soccer culture. Alongside rapid commercialisation and media investment, soccer culture witnessed the emergence of new and vibrant forms of fan culture, characterised in part by the emergence of the fanzine and independent supporter organizations (King, 1998; Taylor, 1991). Facilitated by the social and cultural transformations in the class structures, and the growth of knowledge-based economies in post-industrial Western societies, soccer culture enters a new phase, increasingly dominated by new postmodern patterns of consumption. British soccer's 'new consumption' is, it is suggested, consistent with the rise of a predominantly white-collar, information and technology literate, new middle class (Giulianotti, 1999; King, 1998). The dominance of the 'new middle class' within the post-industrial economic landscape is reflected in the cultural landscape of European soccer culture, which ruptures the traditional cultural and social relationship between sport and the inner city, industrial working-class community. Steve Redhead suggests that:

> The traditional soccer culture of participatory, largely male, fandom of the terraces – threatened by smaller all-seater stadia, steeply rising prices of admission and the embourgeoisement of the sport – has effectively transferred itself to the already existing male 'pub culture' which in part created it in the first place. (Redhead, 1997: 30)

Discussion of the postmodern consumption of sports fan culture tends to accentuate the exclusion of traditional, localised working-class patterns of consumption, to all but the periphery of the political economy of the 'new football'. However, in his study of British ice hockey, Garry Crawford (2004) explicitly rejects the somewhat crude and 'false' opposition between the 'traditional' and 'authentic' fan and the new, ersatz sports consumer. Crawford suggests that this oppositional typology tends towards a romanticisation of particular expressions of fandom which are constructed as 'traditional' and fails to 'locate sports social contexts of an emergent late-modern performance/spectacle society' (Williams, 2007: 130). For Crawford late-modern (or postmodern) sport functions as a source of deep identity construction and opportunity for social performance. This aspect is enhanced, Crawford suggests, especially in the context of the decline in what might be considered as 'traditional' modernist sources of individual and group identity, such as the family, church, community, work, and, we might add, politics. Crawford's study raises a significant question – that maybe it is because of contemporary sport's commodified nature, rather than despite it, that sport functions as a particularly dynamic space for the reinterpretation or re-imagining of identity and belonging.

POSTMODERNITY, PARADOX AND POST-FANDOM

The remaking of fandom, and its current cultural re-centering, gives rise to a notable contradiction whereby postmodern forms and expressions of soccer fan culture have on the one hand become increasingly 'privatised' and 'individuated' through its increasing commodification and mediatisation (Redhead, 1997), yet increasingly 'public' as a cultural practice. Redhead proposes the concept of the 'post-fan', which encompasses the seeming contradiction between the apparent cultural pervasiveness soccer fandom now enjoys, and its commodified and privatised nature. 'Post-fandom' connotes, he suggests:

> not so much the idea simply conceived in the past that a historical period of fandom – mainly male 'terrace' soccer culture, from whatever date is chosen, late nineteenth century, 1950s or mid-1980s – is at an end, more that the fragmentary, self-conscious, reflexive, mediated, 'artistic' (Germain, 1994), 'style-surfing' (Polhemus, 1996) notion of what it means to be a fan of soccer, music and fashion which has always been present is now more pervasive. (Redhead, 1997: 29)

As fandom becomes increasingly pervasive it also becomes an increasingly 'privatised' activity or practice. The 'post-fan', Redhead continues 'does not have to leave the home or the bar to see the object of his/her gaze because television and video provide endless opportunities for "grazing" and "channel surfing"' (1997: 29). Here we encounter perhaps the most ironically significant contradictions of contemporary fandom. Indeed, if it is the case, as Steve Redhead (1997) notes above, that the 'traditional' fan has sought refuge from the embourgoisement of soccer culture in the public house and bar, one might be justified in concluding that far from being a residual counterpoint, 'traditional fandom' is in essence an integral expression of 'post-fandom'.

REFERENCES

Bourdieu, P. (1984) *Distinction: A Critique of the Judgement of Taste*. London: Routledge.

Bourdieu, P. (1986) 'The Forms of Capital', in P. Bourdieu (ed.) *Handbook of Theory and Research for the Sociology of Education*. New York: Greenwood Press. pp. 241–58.

Brick, C. (2004) 'Misers, Merchandise and Manchester United: The Peculiar Paradox of the Political Economy of Consumption', in D.L. Andrews (ed.) *Manchester United. A Thematic Study*. London: Routledge. pp. 101–12.

Crabbe, T. and Brown, A. 'You're Not Welcome Anymore: The Football Crowd, Class and Social Exclusion', in S. Wagg (ed.) *Football and Social Exclusion*. London: Routledge. pp. 71-81.

Cashmore, E. (2002) *Sports Culture: An A–Z Guide*. London: Routledge.

Crawford, G. (2001) 'Characteristics of a British Ice Hockey Audience – major findings of the 1998 and 1999 Manchester Storm Ice Hockey Supporter Surveys', *International Review for the Sociology of Sport*, 36(1): 71–81.

Crawford, G. (2004) *Consuming Sport: Fans, Sport and Culture*. London: Routledge.

Dobbs, B. (1973) *Edwardians at Play: Sport 1890–1914*. London: Pelham Books.

Falcous, M. (1998) 'TV Made it All a New Game: Not Again! A Case Study of the European Superleague', *Occasional Papers in Football Studies*, 1(1): 4–22.

Falcous, M. and Maguire, J. (2005) 'Globetrotters and Local Heroes? Labour Migration, Basketball and Local Identities', *Sociology of Sport Journal*, 22: 137–57.

Germain, J. (1994) *In Soccer Wonderland*. London: Booth-Clibborn.

Giulianotti, R. (1994) 'Social Identity and Public Order: Political and Academic Discources on Football Violence', in R. Guilianotti, N. Bonny and M. Hepworth (eds) *Football Violence and Social Order*. London: Routledge. pp. 153–205.

Giulianotti, R. (1999) *Football. Sociology of the Global Game*. Cambridge: Polity.

Giulianotti, R. (2002) 'Supporters, Fans, Followers and *Flaneurs*: A Taxonomy of Spectator Identities in World Football', *Journal of Sport and Social Issues*, 26(1): 25–46.

Greenfield, S. and Osborn, G. (1998) 'The Legal Regulation of Football and Cricket: "England's Dreaming"', in M. Roche (ed.) *Sport, Popular Culture and Identity*. Aachen: Meyer & Meyer.

Horne, J., Tomlinson, A. and Whannel, G. (1999) *Understanding Sport. An Introduction to the Sociological and Cultural Analysis of Sport*. London: E & FN Spon.

Jensen, J. (1992) 'Fandom as Pathology: The Consequences of Characterization', in L.A. Lewis (ed.) *The Adoring Audience: Fan Culture and Popular Media*. London: Routledge. pp. 9–29.

fandom

King, A. (1998) *The End of the Terraces. The Transformation of English Football in the 1990s*. London: Leicester University Press.

Parry, M. and Malcolm, D. (2004) 'England's Barmy Army', *International Review for the Sociology of Sport*, 39(1): 75–94.

Polhemus, T. (1996) *Style Surfing*. London: Thames Hudson.

Redhead, S. (1997) *Post-Fandom and the Millennial Blues. The Transformation of Soccer Culture*. London: Routledge.

Taylor, I. (1991) 'English Football in the 1990s: Taking Hillsborough Seriously', in J. Williams and S. Wagg (eds) *British Football and Social Change: Getting into Europe*. Leicester: Leicester University Press. pp. 1–15.

Thornton, S. (1995) *Club Cultures: Music, Media and Subcultural Capital*. Cambridge: Polity Press.

Walsh, A.J. and Giulianotti, R. (2001) 'This Sporting Mammon: A Normative Critique of the Commodification of Sport', *Journal of the Philsophy of Sport*, 28: 53–77.

Wheaton, B. (2004) *Lifestyle Sport: Consumption, Identity and Difference, Routledge Critical Studies in Sport*. London: Routledge.

Wheaton, B. (2007) 'After Sport Culture: Rethinking Sport and Post-Subcultural Theory', *Journal of Sport and Social Issues*, 31: 283–307.

Williams, J. (2006) '"Protect Me From What I Want": Football Fandom, Celebrity Cultures and "New" Football in England', *Soccer and Society*, 7(1): 96–114.

Williams, J. (2007) 'Rethinking Sports Fandom: The Case of European Soccer', *Leisure Studies*, 26(2): 127–46.

Feminism

Feminism is a socialist, anti-family, political movement that encourages women to leave their husbands, kill their children, practice witchcraft, destroy capitalism and become lesbians (Pat Robertson, US televangelist, 1992)

I myself have never been able to find out precisely what feminism is: I only know that people call me a feminist whenever I express sentiments that differentiate me from a doormat or a prostitute (Rebecca West)

These two, sharply contrasting observations on feminism give some indication of the controversy that has surrounded male and female roles in Western societies during the last century. In his remark, the ultra-conservative TV preacher and sometime presidential candidate Pat

Robertson derides feminism because, for him, it seeks to undermine Western, capitalist, patriarchal social systems. In his damning of feminism he suggests that it disdains women's roles as heterosexuals, wives and mothers and he implies that women are instead encouraged to take up 'unnatural' ways of being, including witchcraft, anti-capitalism and lesbianism!

Feminism certainly does set out to change women's place in society and this calls for change on many levels. Robertson's polemic may be thought typical of a widespread anti-feminist backlash in that it cites dangers to women's conventional relationships with men, children, capitalism and other women. It is surprising, though, that Robertson doesn't include the claim that 'feminism encourages women to hate men'. It is often assumed that feminism is wholly to do with theory, politics, praxis and/or activism all of which is anti-men. Clearly such a simplistic understanding of feminism is inaccurate. Feminism is not a single discrete theory or politically coherent approach (Wilson, 1986, cited in Whelehan, 1995); it is not one way of living out beliefs and values. It is a complex and dynamic set of theories, politics and praxis. However, feminism does have a focus, which is gender. For sports feminists the concern is with gendered relations to power in sporting contexts, practices and rituals, and as Birrell points out 'it is not to be confused with a focus on "women in sport"' (2002: 61).

The various developments in feminism have been documented in many places and in many ways. Most undergraduate students are aware of a historiography that charts first and second wave feminism in the US, the UK and Europe. Key concepts to emerge from the social movements for women's liberation during the second wave include 'consciousness raising' and the notion that the 'personal is political'. Through localised activism women were able to organise a collective challenge and resistance to sexism, misogyny, sexual harassment and sexual abuse. Such activism was accompanied by a theoretical engagement with how Western societies were organised and arranged primarily to value and benefit men. The term patriarchy emerged as a useful way to explain these arrangements and the many forms of oppression women experienced, because of their gender, in their everyday lives (see Walby, 1990).

For some feminist writers and activists women's experiences are shaped by patriarchy. For others, though, it is a dual system of patriarchy and capitalism and/or class, and for still others it is a triple oppression based on race, gender and class. These different concerns and emphases dominated feminist debate for four decades following the initial emergence of the

Women's Liberation Movement in the 1960s. Feminists have not agreed on the exact details of women's oppression or emancipation, although gender relations endure as a common theme, and debate has meant, at times, schisms within feminism that have not been easy to reconcile. For example, it is middle-class white women who have had their voices heard, which has meant that 'intersecting and mutually constituted forms of oppression' (Ali, 2007: 196) have often been ignored. It is important to remain mindful of Ali's (2007) argument that 'it is not possible to think of all women as simply and only 'oppressed by all men' through a monolithic system named patriarchy' (2007: 196). Feminism is now striving to document and take account of the multiplicity of gender and women's experiences. In this way feminism is more frequently referred to as feminisms.

In sports studies it is possible to identify a range of feminist approaches (see Birrell, (2002) and Scraton and Flintoff (2002) for a detailed and chronological account). For the purpose of this short discussion the different approaches are: feminism and identity politics; profeminism; post-structuralist feminism; post-colonial feminism; and psychoanalytic feminism. Feminism and identity politics encompasses much of the second-wave feminist debate surrounding women's right to equality. Within these debates 'women' emerges as a category and it is the rights of women as a collective that are fought for. During the 1980s and 1990s sports feminists and feminists in leisure studies highlighted the many ways women were ignored and omitted from sport and leisure opportunities and participation, as well as from research agendas and official/academic documentation on active involvement (Hargreaves, 1990). In this way, women's inclusion became a political issue and 'women' a category of identity. However, it soon became apparent that it was impossible to speak of women as a unitary category – a homogeneous group. Women experienced sport and leisure differently according to sexuality, class, race and ability. Despite moves to recognise diversity within the category of 'women', identity politics continued to be a useful way to claim different women's on-going experiences of inequality and exclusion. For example, we became aware of the particular struggles facing lesbians, working-class women, black and South Asian women and disabled women.

Gender relations were further criticised by an emerging profeminist approach, which involved studying in detail how men and masculinity contributed to cultures of sexism, misogyny, homophobia and racism.

Most of this critical work on men is also by men. The tag 'pro' alludes to debate surrounding the claim men have to feminism, given their subjectivity, and, in effect, questions the authenticity of men in feminism. However, it is clear from the substantial critical work presented by writers such as McKay, Messner and Sabo (McKay et al., 2000) that men writing from a feminist perspective – profeminists – can effectively reveal the ways men and masculinity function to promote a dominant (hegemonic) sporting maleness, which marginalises women and 'other' men.

The recent focus on so-called post-structuralist writers, such as Foucault and Butler, by some feminist writers has meant a move to consider discourse, the body, sexuality and regimes of regulation more closely. For example, Foucault's analysis of power has helped feminists understand the complexities of oppression and acts of resistance. For Foucault, individuals are both objects and subjects of power. Gender relations in relation to power (social, cultural, economic and political power) become complex webs, or matrices, and power circulates. There are common configurations, which reflect institutional power and formal discourses. Markula and Pringle (2006) demonstrate how Foucault's work can help an understanding of women's relationships to their bodies, as well as how discourses of exercise and health inform behaviour – a process of defining and disciplining themselves which Foucault calls a technology of the self. (Sykes (1996) and Caudwell (2003) also consider the operation of power and their particular focus is sexuality.) Foucault and Butler are particularly relevant here because both are interested in how sexuality has been identified, defined and given meaning. The concept of heteronormativity has emerged from this kind of post-structuralist feminist analysis.

Finally, post-colonial feminism and psychoanalytic feminism are still to be established in the sociology of sport. Since the second wave, feminists have been more sensitive to issues surrounding 'race'. However within sport studies there are few contributions. There have been numerous calls for more theorising of 'race', ethnicity, whiteness and gender (Birrell, 1989), but, to date, there is a paucity of work in the area. As Ali (2007) points out in her work on feminism and post-colonialism we must remain aware of colonial legacies within academia and how research and resources might be affected in post-colonial society.

Feminist psychoanalysis is well established in feminist film/media theory but does not have a reputation in feminist sports media studies. It has potential to explain desire, spectacle and the gaze. However, feminist analysis of media representations of sport and gender tend to adopt theory from the second wave or from a post-structuralist perspective. Interestingly, Butler's work makes links with some aspects of feminist psychoanalysis, and Davidson's (in Caudwell, 2006) analysis of gay pride and shame is one of the few examples of an engagement with both the social and the psychic domain

To finish with a terse but popular slogan – 'feminism is the radical notion that women are people' – is to oversimplify what feminism is. Although the maxim does provide a reminder of why and how feminism developed, it does not indicate the many nuances of feminism and does not reflect the many debates that have occurred. We can no longer talk of feminism in the singular, instead we must acknowledge feminisms and be aware of the different ways feminists understand gender and/in sport.

REFERENCES

Ali, S. (2007) 'Feminism and Postcolonialism: Knowledge/Politics', *Ethnic and Race Studies*, 30(2): 191–212.

Birrell, S. (2002) 'Feminist Theories for Sport', in J. Coakley and E. Dunning (eds) *Handbook of Sports Studies*. London: Sage. pp. 61–76.

Caudwell, J. (2003) 'Sporting Gender: Women's Footballing Bodies as Sites/Sights for the [Re]Articulation of Sex, Gender and Desire', *Sociology of Sport Journal*, 20: 371–86.

Caudwell, J. (2006) *Sport, Sexualities and Queer Theory*. London: Routledge.

Hargreaves, J. (1990) 'Gender on the Sports Agenda', *International Review for the Sociology of Sport*, 25: 287–308.

Markula, P. (ed.) (2005) *Feminist Sport Studies. Sharing Experiences of Joy and Pain*. Albany: SUNY.

Markula, P. and Pringle, R. (2006) *Foucault, Sport and Exercise: Power, Knowledge and Transforming the Self*. London: Routledge.

McKay, J., Messner, M. and Sabo, D. (2000) *Masculinities, Gender Relations, and Sport*. Thousand Oaks, CA: Sage.

Scraton, S. and Flintoff, A. (eds) (2002) *Gender and Sport: A Reader*. London: Routledge.

Sykes, H. (1996) 'Constr(i)(u)cting Lesbian Identities in Physical Education: Feminist and Poststructural Approaches to Researching Sexuality', *Quest*, 48: 459–69.

Walby, S. (1990) *Theorizing Patriarchy*. London: Blackwell Publishing.

Whelehan, I. (1995) *Modern Feminist Thought*. Edinburgh: Edinburgh University Press.

Pat Robertson's remark can be found at: http://thinkexist.com/quotation/feminism_is_a_socialist-anti-family-political/217913.html (accessed: 8 April 2008).

Rebecca West's observation is in Maggie Humm (ed.) (1992) *Feminisms: A Reader*. Hemel Hempstead: Harvester Wheatsheaf. p. 34.

Gender

Until the early 1960s the word 'gender' was probably most commonly used in relation to the study of language, rather than of human affairs: the French language, for example, designates certain words as 'male' or 'female'. During the 1960s, however, the issue of gender became central to the politics of culture – arguments, in other words, over how we should live – and, since the 1970s, gender has been a central theme in Western sociology. The word 'gender' refers to the social roles and identities typically ascribed to one sex or the other in any given human society. The politicisation of the word over the last 50 years or so has represented an attempt by feminists to do away with the biological determinism of the nineteenth and early twentieth centuries and, thus, to challenge Sigmund Freud's famous assertion that 'Anatomy is destiny'. Gender, in the new view, was *socially constructed*. While feminism is dealt with elsewhere in this book, this short section will discuss briefly how the notion of gender as a social construction has been pursued in relation to sport.

Historically, females were barred from the realms of sport and exercise. When it was mooted that women might compete in the modern Olympics, Baron de Coubertin, the chief architect of the Games, declared that women competing in 'men's' sports 'would be impractical, uninteresting, unaesthetic and improper' (Kort, 2004). Ironically, but, in retrospect perhaps not surprisingly, women's early access to these activities grew out of what would now be called a male chauvinist ideology: Social Darwinism (Abercrombie et al., 2000: 321–2). This doctrine, associated particularly with the philosopher Herbert Spencer (1820–1903), and particularly popular in the United States, adapted Darwin's notion of the 'survival of the fittest' to the understanding of society. The world, in effect, was to the strong – the whites, the upper classes and the males – and women's chief role was to give birth to healthy children: an ethos supported by some of the pioneers of women's physical education, such as the Swedish educationist Martina Bergman Osterberg (1849–1915) (Hargreaves, 1994: 77). Gradually, in the closing years of the nineteenth century, the idea that women should be allowed to play competitive games gained strength, particularly among those females teaching at or attending girls' boarding schools and teacher training colleges (Holt, 1992: 118). Some women's sport was undertaken purely for social reasons – a gentle game of tennis, perhaps, at a suburban club (Holt, 1992: 127) – but some of it, equally, was competitive, and in the 1920s a campaign was mounted to have women admitted to the Olympic athletics events. (Previously, women had only been permitted to enter events deemed compatible with their gender. These were tennis and golf from 1900 and, later, archery, gymnastics, skating and swimming.) An unofficial Women's Olympics was staged in Paris in 1922 and women ran competitively in an Olympiad for the first time at Amsterdam in 1928 (Kidd, 1994; see also Hargreaves, 1994: 211).

Some of the progress made in women's sports continued to be predicated on the traditional distinctions of gender and sexuality. The appearance of the French tennis player Suzanne Lenglen (1899–1938) in the Wimbledon Ladies Singles Final of 1919 wearing lightweight and diaphanous clothing caused outrage. Lenglen, known in the French sports press as 'La Divine' ('The Goddess') played as a professional in the United States in the late 1920s. She became the first of a long line of female sportspeople to trade on her attractiveness and femininity, marketing, among other things, her own perfume, rackets, dolls and clothing (see Engelmann, 1988). However, much political energy has been expended over the last 40 years in trying to downplay traditional differences and gain access for females to sports previously played only, or principally, by males. These efforts have been rooted in *liberal feminism* (in effect, the individualistic, and arguably mainstream, form of feminism which urges women to seek and to take equal opportunities, and calls for legal and political change to assist them in this), and have either sprung from, or inspired, equal opportunities programmes, anti-discrimination legislation or campaigns to boost girls' sporting aspirations. The best example here is probably Title IX. This refers to some Educational Amendments passed by the US Congress in 1972. Title IX, a section of this law, prohibits discrimination against girls and women in federally funded programmes. This includes athletics programmes and has resulted in wider opportunities, e.g. athletic scholarships for women, although enforcement of Title IX faltered during the presidencies of conservative Republicans Ronald Reagan and George H.W. Bush.[1]

Recent discussion in many countries has argued the respective merits of *gender equality* (seeking the same starting line) as against *gender equity* (seeking the same finish line).

The pursuit of gender equality or gender equity in sport continues to be an important subject for research (see e.g. Scraton and Flintoff, 2002) but there is now an increasing focus on power and gender relations in the sociological examination of sport. This research, in essence, concerns the ongoing social construction of gender through sport and it covers at least three main areas.

First, there is considerable literature on the production of ideologies of masculinity and male power through sport. This is a big issue particularly, but not solely, in the United States, where since the late nineteenth century there has been a strong tradition of aggressive male sports and where regular homage is paid to the famous dictum of football coach Vince Lombardi (1913–1970): 'Winning isn't everything. It's the only thing'. He also told his team, the Green Bay Packers: 'Dancing is a contact sport. Football is a hitting sport'.[2] It's widely argued that sports such as American football and boxing, which deploy the human body as a weapon, express a fear of, and distaste for, 'the feminine'. Coaches, it is stressed, often say such things as: 'Screw 'em, but don't marry 'em'; they admonish their players for 'Tackling like a woman'; and sport, generally, is perceived as an anti-gay culture, in which gay sportspeople keep quiet about their sexuality (see e.g. McKay et al., 2000; Messner and Sabo, 1990). Thus, to adopt the popular phrase, sport reproduces women's oppression and men's repression. There is, of course, some resistance to the idea that sports are a key way in which aggressive masculinity is made. Some of this resistance is based ultimately, in socio-biology – that is, the notion that the separate spheres of male and female are rooted in the historic interplay of the *biological* (the body) and the *social* (society/material circumstances). For example, it is often argued that for most of human history men have been fighters, so men are neurally conditioned to be aggressive. Some writers, like the Australian sociologist John Carroll, have related this to sport. Carroll suggested in 1986: 'It is the warrior drive and the warrior ethos that are resurrected in modern team football' (Carroll, 1986: 93, quoted in Humberstone, 1990: 202).

But there are also interesting debates within feminism, and within the paradigm of 'social construction', about masculinity and violence in sport. For instance the American feminist novelist Joyce Carol Oates (1994) has suggested: 'Men fighting men to determine worth (i.e., masculinity) excludes women as completely as the female experience of childbirth excludes men'.[3] Elsewhere in the same book she suggests

gender

that 'Boxing is a celebration of the lost religion of masculinity, all the more trenchant for its being lost'.[4] But there are now a number of writers willing to celebrate boxing as a new facet of women's experience. For example, in a recent book, the writer Leah Hager Cohen (2005) argues strongly for women's right to their own aggression and points out that, in the United States alone there are well over 2,000 registered female boxers (Cohen, 2005: 13).

A second area of debate concerns the reproduction of dominant notions of women through the sports media. The principal areas of concern here have been: the lack of coverage of female sport (its 'symbolic annihilation'); the corresponding trivialisation and marginalisation of women's sport; the (hetero)sexualisation of women athletes; and the construction either of women as unnatural athletes or of athletes as unnatural women (see e.g. Duncan (2006) and Birrell and Theberge (1994)).

In a recent review of the relevant literature Nathalie Koivula argued that 'it is well documented that women receive strikingly less coverage than men, even in sports in which women in fact constitute a majority of the participants' and that female athletes are 'are often marginalized, made invisible, trivialized, infantile, and reduced to sex objects' (Koivula, 1999). As to the heterosexualisation of female athletes and allusions to their 'naturalness' or otherwise, the trend, according to some writers, has been for discussion of this issue to merge with a previously parallel debate about sexuality and the sporting body as sites for defining gender relations. Here we find the invocation of 'third wave feminism'. This is a feminism that, according to some of its exponents, 'is at ease with contradiction' (Gamble, 2000: 52, quoted in Heywood and Dworkin, 2003: 10). The central implication of this is that contemporary female sportspeople and the academic observers of gender politics in sport are now increasingly comfortable with attractive and/or sexualised imagery of the sporting body. There seem to be two central roots to this development. One is the political and intellectual current flowing from the work of Judith Butler who has argued that gender is simply something that we learn to perform. For Butler, and many gender sociologists, the assumption that sex, gender and sexuality are causally related is mistaken. Gender and sexuality should be deconstructed – i.e. broken down and no longer seen as binary opposites. This line of argument has brought cases of transgender to prominence and proffered as evidence that sex, gender and sexuality do not exist as permanent conditions. As an example drawn from the world of sport we can observe the case of Renée Richards, a tennis player born 'male' in 1938, who had sex reassignment surgery in 1975 and was refused admission, as a woman, to the US Open tournament the following year. Assumptions of fixed sex and gender have also been the subtext of anti-drug campaigns. The logic of this (the Butler) position is, in effect, to promote a free market in gender and sexual imagery.

The other factor is the corresponding commodification of sportspeople. The spread of neoliberal, pro-market politics in virtually all the societies in which modern sport is either played or consumed has meant a heavy commercialisation, both of sport and of the people who practise it. This commercialisation, inevitably, encompasses the body and sexuality, but, in the view of a number of contemporary sociologists, this is based on a democracy of signs and preferences. Thus, while the 'babe factor' flourishes in the marketing of female sport/sportspeople, there is nevertheless growing reference to 'female masculinity' in sport and praise for images of sportswomen that combine glamour and physical strength, such as a *Vogue* shoot of the American sprinter Marion Jones in January 2001. (For a full discussion of these issues, see Heywood and Dworkin, 2003: xv–xxiv, 76–99). Moreover, athletes and their advisors are ever more conscious of the commercial possibilities that nuanced sexual imagery can carry, the best example here being the marketing of the 'metrosexual' footballer David Beckham to gay and female audiences.[5] Sociologists such as Toby Miller now write of, and welcome, a symbolic world of 'sportsex', the politics of which 'are far from a functionalist world of total domination by straight, orthodox masculinity because of the niche targets that these commodified signs are directed toward (such as straight women and gay men) ... the beneficial aspect to cataloguing sports is its challenges to gender convention' (Miller, 2001: 10, quoted in Heywood and Dworkin, 2003: 11). Moreover there is a widespread conviction that the new politics of 'sportsex' represent an extension, and a consummation, of the struggles to enforce Title IX. Others are not so sure. The American writer Joanna Cagan wrote in 1999:

> in a lifetime of fluctuating self-esteem and body image, sports has facilitated the few times when I am too happy and preoccupied to run my normal painful analysis of my body and how it rates on the old sexy-meter that drives Hollywood and New York City ... If I pick up a glove, a bat, a basketball, I am judged on what I do with them – not, for once, on how I look doing them.

For Cagan, the media hype surrounding the Women's Soccer World Cup of that year affirmed an old high school truth: 'the pretty girls always win' (Cagan, 1999).

gender

91

NOTES

1. See http://www. feminist.org/sports/titleIXa.asp (accessed: 28 March 2007).
2. See http://www.vincelombardi.com//about/bio2.htm (accessed: 28 March 2007).
3. This extract can be found at http://www.usfca.edu/-southerr/boxing.html (accessed: 29 March 2007).
4. This extract can be found at http://www.brainyquote.com/quotes/authors/j/joyce_carol_oates.html (accessed: 29 March 2007).
5. See Mark Simpson 'Meet the Metrosexual', http://dir.salon.com/story/ent/feature/2002/07/22/metrosexual/index.html (accessed: 30 March 2007).

REFERENCES

Abercrombie, Nicholas, Hill, Stephen and Turner, Bryan S. (2000) *Dictionary of Sociology*. London: Penguin.

Birrell, Susan and Theberge, Nancy (1994) 'The Sociological Study of Women in Sport'; 'Structural Constraints Facing Women in Sport'; 'Ideological Constraints of Women in Sport'; 'Feminist Resistance and Transformation in Sport' – four chapters in D. Margaret Costa and Sharon R. Guthrie (eds) *Women and Sport: Interdisciplinary Perspectives*. Champaign, IL: Human Kinetics Press, pp. 323–76.

Cagan, Joanna (1999) 'Too Hot Mamas? The Problem with Sexualizing Women's Sports'. http://www.nerve.com/Dispatches/Cagan/notMamas/(accessed: 10 December 2008).

Carroll, John (1986) 'Sport: Virtue and Grace', *Theory, Culture & Society*, 3(1): 91–8.

Cohen, Leah Hager (2005) *Without Apology: Girls, Women and the Desire to Fight*. New York: Random House.

Duncan, Margaret Carlisle (2006) 'Gender Warriors in Sport: Women and the Media' in Arthur A. Raney and Jennings Bryant (eds) *Handbook of Sports and Media*. London: Routledge, pp. 231–252.

Engelmann, Larry (1988) *The Goddess and the American Girl: The story of Suzanne Lenglen and Helen Wills*. New York: Oxford University press.

Gamble, Sarah (2000) *The Critical Dictionary of Feminism and Postfeminism*. New York: Routledge.

Hargreaves, Jennifer (1994) *Sporting Females: Critical Issues in the History and Sociology of Women's Sports*. London: Routledge.

Heywood, Leslie and Dworkin, Shari L. (2003) *Built to Win: The Female Athlete as Cultural Icon*. London: University of Minnesota Press.

Holt, Richard (1992) *Sport and the British*. Oxford: Oxford University Press.

Humberstone, Barbara (1990) 'Warriors or Wimps? Creating Alternative Forms of Physical Education', in Michael Messner and Donald Sabo (eds) *Sport, Men and the Gender Order: Critical Feminist Perspectives*. Champaign, IL: Human Kinetics.

Kidd, Bruce (1994) 'The Women's Olympic Games: Important Breakthrough Obscured By Time', *Canadian Association for the Advancement of women and Sport and Physical Activity Action Bulletin*, Spring, http://www. caaws.ca/e/milestones/women_history/olympic_games_Print.cfm (accessed: 28 March 2007).

Koivula, Nathalie (1999) 'Gender Stereotyping in Televised Media Sport Coverage', *Sex Roles: A Journal of Research,* October, http://www.findarticles.com/p/articles/mi_m2294/is_1999_Oct/ai_59426460 (accessed: 29 March 2007).

Kort, Michele (2004) 'Our August Amazons: Women's Sports Reach Olympian', *Ms Magazine, Summer,* http://www.msmagazine.com/summer2004/augustamazons.asp (accessed: 28 March 2007).

McKay, Jim, Messner, Michael and Sabo, Donald (eds) (2000) *Masculinities, Gender Relations and Sport.* Thousand Oaks, CA: Sage.

Messner, Michael and Sabo, Donald (eds) (1990) *Sport, Men and the Gender Order: Critical Feminist Perspectives.* Champaign, IL: Human Kinetics.

Messner, Michael and Sabo, Donald (1994) *Sex, Violence and Power in Sports: Rethinking Masculinity.* Freedom, CA: Crossing Press.

Miller, Toby (2001) *Sportsex.* Philadelphia: Temple University Press.

Oates, Joyce Carol (1994) *On Boxing.* Hopewell, NJ: Ecco Press.

Scraton, Sheila and Flintoff, Anne (eds) (2002) *Gender and Sport: A Reader.* London: Routledge.

FURTHER READING

Cahn, Susan (1994) *Coming on Strong: Gender and Sexuality in Twentieth-Century Women's Sport.* New York: Free Press.

Creedon, Pamela (1994) *Women, Media and Sport: Challenging Gender Values.* London: Sage.

Hargreaves, Jennifer (1994) *Sporting Females: Critical Issues in the History and Sociology of Women's Sports.* London: Routledge.

Heywood, Leslie and Dworkin, Shari L. (2003) *Built to Win : The Female Athlete as Cultural Icon.* London: University of Minnesota Press.

Mangan, J.A. (ed.) (1987) *From 'Fair Sex' to Feminism.* London: Frank Cass.

McCrone, Kathleen (1998) *Sport and the Physical Emancipation of English Women 1870–1914.* London: Routledge.

McKay, Jim, Messner, Michael and Sabo, Donald (eds) (2000) *Masculinities, Gender Relations and Sport.* Thousand Oaks, CA: Sage.

Messner, Michael (2002) *Taking the Field: Women, Men and Sports.* London: University of Minnesota Press.

Messner, Michael and Sabo, Donald (eds) (1990) *Sport, Men and the Gender Order: Critical Feminist Perspectives.* Champaign, IL: Human Kinetics.

Messner, Michael and Sabo, Donald (1994) *Sex, Violence and Power In Sports: Rethinking Masculinity.* Freedom, CA: Crossing Press.

Scraton, Sheila and Flintoff, Anne (2002) *Gender and Sport: A Reader.* London: Routledge.

gender

93

WEBSITES

www.womenssportsfoundation.org
www.feminist.org/sports

Globalisation/
Anti-Globalisation

In recent years the process of globalisation has been identified as a main cause of economic, social, cultural and political change across the world (Robertson, 1992). Although there is fairly unanimous agreement within the social sciences that globalisation is a significant process shaping the world we live in, Rowe (2003) draws our attention to the fact that these processes and their apparent consequences are highly contested. He suggests that theories of globalisation span a wide spectrum of thought, best characterised at one end 'as a technical term describing the greater economic, political, technological and communicative connectivity', and at the other end of the spectrum as a process of transformation 'systematically eroding locally specific structures and practices, and imminently ushering in a common global culture' (Rowe, 2003: 282). Albrow suggests that globalisation refers to 'all those processes by which the peoples of the world are incorporated into a single society, global society' (1990: 9). Key elements within these processes include the increasing internationalisation of financial markets and the rapid advances in communications technology and the internet. These developments, particularly at the level of satellite communications and virtual technologies, have, it is argued, fundamentally transformed societies across the world. Globalisation has, it is suggested, undermined the traditional role played by the state as the key unit of political and economic organisation. Issues previously considered as domestic and very much confined within the boundaries of the nation state, are now perceived as fundamentally global concerns. Issues such as unemployment policy, pollution and the environment, the law, and civil and human rights, have been transformed into global concerns, requiring global solutions. Whilst these issues are at a formal level still subject to legislative and policy interventions at the level of the nation state, they are none the less perceived as being influenced by global, rather than local processes. For example, it is largely agreed that whilst individual national governments might introduce legislation to combat perceived climate change and environmental effects, such interventions are only effective when coordinated through and by globally agreed treaties to reduce pollution.

key concepts in
sports studies

94

However these processes are not complete, and are in a constant state of flux (Cohen and Kennedy, 2007). Moreover, as noted above, globalisation is more than just a network of technical processes, it also involves significant transformations at the level of perception and understanding – of 'thinking globally' (Cohen and Kennedy, 2007). Cohen and Kennedy (2007) introduce the concept of 'globality' as a companion to the processes of globalisation. Globalisation, they suggest, is commonly used to describe an objective, technical process which connects people and places (the globalisation of financial markets, communication networks and labour markets for example). 'Globality' on the other hand 'alludes to the subjective, personal awareness' or development of a global way of thinking about and sharing experience (Cohen and Kennedy, 2007: 7). Not simply a technical development, globalisation is as much about the globalisation of social and cultural connections – images, ideas, values and attitudes have become integral elements of global flows and pathways (Cohen and Kennedy 2007: 7). In recent years it has become increasingly difficult to understand our experiences, even at the most 'localised' and everyday level, without reference to the 'global'.

As a concept, globalisation shares much with the conceptualisation of postmodernity. The themes of fluidity, fragmentation and the emphasis placed upon the transgression of boundaries and structures are principal commonalities between the two concepts. Both emphasise the de-differentiation between social, political, economic and geographical boundaries. Both emphasise the importance of media and communication technology in the reformulation of reality and social experience, and both emphasise the dramatic reconfiguration of the relationships between time and space. Noting the relationship between postmodernity and globalisation Rojek (1993) points to how the development of new virtual and satellite based technological and communication networks enhance the sensation of 'hyperreality' (see **Postmodernism/ Postmodernity**) which, he continues, have fundamentally challenged the way we relate to and experience sport and leisure.

GLOBALISATION AND SPORT

Maguire (1999) has identified three relational interests which he describes as the key forces shaping modern sport. They are: television and media; sporting governing bodies; and commercial and economic interests. He characterises these as the 'Global Sports Nexus'. Increasingly global in form and orientation, they have become more and more dependent upon each other in terms of pursuing and realising their aims, and thus the interests of 'global' sport.

There is widespread agreement that with the development of satellite communication technologies, the media, certainly since the 1960s, have had an increasingly important role to play in the development of sport. In the last decade of the twentieth century the prominence of digital broadcasting platforms has intensified this relationship. 'Media sport' has become a major global business in its own right, particularly in terms of advertising, merchandising and the sale of exclusive television rights to events. One consequence of the increasingly important relationship between sport and media is that as consumers we are able to access more and more global sport product, which on the one hand reflects the increasing diversity of global sport culture, but also throws into sharp relief the often paradoxical and contradictory role that globalisation processes play. In essence, the global sport product we consume through our satellite dishes and digital receivers is the result of a balance between on the one hand an increasing number of choices (greater variety), but on the other, diminishing contrasts. The sports media consumer is able to access an increasingly expansive network of sport from across the globe (diversity and choice), but, however, these increased varieties reflect diminished contrasts, in that the product on offer is increasingly similar in form and content. For example, I am able to watch a diverse array and quality of soccer matches from every continent in the world, much of it live, from the comfort of my armchair. However, it is all still soccer.

HOMOGENISATION, HETEROGENISATION AND HYBRIDITY

The influence of sports media brings to the fore two cultural processes central to the gobalisation debate. Namely the processes of *homogenisation* and *heterogenisation* (or *hybridisation*). *Homogenisation* is a term used to describe a particular form of globalisation whereby one cultural form or expression becomes globally dominant, subsuming and eventually eradicating local or indigenous cultures. This is sometimes referred to as 'cultural imperialism' (see also **Imperialism**) or is more commonly associated with the 'Americanisation thesis' – the formation of a global consumer mono-culture dominated by American influences and practices. Whilst elements of *homogenisation* should not be discounted, Maguire (1999) argues that this somewhat misrepresents the impact globalisation has had, particularly on global sports culture. Firstly, he suggests, the *homogenisation* thesis overstates the degree of uniformity, and, secondly, underestimates how different societies and cultures understand and (re-) interpret global media content. The process at play here is, he suggests, *heterogeneous* or *hybrid* in nature, rather than *homogeneous*. Rather than a dominant global mono-culture, globalisation more accurately reflects processes of cross-cultural differentiation, whereby new identities and cultural formations come in to being. Whilst the emergence of global culture is often perceived as a consequence of the destruction of local, authentic cultures, it actually represents, advocates of the *heterogeneous* thesis suggest, a reformulation and reconstruction of local identities and cultural attachments – hence global culture is characterised by 'otherness' and 'difference' rather than 'sameness'.

Theorist Roland Robertson (1995) has conceptualised the dynamic towards global heterogeneity as *glocalization*. For Roberston, globalisation is not a uniform process, but reflects particular inequalities and cultural differences within which the positions of the 'global' and 'local' are not mutually exclusive. For example, Roberston suggests global markets actively promote and create local traditions on the basis that difference and diversity are sought after commodities within the global market place. For Roberston, the term *glocalisation* best captures the ways in which the processes of *homogenisation* and *heterogenisation* intertwine in often contradictory ways to produce global culture.

RETHINKING TIME AND SPACE

Held et al. (1999) understand globalisation as a set of processes which have transformed, and continue to transform, the temporal and spatial organisation of social life. Globalisation brings into existence a context whereby the relationship between time and space are continually being remade. This is often referred to as *time* and *space compression*. As Maguire (2002: 358) explains, people now experience 'spatial and temporal dimensions differently. There is a speeding up of time and a '"shrinking" of space'. Giddens (1990) suggests that the compression of time and space creates new and accelerated forms of global culture whereby localities, which would hitherto have had little direct connection are now instantly linked to each other. Sport is a telling example of this process. The development of global communications networks and travel has, in effect, shrunk the world. The rapid development of satellite sports media and the global commercialisation of sport has resulted in what might be termed the 'de-territorialisation' of sport, whereby interactions and connections with sport (and leisure) are 'no longer dependent upon simultaneous physical "presence" within specific locations' (Jarvie and Maguire, 1994: 252). Sporting organisations and national bodies such as the English Premier League (soccer) are increasingly aware of the global opportunities to promote and sell their product or brand, thus creating new audience markets and opportunities to accumulate profit. Much is made of the somewhat hackneyed accusation that the supporters of the English soccer club Manchester United are as likely to hail from China or the United States as they are from Manchester, but it none the less illuminates the impact of time space *compression* upon the restructuring of notions of what is meant by the term local, or how we now define local communities. Where we would have once understood the term 'local' or community through the prism of geographical proximity, community is now largely understood as a term which speaks to groupings defined through a sharing of specific values and identities – globalisation as we have noted, enhances the tendency towards the global sharing of cultures, identities and values. Multinational firms and global corporations such as Rupert Murdoch's News International, which owns Sky television, the principal broadcaster of soccer in the United Kingdom, are representative of what Ben-Porat and Ben-Porat (2004) characterise as 'non-territorial forms of power' which operate 'largely beyond the control of states' and which consequently challenge the territorial conceptualisation by which we traditionally understand and organise political, economic and cultural power. Walsh and Giulianotti (2001: 55–6) suggest that a similar process is transforming sporting institutions and clubs. Using Manchester United as their example, they suggest sporting organisations increasingly resemble non-territorial transnational business corporations, seeking out new global 'consumer' orientated markets, pursuing marketing opportunities in, for example, Asia and North America. The process of sporting de-territoralisation results in a fragmentation of the historical and cultural context within which sports were once embedded. Rather than a once strong, traditional communal tie, Walsh and Giulianotti (2001: 55) suggest that the new sporting transnational businesses 'experience an increasingly haphazard and accidental relationship to their old, traditional supporter base in the localities surrounding the club stadium'. As such, traditional indigenous fan communities become marginalised and excluded.

SPORT AND ANTI-GLOBALISATION

The 1990s witnessed the rise of a prodigiously vocal and influential social movement orientated against globalisation. Highly diverse and multifaceted, the 'Anti-Globalisation movement's principal aim is to resist the corporate-led and US-dominated forms of global homogenisation' (Cohen and Kennedy 2007: 2). Bringing together a wide range of concerns, such as fair trade, labour rights, human rights, the environment, feminism, poverty, economic regulation and democracy, the anti-globalisation movement seeks to draw attention to global inequalities and the marginalisation that globalisation causes.

Although not an integral element in the anti-globalisation movement, sport does reflect many of the implicit concerns expressed in the wider debates around globalisation. Sociologists such as Walsh and Giulianotti (2001) and Maguire (2002) have drawn attention to the implicit power imbalances reflected and embedded with the processes that make up global sport. These imbalances have given rise to points of antagonism and contestation within sporting cultures. The rapid commercialisation and commodification of sport, and its growing reliance upon powerful media oligarchies, have, it is suggested, resulted in an increasingly 'Americanized' model of global sports culture (Rees et al., 1998) which have excluded authentic and traditional sporting culture in favour of a *homogenised* global consumer culture (see e.g. Walsh and Giulianotti, 2001). Within the context of British sport, these tensions have taken its most prominent form in soccer culture, as there has been growing disquiet throughout the 1990s and early 2000s at the increasing marginalisation of local, traditional and poorer spectators. This is reflected in the emergence of new fan organisations throughout the 1990s, which are both increasingly independent of official institutions, such as traditional supporters clubs, and much more politically active in attempts to resist what they perceive to be the destructive impact globalisation has upon sport (see e.g. Brick (2001), Brown (1998) and Giulianotti (1999) for a discussion of new independent fan moments that emerged in British soccer in 1990s). This has included, for example, campaigns to resist the implementation of all-seated stadia and reintroduce standing at soccer games and fan/based campaigns to increase supporter involvement in the running of clubs, as well as mounting a challenge to the establishment of media ownership of football clubs, which they argue threatens the traditional ties between sporting institutions and local communities (see e.g. Brown and Walsh's, 1999) account of Manchester United fans' campaign against the proposed BSkyB takeover of the club in 1998–99).

THE LIMITS OF GLOBALISATION?

Globalisation has been identified as the most significant economic, social and cultural dynamic in contemporary societies, and has had a dramatic effect upon the remaking of sport and sporting culture in the late twentieth and early twenty-first centuries. However, sports sociologists have pointed to the danger of over-emphasising the impacts and effects of global flows upon particular aspects of sporting culture. A central argument of the globalisation process is that it has all but negated the role of the nation state in the (re)making of global culture. Rowe (2003) and Andrews and Cole (2002), however, suggest that as both an idea and institutional force the 'nation' plays an increasingly significant role, both in terms of individual and of sporting life. Global mega-media sporting festivals such as the summer Olympic games and the soccer World Cup are often taken as prime examples of the advent of the 'global age' (Rowe, 2003: 281). However, in questioning this assumption Rowe (2003) suggests that sport may effectively repudiate cultural forms of globalisation, since it is largely predicated upon the construction of national difference. In his analysis of the failure of soccer to penetrate North American sporting culture on a significant scale, Veseth (2005) suggests local cultures assimilate global influences and from them reconstruct their own local identities. Maguire (1999) suggests a similar process working through the failure of American Gridiron football to establish any deep roots in British sporting culture during the 1980s. Although initially popular as a media spectacle, Gridiron was unable effectively to penetrate the specific nature of British sports culture to the extent necessary to sustain in the long term. Local and national sporting cultures, whilst not perhaps rejecting global processes, certainly in many ways do resist, reconstruct and repudiate the model of 'Americanized' *homogenised* globalisation. Indeed, as Maguire (2002) suggests, at a time when cultures and identities are experiencing the destabilising effects of globalisation, sport and sport culture often function as 'anchors of meaning' providing a sense of, albeit invented, permanence. National sporting events such as the English FA Cup in soccer and the annual Wimbledon tennis tournament are increasingly represented as uniquely British (or English) in nature, cultural counterpoints to global change and instability. As Maguire (2002: 367) suggests, local (and national) cultures are never completely 'hermetically sealed' but are subject to and shaped by global flows, which in turn shape the processes of globalisation themselves.

REFERENCES

Albrow, M. (1990) 'Globalisation, Knowledge and Society: An Introduction', in M. Albrow and E. King (eds) *Globalisation, Knowledge and Society*. London: Sage. pp. 3–13.
Andrews, D.L. and Cole, C.L. (2002) 'The Nation Reconsidered', *Journal of Sport and Social Issues*, 26(1): 123–4.

Ben-Porat, G. and Ben-Porat, A. (2004) '(Un)Bounded Soccer: Globalization and Localization of the Game in Israel', *International Review for the Sociology of Sport*, 39(4): 421–36.

Brick, C. (2001) 'Anti-Consumption or "New" Consumption? Commodification, Identity and New Football', in J. Horne (ed.) *Leisure, Cultures, Consumption and Commodification*. Eastbourne: Leisure Studies Association. pp. 3–15.

Brown, A. (1998) *Fanatics: Power, Identity and Fandom in Football*. London: Routledge.

Brown, A. and Walsh, A. (1999) *Not for Sale. Manchester United, Murdoch and the Defeat of BSkyB*. Edinburgh: Mainstream.

Cohen, R. and Kennedy, P. (2007) *Global Sociology* (2nd edn). Basingstoke: Palgrave.

Giddens, A. (1990) *The Consequences of Modernity*. Cambridge: Polity Press.

Giulianotti, R. (1999) *Football. A Sociology of the Global Game*. Cambridge: Polity Press.

Held, D., Mcgrew, A., Goldblatt, D. and Perraton, J. (1999) *Global Transformations: Politics, Economics and Culture*. Cambridge: Polity Press.

Jarvie, G. and Maguire, J. (1994) *Sport and Leisure in Social Thought*. London: Routledge.

Maguire, J. (1999) *Global Sport: Identities, Societies, Civilizations*. Cambridge: Polity Press.

Maguire, J. (2002) 'Sport and Globalisation', in J. Coakley and E. Dunning (eds) *Handbook of Sports Studies*. London: Sage. pp. 356–69.

Rees, C.R., Brettschneider, W-D. and Brandl-Bredenbeek, H.P. (1998) 'Globalization of Sports Activities and Sports Perceptions among Adolescents from Berlin and Suburban New York', *Sociology of Sport Journal*, 15(3): 216–30.

Robertson, R. (1992) *Globalisation: Social Theory and Global Culture*. London: Sage.

Robertson, R. (1995) 'Glocalization: Time-Space and Homogeneity-Heterogeneity', in M. Featherstone, S. Lash and R. Robertson (eds) *Global Modernities*. London: Sage. pp. 25–44.

Rojek, C. (1993) 'After Popular Culture: Hyperreality and Leisure', *Leisure Studies*, 12(3): 277–89.

Rowe, D. (2003) 'Sport and the Repudiation of the Global', *International Review for the Sociology of Sport*, 38(3): 281–94.

Veseth, M. (2005) *Globaloney. Unraveling the Myths of Globalization*. Oxford: Rowman & Littlefield.

Walsh, A.J. and Giulianotti, R. (2001) 'This Sporting Mammon: A Normative Critique of the Commodification of Sport', *Journal of the Philosophy of Sport*, 28: 53–77.

globalisation/
anti-globalisation

The term *habitus* is most commonly associated with the French sociologist Pierre Bourdieu, although as Tomlinson (2004) notes, it was first used by the anthropologist Marcel Mauss. Habitus is a pivotal concept in Bourdieu's theoretical framework, along with the associated concepts of *field* and *capital*. The complexity and range of Bourdieu's conceptual work, makes any kind of synthesis difficult (Laberge and Kay, 2002), particularly in this limited space. So my intention here is to give a brief introduction to habitus (and capital), and to outline its relevance to sport sociologists. For a detailed consideration of how habitus (along with *capital*, *field* and *practice*) emerges in Bourdieu's work, how it has been adopted to study sports and physical activity practices and cultures, and how it continues to inform the sociological study of sport see Tomlinson (2004), Brown (2006), Laberge and Kay (2002)[1] and Jarvie and Maguire (1994).

It is claimed that Pierre Bourdieu (who died in 2002) remains one of the most influential social theorists of his generation both in his home country of France, and increasingly throughout the international sociological community (Laberge and Kay, 2002; Tomlinson, 2004). However, his theoretical approach is hard to categorise, not least because his own scholastic influences are extremely wide-ranging. (See Laberge and Kay (2002) who outline the numerous influences on Bourdieu's intellectual project.) While his work has spanned a variety of sociological spheres, he is credited as one of the first mainstream 'fathers' of sociology to take sport and the body seriously. He published 'Sport and Social Class' in 1978 and 'Program for a Sociology of Sport' in 1988, and sport is a major focus in (arguably his seminal work), *Distinction: A Social Critique of the Judgement of Taste* (Bourdieu, 1984). As Tomlinson (2004: 161) details, his ideas have had a profound impact on the 'theoretical and empirical investigations into the social and cultural significance and representation of bodily practices, not solely in sport but also in education, arts and the media'.

Distinction (which was written in the 1960s but published in English in 1984) was essentially a study of 'taste' in French society. The broad question that underpins this work is how do we acquire our tastes or preferences for the different cultural activities, including sports, that become the basis of our lifestyles? (Haywood et al., 1995: 239). *Distinction* provides a

key concepts in sports studies

context for locating Bourdieu's concepts in his theoretical framework, and shows how sport fits into this schema (Tomlinson, 2004). Bourdieu sees taste not just as the result of individualistic choices but as being socially patterned. An individual's upbringing, their family context, education and so on, has a powerful influence upon their leisure consumption choices. Bourdieu sees taste as a key means by which the social distribution of symbolic resources is organised. Taste operates, often in subtle and complex ways, in all forms of consumption from food to clothes, house decor to our postures, gestures and speeches, providing a system of differentiation through which class differences are expressed (Haywood et al., 1995: 241). Definitions of taste, and how they are contested, are therefore tied to the reproduction of class.

However, Bourdieu differs from Marxists in his conceptualisation of class and the way it operates. Bourdieu sees class as a cultural and relative grouping,

> a group of social agents who share the same social conditions of existence, interests, social experiences, and value systems, and who tend to define themselves in relation to other groups of agents ... moreover, social classes can be characterised by any kind of socially constructed trait such as gender, age or ethnicity. (Laberge and Kay, 2002: 241)

He criticises Marxists for seeing *economic capital* (that is, 'wealth and money' (Tomlinson, 2004: 168)), as the only form of power and for seeing culture as secondary to the economic sphere. He argues instead that many forms of power exist (Laberge and Kay, 2002: 240). Bourdieu calls all forms of power 'capital' and discusses different forms of capital such as *cultural capital, symbolic capital, economic capital* and *physical capital*. Cultural capital refers to the 'consumption of cultural goods and the expression of taste' (Tomlinson, 2004: 168). Bourdieu suggests therefore that wealth is not just economic or political but can be symbolic too. Moreover, he contends that these different types of wealth are inherited or accumulated, tend to be unevenly distributed, and form part of a persons '*habitus*'. As Tomlinson notes, the challenge is to consider how these forms of capital interact in the case of specific practices and social classes (Tomlinson, 2004: 168).

Habitus is one of the main 'pillars' in Bourdieu's conceptual framework (Laberge and Kay, 2002: 242). His aim in developing this theoretical approach is to understand the dialectical relationship between social agents and structures in specific empirical contexts, particularly how social agents themselves participate in the process (Laberge and Kay, 2002: 242). Habitus is a 'a system of transposable dispositions' (Haywood et al., 1995: 240) that organises the individual's capacity to act – a kind of socialisation process through which the dominant modes of thought and experiences in the social and physical world become internalised (Haywood et al., 1995). It 'functions as a collection of perceptions, tastes, preferences, appreciations and actions; forming a way of perceiving the world and distinguishing between appropriate and inappropriate activities' (Haywood et al., 1995: 240). It is shaped by childhood experiences, the family, schooling and so on, and internalised within a given set of material conditions. So the habitus is linked to the social surrounding, particularly a person's family group, cultural background and, crucially for Bourdieu, to their class position. He sees each class or class segment as having its own habitus, which represents all of the preferences and tastes that make up their lifestyles, including sport consumption choices (Haywood et al., 1995).

Habitus operates according to a *logic of practice*, that is, it is not just a random set of dispositions, but has a logic (Haywood et al., 1995; Kay and Laberge, 2002a). So our tastes, preferences and dispositions acquired for our different consumption practices, including playing and watching sport activities, are learnt, or developed, in early childhood. Individual tastes and preferences in any one leisure activity are related to, or dependent on, the taste and preferences manifested in all other leisure activities (Haywood et al., 1995). The way habitus operates is therefore the basis by which leisure lifestyles are generated. As our habitus operates unconsciously (and is internalised in early childhood), according to Bourdieu, it cannot be completely overcome (Haywood et al., 1995). While our tastes and activities may change over our life course, for example due to different experiences, Bourdieu argues that our choices are still made according to the 'structural logic of the existing habitus' (Haywood et al., 1995: 240).

As noted above, in *Distinction* Bourdieu discusses how tastes and preferences can be explained in terms of their 'distributional significance'. That is to say, taste is a marker of distinction and a signifier of identity of a group, setting out and maintaining similarities and differences between themselves and 'others'. These choices are made in relation to the social distribution of activities or styles or spaces – for example, whether it is common and easily accessible or rare and exclusive. Accessibility is related not just to material factors – their cost (*economic capital*) – but also the *cultural capital* they require (Haywood et al., 1995: 240), that is, the particular and distinctive cultural knowledge they demand. Consider, for example, the tastes involved with watching football or going to the opera. The economic cost of an opera ticket is not dissimilar to one for a Premiership football match. However, to appreciate and enjoy the two activities requires different cultural competencies. Through 'the formation of habitus individuals acquire a range of cultural competencies or cultural capital which makes particular activities more or less accessible for them' (Haywood et al., 1995: 240). The opera is considered to be less mundane and common, and associated with a more middle- and upper-class habitus. Habitus can therefore be thought of as the basis upon which sport consumption choices are based.

> Class habitus defines the meaning conferred on sporting activity, the profits expected from it; and not least of these profits is the social value accruing from the pursuit of certain sports by virtue of the distinctive rarity they derive from the class distribution. (Bourdieu, 1978: 835)

Sport acts as a taste signifier in a constant struggle to gain or maintain distinction. 'Social groups express distaste for the taste of other groups; taste is seen as an expression of the symbolic dimensions of class relations' (Laberge and Kay, 2002: 246).

BODY HABITUS

For Bourdieu, 'the appeal of sport and leisure practices to social groups lies in the distinctive uses of the body' – that is, our body habitus (Jarvie and Maguire 1994: 184).

Habitus is not just about our taste/sense of style/knowledge but it is inscribed and internalised in the individual's body; it is embodied (see **The Body**). External structures are, in effect, applied to the body and become part of the taken-for-granted ways in which we use our bodies, and the meaning we give to our bodily practices (Shilling, 1993, 1997). So our body size, shape, posture, way of walking, gestures, way of eating, drinking – even our speech or accent – are part of our body habitus.

Bourdieu used body habitus to help explain how we learn sports and games:

> The habitus as the feel for the game is the social game embodied and turned into second nature … The habitus, as written into the body, into the biological individual, enables the infinite number of acts of the game … to be produced. (Bourdieu, 1990: 63, cited in Jarvie and Maguire 1994: 190)

habitus

105

Jarvie and Maguire (1994) illustrate this 'development of a body habitus' in the context of how a boxer acquires 'the knowledge of what it is to be a boxer'. 'Here lessons are absorbed about manners, customs, style and deportment that become so engrained in the boxer that they are forgotten in any conscious sense' (Jarvie and Maguire, 1994: 189).

Not everyone has the same habitus, but people who occupy similar positions in the social world will have a similar habitus (Jarvie and Maguire, 1994: 189). Body habitus is therefore part of the class habitus; 'the body is the most indisputable materialisation of class taste' (Jarvie and Maguire, 1994: 205):

> it is the relationship to one's own body, a fundamental aspect of the habitus, which distinguishes the working classes from the privileged classes, just as, within the latter, it distinguishes fractions that are separated by the whole universe of a lifestyle. On the one side, there are the instrumental relations to the body which the working classes express in all the practices centred on the body, whether in dieting or beauty care ... which is also manifest in the choice of sports requiring a considerable investment of effort, sometimes pain and suffering (e.g. boxing) ... on the other side, there is a tendency of the privileged classes to treat the body as an end in itself. (Bourdieu, 1978: 819–40, cited in Jarvie and Maguire, 1994: 202)

The body habitus of male members of the working classes tends to be quite physical, as in forms of manual labour. This translates to their sport practices; activities like boxing, football, rugby league and so on, traditionally popular among working-class men, tend to involve physical exertion and often bodily contact (Shilling, 1997). However, for the male members of the middle classes the body habitus is less associated with the large and strong body, and they are more likely to see the body 'as an end in itself' (Bourdieu, 1978: 838; Laberge and Kay, 2002: 250). Hence, the popularity of activities to keep the body 'healthy' slim and fit, such as keep-fit, yoga, squash and tennis (Jarvie and Maguire, 1994).

Habitus is clearly useful in understanding how 'the differential appeal of different sports and physical activity practices is linked to the differentially acquired bodily dispositions' (Laberge and Kay, 2002: 248). Wacquant's (1995) study of boxing in a ghetto gym in Chicago used Bourdieu's concept of habitus to examine how boxing was linked to the living conditions of the young black men and their distinctive body habitus. Moreover, women and men also have a different body habitus, as explored in Laberge's research (Kay and Laberge, 2004; Laberge,

1995; Laberge and Sankoff, 1988). Joanne Kay's research on adventure racing (The Eco-Challenge) provides another excellent example of the application of Bourdieu's concepts to the understanding of the emergence and meaning and the social dynamic and power structure of this new 'lifestyle' sport (see **Extreme Sport**) (Kay and Laberge, 2002a, 2002b). For details of other studies that have used habitus to examine sporting practices see Laberge and Kay (2002), Brown (2006), Laberge and Sankoff (1988) and Tomlinson (2004).

A number of criticisms of Bourdieu's intellectual project prevail (see e.g. Jarvie and Maguire, 1994: 206–7; Laberge and Kay, 2002: 262; Tomlinson, 2004: 171). In summary, however, Bourdieu's concepts help us to understand the embodied process in learning sport, the ways in which both conscious and unconscious processes are combined, and how these skills and processes become embodied in a person's habitus (Jarvie and Maguire, 1994: 205). However, a person's habitus is also influenced by their social location, both within the specific *field* (as Bourdieu calls it), and more widely in their own social and political location. In particular, class underpins the person's habitus, so, for Bourdieu, choice about which sports to participate in is not freely made but 'reflects and embodies class disposition, a body habitus' (Jarvie and Maguire, 1994: 205). 'Within Bourdieu's project, the sport setting is a rich context for the analysis of the relation between body habitus and the moment of individual choice' (Jarvie and Maguire, 1994: 205).

NOTE

1. Laberge and Kay (2002) also cite Defrance (1995) and Shilling (1993).

REFERENCES

Bourdieu, P. (1978) 'Sport and Social Class', *Social Science Information*, 17.
Bourdieu, P. (1984) *Distinction: A Social Critique of the Judgement of Taste*. London: Routledge and Kegan Paul.
Bourdieu, P. (1988) 'Program for a Sociology of Sport', *Sociology of Sport Journal*, 5.
Bourdieu (1990) *In Other Words: Essays Towards a Reflexive Sociology*. Cambridge: Polity Press.
Browne, D. (2006) 'Pierre Bourdieu's "Masculine Domination" Thesis and the Gendered Body in Sport and Physical Culture', *Sociology of Sport Journal*, 23: 162–88.
Defrance, J. (1995) 'The Anthropological Sociology of Pierre Bourdieu: Genesis, Concepts, Relevance', *Sociology of Sport Journal*, 12: 121–31.

Haywood, L., Francis, K., Peter, B., John, S., John, C. and Ian, H. (eds) (1995) *Understanding Leisure*. Cheltenham: Stanley Thornes (Publishers) Ltd.

Jarvie, G. and J. Maguire (1994) 'Fields of Power, Habitus and Distinction', in *Sport and Leisure in Social Thought*. London: Routledge. pp. 183–210.

Kay, J. and Laberge, S. (2002a) 'Mapping the Field of "AR": Adventure Racing and Bourdieu's Concept of Field', *Sociology of Sport Journal*, 19: 25–46.

Kay, J. and Laberge, S. (2002b) 'The "New" Corporate Habitus in Adventure Racing', *International Review for the Sociology of Sport*, 37(1): 17–36.

Kay, J. and Laberge, S. (2004) '"Mandatory equipment": women in adventure racing', in B. Wheaton (ed.) *Understanding Lifestyle Sports: Consumption, Identity and Difference*. London: Routledge. pp. 154–74.

Laberge, S. (1995) 'Towards an Integration of Gender into Bourdieu's Concept of Cultural Capital', *Sociology of Sport Journal*, 12: 132–46.

Laberge, S. and Kay, J. (2002) 'Pierre Bourdieu's Sociocultural Theory and Sport Practice', in J. Maguire and K. Young (eds) *Theory, Sport and Society*. Oxford: JAI. pp. 239–66.

Laberge, S. and Sankoff, D. (1988) 'Physical Activities, Body Habitus and Lifestyles: Towards an Integration of Gender into Bourdieu's Concept of Cultural Capital', in J. Harvey and H. Cantelon (eds) *Not Just a Game: Essays in Canadian Sport Sociology*. Ottowa: University of Ottowa Press. pp. 267–88.

Shilling, C. (1993) *The Body and Social Theory*. London: Sage.

Shilling, C. (1997) 'The Body and Difference', in K. Woodward (ed.) *Identity and Difference*. London: Sage, in association with the Open University. pp. 63–120.

Tomlinson, A. (2004) 'Pierre Bourdieu and the Sociological Study of Sport, Habitus, Capital and Field', in R. Giulianotti (ed.) *Sport and Modern Social Theorists*. Basingstoke: Palgrave. pp. 161–71.

Wacquant, L.J.D. (1995) 'Pugs at Work: Bodily Capital and the Bodily Labour Among Professional Boxers', *Body and Society*, 1: 65–94.

Hegemony

Hegemony is a term that has had increasing currency in British sociology since the 1970s. It has also, for reasons that this section should make plain, now become widely used in sports studies. It grew more acceptable and attractive as a term as the concept of 'ideology' became less so. This means that, to an extent, a review of the recent history of the two terms is necessary to explain 'hegemony'.

Ideology is defined and explained at greater length elsewhere in this book (see **Ideology**). Here we can take it simply to be a set of beliefs and values comprising a view of the world that is false, distorted or partial. Intentionally or not, this view of the world will serve the interests of a particular group. The term is usually linked to Marxist analysis, but other sociologists and philosophers use the concept, or a similar one.

Two major and enduring intellectual issues arise out of the study and use of the concept of ideology. Firstly, can there be a view of the world that *is not* ideological – that is, one that is neither partial nor distorted, but *true*. And, secondly, how is ideology 'made'? Marxists, for example, have often asked: 'Where do ruling ideas come from?'

The word 'hegemony' – uncommon, but not unknown, in everyday parlance – derives from the Greek 'hegemon', meaning leader. 'Hegemony' means 'leadership or dominance'. Leadership here is *moral* leadership. 'Hegemonic', therefore, means 'ruling' or 'supreme'. Sociologists invariably speak either of hegemonic groups or of hegemonic ideas, or both.

The word 'hegemony' carries with it the notion of *contestation* – a battle over ideas with the assumption that these ideas can be changed, modified or replaced – an assumption not widespread in Western Marxism during the 1960s and 1970s, arguably its heyday in European universities. The preferred interpretation of Marx's key ideas at this time was the so-called Base/Superstructure model. This model was rooted in a quite rigid understanding of Marx's theory of the origin of ideas in human societies. This holds that the prevailing ideas in a society are generated by the relations of production in that society – in other words, by the organisation of economic life – the economic *base*. These ideas then came to inform life in all of the institutions – the education system, the family, religion…and, of course, sport – within that society. These institutions are known as the 'superstructure'. One of the most influential Marxists of the time was the French philosopher Louis Althusser (Abercrombie et al., 2000: 13–14). His rendering of the Base/Superstructure model is among the most inflexible. In his view ruling ideas were urged on the masses through ideological state apparatuses (the schools, the media…) and backed up by the repressive arm of the state (the police, the courts…). In this view, sport would be seen as yet another theatre in which members of a particular society became drenched in the ideas of its ruling class. In an advanced capitalist society, the like of which will be inhabited by many readers of this book, members of that society would imbibe the key values of sport: competitiveness, team spirit, discipline, respect for rules and records, and so on. And, indeed, accounts of sport from broadly this perspective have been written – notably one by the French Marxist Jean-Marie Brohm (1989) But, for many sociologists and others, Althusser's approach was increasingly seen as crude, over-deterministic and 'top-down'. (These spatial metaphors can be confusing. The phrase 'top-down' refers to the class structure, whereas the economic 'base' is, for Marxists, the source and context of ruling-class power.)

Critics of the Althusserian approach included (then) Marxist sociologists such as Stuart Hall and Marxist historians such as Raymond Williams and E.P. Thompson. Thompson's (1995) essay 'The Poverty of Theory' in his book of the same name was particularly influential in the turning of the intellectual tide here. So was the Centre for Contemporary Cultural Studies at Birmingham University. Founded in 1964 by the eminent cultural critic Richard Hoggart, and directed between 1969 and 1979 by the charismatic Jamaican Marxist Stuart Hall, the CCCS was noted for its interest in popular culture and for its unwillingness to reduce, say, popular music, fashion or sport to 'ideology' or to 'false consciousness'. At this centre, and in sympathetic university departments around the world, sociologists and historians now began to study a range of popular cultural forms – including, of course, sport – and for a conceptual framework in which to do so many of them turned to the work of Italian Marxist Antonio Gramsci.

Gramsci had been imprisoned by Italian fascist leader Mussolini and was best known for his *Prison Notebooks*, written between 1929 and 1935 (Gramsci, 2003). Gramsci argues that ruling ideas enjoy a *hegemony*, which is never complete, never final and is always *contested*.

Let's spell out the implications of this shift in intellectual thought. Firstly, Gramsci goes beyond the cruder conceptions of society (e.g. the two-class model adopted in much sociological writing). What might be called a 'ruling class' in modern society is actually, according to Gramsci, composed of different groups or 'fractions' (e.g. finance capitalists and manufacturing capitalists). There may be hegemonic struggles, be it within each ruling fraction, between them or between them and subordinate classes.

The notion of hegemony involves the 'colonisation of common sense'. Popular culture – the customs and pleasures of the common people – is seen as being shaped by dominant ideology, but also as resisting and re-shaping it: this is hegemonic struggle. Successful – that is, ruling or hegemonic ideologies – may promote the idea of an 'imagined community' (Benedict Anderson's (1991) phrase to describe a nation).

These ideologies often fuse economic and social practices with ideas of group identity, rooted, perhaps, in religion or in ideas of nation. Moreover this dominant ideology is often best promoted when apparently menaced by an alien Other. In the UK these might be represented as 'threats to our British way of life'. In the lifetime of many readers of this book, these Others might include communists (during the period of the 'Cold War', roughly 1950 to 1990), trade unionists (the 'enemy within' of the 1980s), or asylum seekers and terrorists (as in the 'war on terror'). Similarly, examples of hegemonic ideologies in the modern world would include 'Thatcherism' (corresponding to 'Reaganomics' in the United States and now known, more generally, as neoliberalism), the 'Third Way' (espoused by President Bill Clinton, and British Prime Minister Tony Blair in the late 1990s) and Islamic fundamentalism – a vexed and contested term, like all the preceding ones. It can be argued that popular culture is a key area in which hegemony is established and nurtured. It is, after all, about winning the hearts and minds of the people and where better than in those social realms where those hearts and minds are apt to wander. Certainly there is now much writing and argument that links hegemony to sport. This has been done principally in two ways.

Firstly, modern sport has been seen by some writers as being linked to ruling-class hegemony. Up to the 1970s the popular academic view had been that modern sport was a product of *modernisation*. That's to say, it emerged out the decline of tradition and the forging of a new modern society. It was seen, therefore, as a natural by-product of modernising processes: *industrialisation, rationalisation, urbanisation, individualism* and *technological advance*.

These processes went, in the conventional view, to make up 'progress' – which was, of course, a neutral or 'good' thing. In sport these processes brought a transition from *traditional sport*, which was *periodic, unorganised, localised* and rooted in *ritual* to modern sport – a *bureaucratised, specialised, individualised* and *institutionalised* affair. For an exposition of roughly this view see, for example, Allen Guttmann's *From Ritual to Record* (1979).

But, Canadian Marxist Richard Gruneau countered this thesis, suggesting instead that sport must be understood in relation to power and cultural struggle, that it should be seen in the context of capitalist society and it should be linked therefore to ideology and to the dominant class. Capitalist social relations, he argued, set limits, but there was always struggle.

So we must speak of sport and *hegemony*. That is, sport promotes the dominant ideology of a modern capitalist society, but that ideology is challenged and never wholly accepted (Gruneau, 1982). For example, when modern sport became entrenched in the 1920s and 1930s it was nationalistic, increasingly competitive and dominated by gentleman amateurs. But this ideological pattern had many dissenters from within the world of sport – notably the workers' sport movement which, for a period, organised its own Olympics (Riordan, 1984, 2006). Similarly, in the United States, American or Gridiron football, seen by many Americans as a key expression of the nation's inherent competitiveness, is nevertheless opposed by millions of parents, who want their children, boys or girls, to play less violent games – hence the 'Soccer Moms' of legend.

Secondly, sport is seen to promote other, non-economic ideologies. There are ideologies, for instance, of gender, of sexuality, of the body, and so on. There are therefore hegemonic masculinities and femininities – ways of being male and female accepted as conventional – and there are (often racialised) ethnicities, sexualities and body types.

Sport, and the sports media, will, it is argued, help to strengthen hegemonic notions of maleness, femaleness, ethnicity, sexuality and the body. Sports culture has thrown up and celebrated flamboyant heterosexual icons – George Best, for example – and gay sportspeople, particularly male ones, have generally had to hide their sexuality. But, once again, there is plenty of room for challenge. There are, of course, now Gay Olympics, begun in San Francisco in 1982. Women's tennis is another good example of a sport in which important contestations have taken place. Here, although the Russian Anna Kournikova has continued to represent conventional female glamour, hegemonic notions of female sexuality have been successfully contested by the Czech American Martina Navratilova and the French player Amelie Mauresmo, both of whom are openly gay. Similarly, Mauresmo, along with the African Americans Venus and Serena Williams, have, through their strong physiques, contested hegemonic notions of the female body and how it should look.

In these apparently new times, when the adoption of the prefix 'post-'(postmodern, post-structuralist…) has become so pervasive, it might be thought that the concept of hegemony was losing currency. But two leading British sociologists of sport recently argued for its continued importance. It 'would be folly', wrote John Sugden and Alan Tomlinson,

to abandon a notion of hegemony that illuminates the nature of the contest and struggle over resources, the conditions whereby consent is secured by the dominant, and the persisting significance of the economic in the constitution of the relations of political economy. (Sugden and Tomilson, 2002: 9)

REFRENCES

Abercrombie, Nicholas, Hill, Stephen and Turner, Bryan S. (2000) *The Penguin Dictionary of Sociology*. London: Penguin.

Anderson, Benedict (1991) *Imagined Communities*. London: Verso.

Brohm, Jean-Marie (1989) *Sport: A Prison of Measured Time*. London: Pluto Press.

Gramsci, Antonio (2003) *Selections from the Prison Notebooks*. New York: International Publishers.

Gruneau, Richard (1982) 'Modernization or Hegemony: Two Views of Sport and Social Development' in Hart Cantelon, and Richard Gruneau (eds) *Sport, Culture and the Modern State*. Toronto: University of Toronto Press. pp. 1–38.

Guttmann, Allen (1979) *From Ritual to Record*. New York: Columbia University Press.

Riordon, James (1984) 'The Workers' Olympics', in Alan Tomilson and Garry Whannel (eds) *Five Ring Circus: Money, Power and Politics at the Olympic Games*. London: Pluto Press. pp. 98–112.

Riordan, James (2006) 'Amateurism, Sport and the Left: Amateurism for All Versus Amateur Elitism' *Sport in History*, 26 (3): 468–83.

Sugden, John and Tomlinson, Alan (2002) 'Theory and Method for a Critical Sociology of Sport' in John Sugden and Alan Tomlinson (eds) *Power Games: A Critical Sociology of Sport* .London: Routledge. pp. 3–21.

Thompson, E.P. (1995) *The Poverty of Theory*. London: Merlin Press.

FURTHER READING

Bocock, Robert (1986) *Hegemony*. Chichester: Ellis Horwood.

Gramsci, Antonio (2003) *Selections from the Prison Notebooks*. New York: International Publishers.

Harris, David (1992) *From Class Struggle to the Politics of Pleasure: The Effect of Gramscianism on Cultural Studies*. London Routledge.

Sugden, John and Tomlinson, Alan (2002) 'Theory and Method for a Critical Sociology of Sport' in John Sugden and Alan Tomlinson (eds) *Power Games: A Critical Sociology of Sport*. London: Routledge. pp. 3–21.

history

History

Few academic subjects have lent themselves so readily to pithy quotation as the discipline of history.[1] Some historians, the eminent historian Arnold Toynbee once suggested, 'hold that history is just one damn thing after another'. History is, after all, the study of the past – 'a foreign country' according to the novelist L.P. Hartley – and the things that happened there. It sounds simple enough, but it's possible that the writing of history has never been a more contentious matter than it is today. The question of what constitutes history has become increasingly difficult to answer and it is now linked to a second question – whether history, in the sense that that word has commonly been understood, is possible at all.

Fifty years ago the subject matter of history at least seemed clear. History, to the people who wrote it, studied it or had, however reluctantly, to do it at school, meant 'kings and queens'. This, in turn, meant establishing or learning facts about past affairs of state – battles, acts of parliament, the odd popular protest and the doings of leading statesmen. Arguments among historians tended to concentrate upon the reliability of these 'facts' and on the question of whether, indeed, facts about the past could ever be determined.

Facts were, as they remain, symbols of modernism and the rise of science. The positivists among social thinkers have always held that society, past or present, could be studied by scientific method. The British historian R.G. Collingwood was one of a number of his profession who embraced modernism and science for their discipline. History, he wrote, was 'a science whose business is to study events not accessible to our observation and to study these events inferentially'[1] (Collingwood, 1993, quoted in Hughes-Warrington, 2000: 42). The idea of history as a scientific discipline in confident pursuit of facts held sway in the early twentieth century and was expounded by a number of leading historians – notably Lord Acton and G.R. Elton. Acton believed in 'ultimate' or 'universal' history – an agreed version of the facts that transcended all political or social biases. For example, in his instructions to the compilers of the *Cambridge Modern History* he called for an account of the Battle of Waterloo 'that satisfies French and English, German and Dutch alike' (i.e. all the main protagonists and the historians of their nations) (quoted in Carr, 1990: 9). Similarly, Elton asserted that there is 'truth to be discovered if only we can find it' (Elton, 1967: 73–4, quoted in Hughes-Warrington, 2000: 83). Indeed, in the twentieth century most Western historians probably agreed with the contention of the philosopher Sir Isiah Berlin that 'the case against the notion of historical objectivity…does not exist'.[2]

Other historians, however, have been trenchantly critical of this notion of history as the rigorous uncovering of 'facts'. Chief among these was E.H. Carr who spent much of his career at Balliol College, Oxford. Carr was a Marxist and his book *What is History?* is the leading text in the case against positivist history. Carr argued for a relativist view of history and a less reverential view of facts. Facts, Carr argued, were only a starting point. It was no doubt important, he wrote, to know that the Battle of Hastings

> was fought in 1066 and not in 1065 or 1067, and that it was fought at Hastings and not at Eastbourne or Brighton ... The facts speak only when the historian calls on them; it is he who decides to which facts to give the floor ... the only reason we are interested to know that the battle was fought at Hastings in 1066 is that historians regard it as a major historical event. (Carr, 1990: 10–11)

Not surprisingly for a Marxist, Carr was also dismissive of the 'great men' theory of history – the idea that history was simply something that had been brought about by outstanding and/or charismatic individuals like Napoleon, Lenin or Adolf Hitler. 'The view which I would hope to discourage is the view which places great men outside history and sees them as imposing themselves on history in virtue of their greatness' (Carr, 1990: 54). Marx, after all, had once famously suggested that, far from being the story of influential individuals, 'the history of all hitherto existing society' was 'the history of class struggle' (Marx and Engels, 1970). Indeed, there have been a number of distinguished Marxist historians in British academia, many of them, such as A.L. Morton, Christopher Hill and Rodney Hilton, members of the Communist Party History Group. But, of course, not all social history is Marxist. In general over the last 50 years we have seen an increased conjoining of sociology and history, with history being seen as process – Norbert Elias' *The Civilising Process* (2000) would be a good example. Moreover, the increasing reluctance to reduce history to affairs of state or to the doings of 'great men' has led to a growing acceptance that there is no history, only histories – a view expressed by, among others, the liberal philosopher Karl Popper. Thus we have seen a proliferation of women's history, black history, queer history (the history of homosexual culture), and so on. Much of this is history of groups previously, in the memorable phrase of the feminist historian Sheila Rowbotham, 'hidden from history'. Attempts to salvage the lives of ordinary, powerless people who lived in times past have often been called 'history from below'.

However, history itself – be it Whig, scientific, Marxist, processual, from below, or some combination of these – has lately been called into question. This is widely known as 'the linguistic turn' – a phrase coined by the American philosopher Richard Rorty – and it involves the belief, central to postmodernism (see **Postmodernism/Postmodernity**), that the past consists only in the language and texts which are used to describe it. For these writers, there is only discourse. Principal exponents of this view include Patrick Joyce, Professor of History at Manchester University in the UK, and the burgeoning postmodern critique has begun to put those historians who believe in a social reality to which language refers on the defensive. In 1997, for example, Richard J. Evans, Professor of Modern History at Cambridge University, published a book called *In Defence of History*, speaking up for the discipline variously defined by Carr and Elton. Addressing the postmodern critics, he concludes

> I will look humbly at the past and say despite them all: it really happened, and we really can, if we are very scrupulous and careful and self-critical, find out how it happened and reach some tenable though always less than final conclusions about what it all meant. (Evans, 1997: 253).

Many of these trends and disputes can be seen in the comparatively new field of sports history. Before academics became involved – and historians have not been writing about sport in any numbers for more than a quarter of a century – it's fair to say that the history of sport leaned heavily upon the 'great men' and positivist traditions. That's to say that the history of sport took the form principally of the factual recording of sporting events and institutions: the who, when and where, perhaps, of a World Cup tournament or an Olympiad. Much sports history was written by freelance writers and journalists and has often had the sanction of the sporting organisation whose past was being chronicled. *Times* football correspondent Geoffrey Green, for instance, wrote the official history of the Football Association, published in 1954 and followed that with the official centenary history of Manchester United Football Club in 1978. It's fair to say that these books, and the many like them, never strayed far from the paradigm of history writing deemed inadequate by E.H. Carr: the history of sport was rendered as the history of great deeds by great sportsmen, managers and administrators. The sports with which they were associated had no social context. Moreover, female, ethnic minority and other sportspeople and others seemed to have no history at all. It is also important to note that, despite its historical importance in the lives of all social classes, sport was seldom mentioned in conventional social histories.

This pattern changed in the 1970s and early 1980s when sport, itself hitherto largely hidden from professional history, began to be the subject of books by academic historians. Two key texts here are James Walvin's *The People's Game* (1975) and *Association Football and English Society* by Tony Mason (1983). Both men were seasoned historians who had researched other areas – Walvin had written on slavery, among other things, and Mason was a respected labour historian. Both now produced academic social histories of association football – the first of their kind – and, though both books were short of the kind of sociological analysis that Carr would have favoured, they were based on extensive archival research (especially Mason's) and thus provided the basis for a new, scholarly sports history. Other books were meanwhile appearing and, this time, albeit from differing perspectives, the sense of the social context of sport was stronger. Using Elias' civilising process as a framework, Christopher Brookes wrote a history of English cricket (1978) and Eric Dunning and Kenneth Sheard used the same theory to chart the history of rugby football (1979). Stephen Wagg's (1984) history of the English football world, which appeared the year after Mason's, is, arguably, more materialist.

The 1980s saw the publication of more general texts, such as *Sport and the British* by the Oxford-educated historian Richard Holt and in 1994 feminist history of sport received a fillip when Jennifer Hargreaves' seminal text *Sporting Females* arrived on the shelves. Similarly black sportspeople had their own historians – see, for example, the two volume history of Caribbean cricket by Hilary Beckles, Professor of History at the University of West Indies (1998) and Mike Marqusee's (1999) *Redemption Song*, an account of the career of Muhammad Ali, perhaps the most charismatic sportsman of them all, which places Ali in the political and social history of his time.

Sport history is now established in the academic life of the English-speaking world, with its own journals, conferences and associations. There are signs too that the greater regard that academics have for sport is reciprocated by the sports themselves: a number of notable official histories – for instance of the Welsh rugby union (Smith and Williams, 1980) and of FIFA (Lanfranchi et al., 2004) – have been written by scholars and not by journalists.

NOTES

1. The website of History News Network (http://hnn.us/articles/1328.html) at George Mason University in Virginia, USA carries a long list of sayings about History, compiled by Ferenc Szasz, Professor of History at the University of New Mexico. I have drawn on it for this section.
2. History News Network website, http://hnn.us (accessesed: 11 November 2006).

REFRENCES

Beckles, Hilary McD. (1998) *The Development of West Indies Cricket, Vol.1 The Age of Nationalism, Vol. 2 The Age of Globalization.* London: Pluto Press.

Brookes, Christopher (1978) *English Cricket: The game and its players through the ages.* London: Weidenfeld and Nicolson.

Carr, E.H. (1990) *What is History?* (2nd edn) R.W. Davies (ed.). London: Penguin. Originally published 1961.

Collingwood, R.G. (1993) *The Idea of History* (revised edn), W.J. van der Dussen (ed.). Oxford: Oxford University Press. Originally published 1946.

Dunning, Eric and Sheard, Kenneth (1979) *Barbarians, Gentlemen and Players.* Oxford: Martin Robertson.

Elias, Norbert (2000) *The Civilising Process: Sociogenetic and Psychogenetic Investigations* (Revised edition edited by Eric Dunning, Johan Goudsblom and Stephen Mennell). Oxford: Blackwell.

Elton, G.R. (1967) *The Practice of History.* London: Fontana.

Evans, Richard J. (1997) *In Defence of History.* London: Granta Books.

Green, Geoffrey (1954) *The History of the Football Association.* London: The Naldrett Press.

Green, Geoffrey (1978) *There's Only One United.* London: Hodder and Stoughton.

Hargreaves, Jennifer (1994) *Sporting Females: Critical Issues in the History and Sociology of Women's Sports.* London: Routledge.

Holt, Richard (1989) *Sport and the British: A Modern History.* Oxford: Clarendon Press.

Hughes–Warrington, Marnie (2000) *Fifty Key Thinkers on History.* London: Routledge.

Lanfranchi, Pierre, Eisenberg, Christiane and Mason, Tony (2004) *100 Years of Football: The FIFA Centennial Book.* London: Weidenfeld and Nicolson.

Marqusee, Mike (1999) *Redemption Song: Muhammad Ali and the Spirit of the Sixties.* London: Verso.

Marx, Karl and Engels, Friedrich (1970) *The Communist Manifesto.* Harmondsworth: Pelican.

Mason, Tony (1983) *Association Football and English Society 1863–1915.* Brighton: The Harvester Press.

Smith, David and Williams, Gareth (1980) *Fields of Praise: Official History of the Welsh Rugby Union 1881–1981.* Cardiff: University of Wales Press.

Wagg, Stephen (1984) *The Football World: A Contemporary Social History.* Brighton: The Harvester Press.

Walvin, James (1975) *The People's Game.* London: Allen Lane.

FURTHER READING

Carr, E.H. (1990) *What is History?* (2nd edn) R.W. Davies (ed.). London: Penguin. Originally published 1961.

Evans, Richard J. (1997) *In Defence of History.* London: Granta Books.

Identity and Difference

Identity is about belonging, about what you have in common with some people and what differentiates you from others. At its most basic it gives you a sense of personal location, the stable core to your individuality. But it is also about your social relationships, your complex involvement with others. (Weeks, 1990: 88, quoted in Rutherford, 1990: 88)

WHAT IS IT?

Identity is a widely used term across the social sciences and humanities, referring in the broadest sense to who we are, and the ways in which an individual understands him or herself as a being. However, its use, meaning and theorisation differ considerably between disciplines. For example, psychologists tend to be interested in personal identity – that is, our construction of self and how we see ourselves as unique individuals (Bradley, 1996). As sociologists we tend to be more interested in our social or cultural identities. According to Bradley (1996), social identity is 'how we locate ourselves in the society in which we live and the ways in which we perceive others as locating us' (Bradley, 1996; 24). It derives from the sets of lived relationships in which we are engaged, and, particularly, broader societal dynamics of power and inequality (Bradley, 1996). Thus identity is formed in the relationship between 'social structure' and an individual 'subjectivity' (Hughson et al., 2005: 110).

A further distinction is made between *identity* and *subjectivity*, terms which are sometimes used interchangeably. Woodward (1997) suggests that subjectivities involve both conscious and unconscious thoughts about who we are. However, our subjectivity is experienced in social contexts where 'language and culture give meaning to our experiences of ourselves and where we adopt an identity' (1997: 39).

In the contemporary world our identity comes from multiple and, at times, contradictory sources, including our nationality, where we live, our ethnicity, gender, sexuality, social class, community and sport preferences. Identity therefore points to a series of relationships – between individuals and variously formed collectivities – and to the ways in which they are similar and different (Jenkins, 1996). In sociology (as well as history, politics and related (inter)disciplinary fields) individuals' labelling of themselves – their expression of identity – tends to be based on membership of, or inclusion in, particular groups. These groups or collectivities range in scale from nations to subcultures, and include social classes, ethnicities, genders, sexualities, and so on. However, identity is often most clearly defined by what it isn't, that is by *difference* (Woodward, 1997: 2). Difference marks who is an insider and an outsider to a particular group, it marks 'us' and 'them', whether that group membership and identity is based on subculture, such as among football fans, or as in the ways difference works to include and exclude groups of people in nationalist or ethnic conflicts. Moreover, identities are often constructed in terms of oppositions or binaries inscribed in and though language, such as male/female, black/white and straight/gay (Woodward, 1997: 2). (See also **Feminism; Discourse and Post-Structuralism**.)

Closely related to social identity is the idea of cultural identity – that is, our 'sense of belonging to a particular culture, past or present' (Bradley, 1996: 24). Stuart Hall is one of the most prominent contemporary cultural theorists to have written about cultural identities, which he sees as particularly relevant to communities of ethnic minorities who have migrated away from their original homelands. Discussing the complexity of (representing) identity for Caribbean identity in the African diaspora, Hall discusses two different ways to 'think about' cultural identity. Firstly, that it is a single shared culture reflecting 'common historical experiences and shared cultural codes' providing 'stable, unchanging and continuous frames of reference and meaning' (Hall, 1997: 51). Secondly, however, he recognises that as well as many similarities there are also significant differences that 'constitute what we really are'. In this sense cultural identities are not fixed, but are continually evolving, suggesting that identity is a process that is about 'becoming as well as being' (Hall, 1997: 52). Hall emphasises that although our cultural identities are part of our history, they are not essentialised or fixed, but are 'subject to the continuous play of history, culture and power' (Hall, 1997: 52) .

WHY IS IDENTITY IMPORTANT?

Because identity has become so important in understanding who we are and how we fit in to the world, by the 1990s identity was one of the central concepts in contemporary sociological and cultural theory, and provoked widespread discussion across the social sciences and humanities. Exploring the concept and representation of identity raises fundamental questions about the world in which we live; as Woodward explains in the introduction to *Identity and Difference*, 'Identity gives us a location in the world and presents the link between us and the society in which we live ... as a conceptual tool with which to understand and make sense of social, cultural, economic and political changes' (Woodward, 1997: 1).

It is not surprising, therefore, that a vast amount of literature has been written about a concept which has been seen as a metaphor for changing Western societies. In contemporary 'postmodern' culture, new and multiple sources of identities have emerged, while, at the same time, we have seen the resurgence of old identities. Much has been written about the new politics of identity. This writing encompasses (but is not limited to) the relationship of identity to gender, sexuality, race, ethnicity, nationalism, class, and so on – sources which may 'lead to contradictory fragmented identities' (Woodward, 1997: 1). There are also diverse theoretical perspectives on different identities from diasporic and cosmopolitan identities to new forms of leisure identities. But here I will point to some of the ways identity has been understood by, and the questions it has raised among, sport sociologists. (For a comprehensive discussion see the special issue of the *Sociology of Sport Journal* on identity, King and McDonald, 2007).

Another related term that has emerged in the context of cultural identity is *identity politics*. This involves 'claiming one's identity as members of an oppressed or marginalized group as a political point of departure' (Woodward, 1997: 24). Thus identity 'becomes a major factor in political mobilisation' (Woodward, 1997: 24). This mobilisation has often been around the conviction that 'the personal is political' (see **Feminism**). Common examples of these new social and political initiatives, many of which emerged in the West in the 1960s, include the movements for women's rights, civil rights for African Americans, protection of the environment and gay and lesbian rights. Identity politics involves a celebration of the group's uniqueness as well as an analysis of its particular oppression. However, as Woodward surmises, while some aspects of new social movements challenged fixed essentialised identities of 'race', class, gender and sexuality, and subverted biological certainties, others asserted the primacy of different essential categories (Woodward, 1997: 28).

CRISIS OF IDENTITY?

In political terms, identities are in crisis because traditional structures of membership and belonging inscribed in class, party and nation-state have been called into question. (Mercer, 1992: 242, quoted in Woodward, 1997: 26)

The notion of an identity crisis is widespread in the literature on contemporary identity, and is seen as an important characteristic of changing Western societies. This crisis is seen to be driven by a number of social processes, including the intensified process of globalisation, particularly the global movement of capital and labour. The wide-ranging consequences of these processes include the breakdown of old structures of nation states and communities. These processes have led to the emergence of new more fluid and transnational identities and paradoxically, as I observed earlier, to a concurrent resurgence of old ones – for example as seen in renewed forms of nationalism around the world. These nationalisms and other resurgent traditional identities are, of course, often played out in the culture of sport. Likewise on a political level we have witnessed 'large-scale political upheavals' such as the fall of the Berlin Wall and break-up of the USSR, and a re-emergence of older forms of ethnic, religious and national identifications in the former Eastern European countries to 'fill the void' left by the 'break-up of communism' (Woodward, 1997: 17). The acceleration of migration in the global economy, combined with increasing multiculturalism in post-colonial Europe and the USA, has produced plural and contested identities.

FRACTURED IDENTITIES

It is now commonplace that the modern age gave rise to a new and decisive form of individualism, at the centre of which stood a new conception of the individual subject and its identity. (Hall, 1994: 119)

These economic and social changes that have taken place on a global level are also reflected in identity formation, resulting in a new conception of identity – what Hall calls the 'post-modern subject'. Kellner (1992, 1995) explains this 'fracturing' of identity in the transition from traditional to postmodern society. In traditional society identity was relatively fixed and stable, whereas in modernity it became 'more mobile, multiple, personal, self-reflexive, and subject to exchange and innovation' (Kellner, 1992: 141). Although the possibilities of different sources of identification expanded, identities remained relatively fixed. However, in postmodern culture the 'self' or 'subject', is said to be 'de-centred', rupturing the basis of self-authenticity (cf. Baudrillard, 1985), and replacing identity formation with a more fleeting, and media driven self-representation. However, not all commentators on late-modernity/postmodernity take such a radical position, suggesting instead that the pace, scale and complexity of the fragmentation of identity accelerates and viewing identity as an 'on-going project' (see the discussion of *body projects* in the section on **The Body**) and emphasising that we 'function as active agents in the construction of our identities' (Bradley, 1996: 212). Contrary to the theories of orthodox Marxism which saw work and production as central sites for identity formation, in postmodern consumer culture growing segments of the population draw their sense of identity from a broad range of material and symbolic sources, including consumption practices and sport and leisure lifestyles (e.g. Bocock, 1993; Featherstone, 1991; Horne, 2006; Lury, 1996; Tomlinson, 2001):

> Consumption has been seen as epitomising this move into postmodernity, for it implies a move away from productive work roles being central to people's lives, to their sense of identity, of who they are. In place of work roles it is roles in various kinds of family formations ... in leisure time pursuits, in consumption in general, which have come to be seen as being more and more significant for people. (Bocock, 1993: 4)

The importance of sport and leisure as a source of identity is certainly not a 'postmodern' development; however in postmodernity the importance of leisure seems to have intensified, with some even arguing that work has become a means of extending the non-work sphere. Bauman (1988), for example, suggests that the 'work ethic' has been superseded by the 'consumer' ethic. He states that 'The same central role which was played by work, by job, occupation, profession, in modern society, is now performed by consumer choice' (Bauman, 1992: 223).

In sport and its associated cultural imagery we can see vivid examples of these trends, ranging from the numerous studies of identity construction in sporting subcultures (boxing, baseball, surfing and bodybuilding to name a few) and the multiple and shifting ways identities are expressed in sport fandom, such as among football supporters (from team strips and paraphernalia, to membership of supporter networks and fanzines), to new sites such as sport video games and online communities. As research across many different contexts has illustrated, identities are constructed in and through sport in a myriad of ways. However, it is misleading to see identity as just a matter of personal choice. While it is undeniable that the sites for identity construction through sport and popular culture have proliferated, these are always constrained by social structures – in particular of gender, class, 'race' and sexuality. As Tomlinson (2005) argues,

> many collectively experienced and consumed popular cultural forms are far from a matter of personal choice. Their meaning and impacts can be bound up with the political dynamics within and between societies. For example, the 'reflexive project of the self' or the 'constant transformation' of cultural identity is not an easy or even available option to the individuals born into the sectarian culture of Northern Ireland or the black majority of a South African township. (Tomlinson, 2005: 38)

Nevertheless, sport, even in these kinds of contexts, does provide important sites for examining the multiple meanings and non-essential character of contemporary identities. This is particularly evident in the context of the expression of hybrid 'race' and ethnic identities, for example where young people from non-host ethnic backgrounds draw on aspects of both their parent and host cultures to create collective identities. Hughson's study of young male football fans of Croatian background living in Australia and who support the Sydney United (formerly Sydney Croatia) football team, is a vivid example of this process (cited Hughson et al., 2005). 'The young men were able to construct their own hybrid identity from the range of cultural insignia and practices that were familiar to them in their lives as the progeny of Croatians living in Australia' but one that denied an 'essentialist Croatian identity ... at the hub of this interpretation of identity is a shift from an essentialist to a non-essentialist understanding of ethnicity' (Hughson et al., 2005: 111). In summary, while it is clear that identities are constructed, and that sport is an important site for identity formation, both in its embodied performance (see **The Body**), as fans and consumers, and as a significant site for marking gender, race, sexuality and national identity, important questions remain about how these identities are constructed, 'from what, by whom and for what purpose?' (Horne, 2006: 126).

REFERENCES

Baudrillard, J. (1985) 'The Masses: The Implosion of the Social in the Media', in M. Poster (ed.) *Jean Baudrillard: Selected Writings*. Cambridge: Polity Press. pp. 207–19.

Bauman, Z. (1988) 'Is there a Postmodern Society?', *Theory Culture & Society*, 5: 217–37.

Bauman, Z. (1992) *Intimations of Postmodernity*. London: Routledge.

Bocock, R. (1993) *Consumption*. London and New York: Routledge.

Bradley, H. (1996) *Fractured Identities: Changing Patterns of Inequality*. Cambridge: Polity Press.

Featherstone, M. (1991) *Consumer Culture and Postmodernism*. London: Sage.

Hall, S. (1994) 'The Question of Cultural Identity', in *The Polity Reader in Cultural Theory*. Oxford: Polity Press. pp. 119–25.

Hall, S. (1997) 'Cultural Identity and Diaspora', in K. Woodward (ed.) *Identity and Difference*. London: Sage, in association with the Open University. pp. 51–9. Originally published 1990.

Horne, J. (2006) *Sport in Consumer Culture*. Basingstoke: Palgrave Macmillan.

Hughson, J., Inglis, D. and Free, M. (2005) *The Uses of Sport: A Critical Study*. London: Routledge.

Jenkins, R. (1996) *Social Identities*. London: Routledge.

Kellner, D. (1992) 'Popular Culture and the Construction of Postmodern Identities', in S. Lash and J. Friedman (eds) *Modernity and Identity*. Oxford, UK and Cambridge, USA: Blackwell. pp. 141–77.

Kellner, D. (1995) *Media Cultures: Cultural Studies, Identity and Politics between the Modern and the Postmodern*. London and New York: Routledge.

King, S. and McDonald, M. (2007) '(Post) Identity and Sporting Cultures: An Introduction and Overview', *Sociology of Sport Journal*, 24: 1–19.

Lury, C. (1996) *Consumer Culture*. Cambridge: Polity Press.

Mercer, K. (1992) 'Back to My roots: A postscript to the 80's', in D. Bailey and S. Hall (eds) *Critical Decade: Black British Photography in the 80's, Ten-8*, pp. 32–9.

Tomlinson, A. (2001) 'Sport, Leisure and Style', in D. Morley and K. Robins (eds) *British Cultural Studies: Geography, Nationality, and Identity*. Oxford: Oxford University Press. pp. 399–415.

Tomlinson, A. (2005) *Sport and Leisure Cultures*. Minneapolis: University of Minnesota Press.

Weeks, J. (1990) 'The Value of Difference', in J. Rutherford, (ed.) *Indentity: Community, Culture, Difference*'. London: Lawrence and Wishart. pp. 88–100.

Woodward, K. (ed.) (1997) *Identity and Difference*. London: Sage, in association with the Open University.

identity and difference

FURTHER READING

Carrington, B. (2007) 'Merely Identity: Cultural Identity and the Politics of Sport', *Sociology of Sport Journal*, 24: 49–66.

King, S. and McDonald, M. (2007) '(Post) Identity and Sporting Cultures: An Introduction and Overview', *Sociology of Sport Journal*, 24: 1–19.

Tomlinson, A. (2005) *Sport and Leisure Cultures*. Minneapolis: University of Minnesota Press.

Woodward, K. (ed.) (1997) *Identity and Difference*. London: Sage, in association with the Open University.

Ideology

'Ideology' is an important word in the vocabulary of political and social commentators and first entered this vocabulary around the time of the French Revolution of 1789. It has two principal meanings.

Firstly, it can describe a particular set of attitudes, beliefs or views of the world. These might attach to, and help to define, a particular social group – for example, a class, a gender group, a political movement or a nation. Examples here might include 'communist ideology', 'Thatcherism', sexism and racism. In the world of sport, similarly, there have been many ideologies: 'Muscular Christianity', amateurism and Olympism among them.

Secondly, 'ideology' can refer to ideas which are regarded as false or distorted and which, thus, work to mask social, economic or political interests. So, when people say 'That is an ideological statement', what they mean is that, in their opinion, the statement is slanted or inaccurate. (This, of course raises the question of whether statements can ever be free of bias – and therefore *un*-ideological.)

As students of sport we can see that there are identifiable ideologies (or philosophies) of sport and that these ideologies are often linked – or perceived to be rooted in – wider philosophies or national cultures. We are all likely, for example, to have heard reference to an American Gridiron football team for whom 'winning is all that matters', or of 'the calypso cricket of the Caribbean' or of how English sportspeople represent a 'nation of losers' suffering from 'Eddie the Eagle syndrome'.

When the word 'ideology' is used to describe a cluster of attitudes and beliefs it tends to divide political commentators. Some rejoice in a world where a range of ideologies is 'on offer'. This is essentially a liberal position and those who adopt it accept, and perhaps welcome, the notion that people think and speak from different perspectives. For them every thing is relative. As Bob Dylan once wrote: 'You are right from your side, and I am right from mine' (in his song 'One Too Many Mornings').

Other writers take the term 'ideological' to be derogatory. For them it means a rigid adherence to some doctrine and it clearly assumes the possibility of seeing the world in a *non*-ideological way. A good example here is the accusation, often made in the mid-twentieth century, that particular people were 'bringing politics into sport'. Historically, this accusation was most often made against East European countries, where coaches were popularly held to impose 'communist ideology' on sportspeople. But, interestingly, it was widely made against US President Jimmy Carter and British Prime Minister Margaret Thatcher when, in protest against the Soviet Unions occupation of Afghanistan, they tried to discourage athletes from competing in the Moscow Olympics of 1980.

The second sense of the notion of ideology (ideology as social control) has been developed most rigorously within the Marxist tradition of critical theory and it generally refers to all the ways in which dominant political groups manage to secure and maintain their social, cultural and economic power. Such power is secured, Marxists argue, through a variety of measures which range from the dissemination of misleading ideas about the nature of society (e.g. the idea that hard work leads to achievement or success in life), to the material practices of reality itself which are said to contain a subliminal or unconscious 'practical' ideology. So, ideology may work through the deployment of seductive ideas and slogans which filter into people's consciousness, or it may work through the routine practices of day-to-day life like shopping, drinking or playing or watching sport.

To simplify then, we might say that there are two key senses of the term ideology within Marxist critical thought:

(a) ideology as 'false' or distorted ideas that mask forms of economic and social inequality;
(b) ideology as ideas embodied and lived out 'unconsciously' or 'habitually' in the 'reality' of capitalist society.

Some writers have applied these arguments to sport. The early work of Bero Rigauer (for instance, *Sport and Work*, 1981) makes reference to the concept of ideology when he criticises theorists of play who remove sport from the domain of the economic, in order to foster the illusion that sport is autonomous from the 'work' structures of industrial capitalism. The work of Jean-Marie Brohm (principally, *Sport: A Prison of Measured Time*, 1976) has drawn on some of these Marxist arguments to assert that the seeming autonomy of sport as a social practice displaces our attention from the nature of social reality and perpetuates the myth of capitalist progress. Hence, for Brohm, we get the 'ideology' of linear progression in sport: sport embodies a

ideology

belief that things are always getting better with the perpetual breaking of records, and so on.

A further example Brohm uses is the way sport 'idealises' modes of natural selection. Through sporting competition, it seems, there is the survival of the fittest. Thus capitalism is presented as a natural system which expresses the true nature of human beings. In its seeming 'autonomy' from politics and society, sport (Brohm maintains) provides an important ideological service for the maintaining of capitalist social relations. Aspects of sport function ideologically for capitalism through 'repressive socialisation' – a socialisation process which instills acceptance of defeat, injustice or inequality. This phenomenon is neatly summed up by Theodor Adorno's remark that sport provides 'a training for life when things go wrong' (Adorno, 2001).

THE CRITICS

As a concept, ideology has been attacked by a number of contemporary postmodern theorists. For instance, the notion of ideology as 'false', 'distorted' or 'misleading' ideas and practices has been challenged by writers influenced by the French historian of ideas Michel Foucault. Foucault's conception of power has been seen as a significant theoretical advance on the notion that we can reveal and undermine ideology through identifying reality. Foucault's notion of power resists the idea that there can be a form of thought or action that is outside the production of power differentials. For Foucault, there is no reality that is outside of attempts to describe it – an increasingly popular view in the social sciences, often referred to as the 'linguistic turn'. Ideology, for Foucault, always stands in relation to some conception of truth and this is where it should be replaced by a conception of power which admits to no ultimately legitimate or truthful 'outside'.

Similarly, the concept of *hegemony* as developed in Cultural Studies (see **Hegemony**) has been regarded by some (such as Raymond Williams in his *Marxism and Literature*, 1977) as offering a broader, more nuanced and sophisticated account of the workings of political power and domination. Hegemony, its proponents such as Ernesto Laclau and Chantal Mouffe claim, (Laclau and Mouffe, 1985) avoids both the truth/falsity trap of much Marxist theorising on ideology and allows the notions of political agency and resistance to play a more significant role in the elaboration and contestation of power relations.

REFERENCES

Adorno, Theodor W. (2001) *The Culture Industry: Selected Essays on Mass Culture*. London: Routledge.

Brohm, Jean-Marie (1976) *Sport: A Prison of Measured Time*. London: Pluto.

Laclau, Ernesto and Mouffe, Chantal (1985) *Hegemony and Socialist Strategy*. London: Verso.

Rigauer, Bero (1981) *Sport and Work*. Colombia: Colombia University Press.

Williams, Raymond (1977) *Marxism and Literature*. Oxford: Oxford University Press.

FURTHER READING

Marcuse, Herbert (1978) *The Aesthetic Dimension*. London: Routledge and Kegan Paul.

Imperialism/ The Post-Colonial

Imperialism is the 'imposition of the power of one state over the territories of another, normally by military means, in order to exploit subjugated populations and extract economic and political advantages' (Abercrombie et al., 2000: 173). With regard to the analysis of sport as a social and historical phenomenon, the most important empire was the British, fashioned, like other European empires, largely in the nineteenth century (see e.g. Kiernan, 1982). By the beginning of the First World War, these empires controlled over four-fifths of the world's land mass. In the British instance, as with other European empires, imperialism ordinarily took the form of *colonialism*: that is, territories were governed directly by an administrative class imported from the imperial power, which imposed its own law, administration and, to a degree, culture, on the indigenous population. The most explicitly imposed forms of culture encompassed such vital elements as the official language of the country and the nature of its education system. Sport is plainly another significant aspect of the cultural legacy of imperialism, although, as we have seen elsewhere in this book (see **Culture; Globalisation**), there has been debate over the precise role of sport in the imperial project.

European nations relinquished most of their colonies in the 1960s, sometimes voluntarily, more likely as a result of wars of national liberation fought by subject peoples. Many scholars and other commentators argue, however, that these territories have remained under the political and economic domination both of the former imperial nations of Europe and of the United States, the principal world power of the post-colonial era. This perceived situation is widely referred to as *neo-colonialism*. This term now has wide currency among academics of the left, but it was in use even as the European empires were being dismantled, one of its first exponents being the African intellectual Kwame Nkrumah, who became the first president of independent Ghana (formerly the Gold Coast, a British colony) in 1960 (Nkrumah, 1965).[1]

Sport can be seen to have been an important element in the resistance of indigenous peoples to imperial rule and, similarly, it is argued that the colonial experience has continued to inscribe sport culture in the former colonies.

Finally, there is now discussion over whether, despite the claims of its own government and notwithstanding the fact that it has never established formal colonial administrations, the United States should be seen as an imperial power. Some academics, convinced that it should, have therefore begun to discuss the place of sport in US imperialism.

SPORT AND THE BRITISH EMPIRE

Historically, the British Empire had two main segments. There were the dominions, governed by 'white' settler minorities – principally Canada, Australia, New Zealand and South Africa – which were effectively self-governing from the early years of the twentieth century. And there were the colonies, territories whose populations were defined effectively through their 'race' (they were darker skinned than Europeans) and whose independence wasn't granted until after the Second World War. These two segments are today generally styled as the 'Old' and 'New Commonwealth'.

Outside of the British Isles – bearing in mind that Wales, Ireland and Scotland were annexed by England in the thirteenth, seventeenth and eighteenth centuries, respectively – America was the first major British colony. But most of the British Empire was acquired after the American declaration of Independence in 1776, the period of its greatest growth being between the 1830s and the 1880s. British imperialism carried with it a powerful cultural hegemony, but this was never uncontested; sometimes, indeed, it was contested by rival 'white' settler groups – as in Canada, where there was political division between French- and British-descended groups and in South Africa, where politics was dominated by Dutch-descended Afrikaners and commerce by British descended entrepreneurs.

Sport has been linked to imperialism in various ways. Firstly, the historian Richard Holt has argued that sport in the British empire was an important means for the *transmission of imperial and national ideas* – ideas of 'Britishness', such as 'fair play'. This began in the British public schools, the headmasters of which were sometimes devout imperialists and invariably taught that it was better to be a poor scholar than a poor sportsman. 'In the history of the British Empire', wrote J.E.C. Welldon, headmaster of Harrow, 'it is written that England has owed her sovereignty to her sports' (quoted in Holt, 1992: 205).

Secondly, sport provided a cultural home from home for the colonial elite, strengthening their solidarity, buttressing their identity and preserving their exclusiveness while away from Britain. Lawn sports, such as tennis, house sports, such as snooker, and modern sports of the British elite, such as horseracing, cricket and rugby football all flourished in the imperial territories.

Thirdly, imperial sport often reflected a high military presence (a third of the British army was stationed in India in the late nineteenth century) and promoted the honing of military skills, such as shooting and horsemanship: pigsticking and polo are examples here.

Fourthly, sport was a means to the building of cultural bridges. Vast territories such as India could not be governed successfully by a foreign power without the acquiescence of local elites. For example, Indian princes regularly hunted and played polo with colonial administrators and several of them played cricket for England – notably Prince K.S. Ranjitsinhji, later a Maharajah, who played 15 tests for England between 1896 and 1904.

Moreover, sports such as cricket helped to promote the loyalty of the 'white' territories, reconciling nationalism and empire loyalty in the form of what was widely referred to as 'colonial nationalism' (see e.g. Eddy and Schreuder, 1988). As Holt observes: 'Affection for the "Old Country" was tinged with a sharply democratic "Jack's as good as his master" attitude' (Holt, 1992: 232).

Sport gave confidence to the imperialists that the empire was an essentially voluntary, family arrangement. In 1927 Sir Theodore Cook, editor of the gentleman's journal *The Field* and former captain of the British fencing team, wrote:

> English cricketers are playing against Parsees and Mohammedans at Karachi while a team of Maoris are testing the best of our rugby footballers at home. By such threads are the best bonds of union woven. For the constitution of the British Empire, unexpressed and inexpressible, does not depend on force. (Cook, 1927: 321, quoted in Mangan, 1992: 9)

Indeed such confidence helped to inspire the first Empire Games in Hamilton, Ontario in 1930 (see Moore, 1992). But history shows that sport was as big a factor in resisting imperialism and in the breaking of imperial bonds as it was in promoting the amity of colonial nations. In Ireland, for example, resistance to occupation and annexation by Britain was led by, among others, the Gaelic Athletic Association, who promoted indigenous Irish sports and boycotted those designated as British (Cronin, 1999). Moreover, in the divided society left behind after the partition of Ireland in 1921 sport remained – as it remained in many similarly divided post-imperial territories – a key indicator of inter-communal strife (see e.g. Sugden and Bairner, 1993, 1999).

Sport also helped to fire independence movements, particularly in the Caribbean, where leading nationalists such as C.L.R. James were also devotees of cricket and helped to turn the West Indies cricket team into a flagship for the nationalist movement. In these struggles it seems clear that nationalist campaigners had been directly inspired by the 'fair play' ethic that the British had been so keen to evangelise (McDevitt, 2004). In sport the dominions and the colonies alike judged the British by their own standards and they knew as well as the imperial masters when something was 'not cricket'. The 'Bodyline' controversy of the early 1930s was a good case in point: when the British practised 'bodyline' bowling, they were impatient with Australian complaints, but when the West Indians did it, they were affronted (Beckles and Stoddart, 1995). Sport – or rather the withholding of it, via an international boycott for much of the 1970s and 1980s – was also an important factor in combating one of the ugliest of post-colonial residues: South African apartheid.

THE POST-COLONIAL OR THE NEO-COLONIAL?

For many, the term 'post-colonial' assumes that colonialism has gone. Officially it has. This, as we have seen elsewhere in this book (see **State, Nation and Nationalism**) is the age of the nation state and one in which the 'end of history' – that is, the demise of alternative political systems to liberal democracies – is proclaimed (most notably by Fukuyama, 1992). The passing of formal colonialism, at least as a form of official cultural subjugation, is acknowledged in the growth of post-colonial studies, chiefly in the universities across what was the British Empire. Post-colonial studies are widely held to have been inspired by the publication in the late 1970s of Palestinian intellectual Edward Said's (1979) book *Orientalism*, a principal argument of which is that writing and theorising about the East by Western writers was riddled with assumptions about the people of Eastern countries that constituted them as 'the Other'. Much of the debate within post-colonial studies has concerned itself with literature and the question of whether writers in the ex-colonies can transcend their historic 'subaltern status' and write, so to speak, outside the colonial consciousness in which their countries' cultures have for so long been steeped: as a prominent writer in post-colonial studies once asked: 'Can the subaltern speak?' (Spivak, 1988). Comparatively little, though, has been written about sport from a post-colonial perspective, despite its prominence in the culture of ex-colonies. John Bale and Mike Cronin are among the few academics who have sought to remedy this. In their *Sport and Postcolonialism* (2003) they pose three sets of questions which should be asked about post-colonial sport:

(i) *Questions of When?* Questions of when post-colonial sport began are deceptively difficult – as shown by Stuart Hall in an essay of 1996. In post-colonial studies, 'Post-colonial' begins, variously, with the first European exploitation of 'Third World' countries; with the formal colonisation of these countries; or with their *de*colonisation. As Bale and Cronin point out, adopting what seems to be the first of these premises, '[p]ost-colonial sport could be said to have arrived when the first "Third World" sports workers arrived in "First World' sport" (Bale and Cronin, 2003: 3).

(ii) *Questions of What?* On the matter of what forms of sport relate to the post-colonial, Bale and Cronin propose a range of different sport forms, including: pre-colonial body cultures that survived colonialism intact; indigenous games that were transformed by colonisation (like lacrosse, which originated among North American Indians and is now Canada's official summer sport); sports that emerged in former colonies (like baseball and basketball in the United States); colonial sports fashioned by former colonies into 'national sports', such as Australian Rules Football; sport diffused by empires and adopted without rule changes in colonised countries, such as cricket and rugby; and 'hybrid' sports, such as the cricket game played in the Trobriand Islands (now known as the Kiriwina Islands) of Papua New Guinea (Bale and Cronin, 2003: 4–5). In the study of the various forms of sport, hybridity and resistance have been important and recurrent themes.

(iii) *Questions of How?* These are matters of method and the principal task, following Said, is to provide 'alternative readings of conventional colonial wisdoms and dominant meanings' in relation to post-colonial sport (Bale and Cronin, 2003: 7).

As we observed earlier, however, a number of writers refuse to accept the 'post' in 'post-colonial' and assert instead that we have simply moved from an era of formal colonial rule into a period of neo-colonial exploitation, wherein stronger countries continue, by other means, to dominate the politics, economies and cultures of weaker ones. This perspective has been applied to sport, a good example being the work of the sociologist Paul Darby on African football. Darby (2000) has pointed out that, in what he calls 'the new scramble for Africa', most of the best African players have moved to play in France, England or Belgium – the principal colonisers of Africa in the nineteenth century. In a number of African countries, this has weakened both the national game – through a lowering of standards – and the national team – through the unavailability of top players for matches and training camps.

Finally, a word about the United States – widely acknowledged to be the world's only remaining superpower, and, because of its frequent intervention in the affairs of other countries, popularly seen as a/the chief agent of neo-imperialism. Although there is little support for the idea that sport in global society is being Americanised, as has been argued elsewhere in this book (see **Culture**; **State, Nation and Nationalism**), there has been comparatively little attention paid to the fact that the United States has an imperial past. American academic Gerald Gems (2006) recently wrote about the role of sport in the building of the American empire. Gems argues that American imperialism was impelled by racism, Social Darwinism and the notion of 'Manifest Destiny'. This last is a patriotic vision of the country's mission to spread democracy, or, as some historians argue, an ideology developed to justify westward territorial expansion. Having taken Texas, formerly part of Mexico, in 1845, the United States went on to annexe territory in Hawaii, the Philippines, Puerto Rico, Cuba and the Dominican Republic, and in each of these territories, Gems argues, there was a policy of cultural imperialism with sport at its heart. As with other imperial projects, the story of this policy was one of some assimilation, some hybridity and some resistance. American sports such as baseball were established in these countries, but not always on terms that suited the imperial power. For example, Jackie Robinson, later (in 1947) to become the first African American to play Major League baseball in the United States, played for the Honolulu Bears in 1941 because Hawaiian baseball had no colour bar (Gems, 2006: 78). Similarly, although baseball became a national sport in Cuba, and Fidel Castro, political leader of Cuba between 1959 and 2006, is a former pitcher, the country established an anti-capitalist sport culture following the overthrow of an American-backed dictatorship in 1959. Imperialism, said Castro, 'has tried to humiliate Latin American countries, has tried to instil an inferiority complex in them; part of the imperialists' ideology is to present themselves as superior. And they have used sport for that purpose' (Gems, 2006: 97–8).

NOTE

1. See http://www.marxists.org/subject/africa/nkrumah.neo-colonialism (accessed: 1 May 2007).

REFERENCES

Abercrombie, Nicholas, Hill, Stephen and Turner, Bryan, S. (2000) *Dictionary of Sociology*. London: Penguin Books.
Bale, John and Cronin, Mike (eds) (2003) *Sport and Postcolonialism*. Oxford: Berg.
Beckles, Hilary and Stoddart, Brian (eds) (1995) *Liberation Cricket: West Indies Cricket Culture*. Manchester: Manchester University Press.
Cook, Sir Theodore (1927) *Character and Sportsmanship*. London: Williams and Norgate.
Cronin, Mike (1999) *Sport and Nationalism in Ireland: Gaelic Games, Soccer and Irish Identity since 1884*. Dublin: Four Courts Press.
Darby, Paul (2000) 'The New Scramble for Africa: African Football Labour Migration to Europe', *The European Sports History Review*, 3: 217–44.

imperialism/
the post-colonial

135

Eddy, John and Schreuder, Deryck (eds) (1988) *The Rise of Colonial Nationalism*. London: Allen and Unwin.

Fukuyama, Francis (1992) *The End of History and the Last Man*. London: Penguin.

Gems, Gerald R. (2006) *The Athletic Crusade: Sport and American Cultural Imperialism*. London: University of Nebraska Press.

Hall, Stuart (1996) 'When was "the Postcolonial"? Thinking at the Limit', in Iain Chambers and Lidia Curti (eds) *The Post-Colonial Question: Common Skies, Divided Horizons*. London: Routledge. pp. 242–60.

Holt, Richard (1992) *Sport and The British*, Oxford: Oxford University Press.

Kiernan, V.G. (1982) *European Empires from Conquest to Collapse, 1815–1960*. London: Fontana.

Mangan, J.A. (ed.) (1992) *The Cultural Bond: Sport, Empire, Society*. London: Frank Cass.

McDevitt, Patrick F. (2004) 'Defending White Manhood: The Bodyline Affair in England and Australia' in *'May the Best Man Win': Sport, Masculinity and Nationalism in Great Britain and the Empire 1880–1935*. Basingstoke: Palgrave Macmillan. pp. 81–137.

Moore, Katharine (1992) 'The Warmth of Comradeship: The First British Empire Games and Imperial Solidarity', in J.A. Mangan (ed.) *The Cultural Bond: Sport Empire, Society*. London: Frank Cass. pp. 20–10.

Nkrumah, Kwame (1965) *Neo-Colonialism, the Last Stage of Imperialism*. London: Thomas Nelson.

Said, Edward (1979) *Orientalism*. New York: Vintage Books.

Spivak, Gayatri Chakravorty (1998) 'Can the Subaltern Speak?', in Cary Nelson and Lawrence Grossberg (eds) *Marxism and Interpretation of Culture*. Urbana: University of Illinois Press. pp. 271–313.

Sugden, John and Bairner, Alan (1993) *Sport, Sectarianism and Society in Divided Ireland*. Leicester: Leicester University Press.

Sugden, John and Bairner, Alan (eds) (1999) *Sport in Divided Scoeities*. Aachen: Meyer and Meyer.

Further Reading

Allen Guttmann's *Games and Empires* (New York: Columbia University Press 1996) is a good introduction to the topic of sport and imperialism. John Bale and Mike Cronin's (2003) *Sport and Postcolonialism* (Oxford: Berg) is similarly useful for beginning to think about sport and the postcolonial.

J.A. Mangan (ed.) (1992) *The Cultural Bond: Sport, Empire, Society* (London: Frank Cass) is an interesting series of case studies of the relationship between sport and empire. The title of Patrick McDevitt's *'May the Best Man Win': Sport, Masculinity and Nationalism in Great Britain and the Empire 1880–1935* (Basingstoke: Palgrave Macmillan) is self explanatory; the book is very informative and well written, as is Gerald R. Gems' (2006) *The Athletic Crusade: Sport and American Cultural Imperialism* (London: University of Nebraska Press).

Paul Dimeo and James Mills' (2001), *Soccer in South Asia* (London: Frank Cass) is a collection of essays on the ways in which a British sport is now practised in a post-colonial society.

Marxism

(see also Capitalism; Hegemony)

Marxist theory understands human societies as being organized into classes which are shaped by divisions and conflicts of interest. These conflicts arise out of the general organisational form (mode) of production in any given historical period. In the capitalist epoch this is reflected in the two major class groups: the working class (proletariat) who are forced to sell their labour in order to survive; and the capitalist class (bourgeoisie) who own the means of production and gain profit through the exploitation of the working class.

Karl Marx, philosopher, political economist and revolutionary, was born in Germany in 1818 and died in exile in England in 1883. He is buried in Highgate Cemetery. Although considered one of the pillars of classical nineteenth-century sociology alongside Emile Durkheim (1858–1917) and Max Weber (1864–1920), Marx does not fit the stereotypical picture of the academic sociologist. Alan Ingham (2004) suggests that the term Marxist sociology is itself a contradiction in terms. Marx professed that it was not enough to understand the world in which one lived; the point, he concluded, was fundamentally to change it.

The progressive collapse of the Soviet Union during the late 1980s and early 1990s and the subsequent retreat of left-wing political organisations and intellectual thought, has led to the almost universal condemnation of Marxism as a form of social organisation and social theory. The Marxist tradition has seemingly been engulfed by the rise of post-modernism. Many former Marxist theorists have allied themselves with the new anti-Marxist intellectual trend. However, despite this, Marx and Marxist ideas still play a very important role in shaping the sociological imagination and the mapping of cultural enquiry. This is nowhere more so than in the social analysis of sport. This contribution focuses primarily upon the influence of classical Marxism (the development of Marxist theory prior to the outbreak of World War One in 1914) and its influence upon the development of the social analysis of sport (for neo-Marxist analysis of sport see **Hegemony**). The principal exponents of this form of analysis in sports studies include Paul Hoch, Jean-Marie Brohm and Bero Rigauer.

As a student of Hegelian philosophy in Berlin, Marx became involved in a group of leftist radicals and intellectuals called the Young Hegelians. The Young Hegelians were involved in an intellectual project devoted to a systematic critique of aspects of Hegel's metaphysical materialist approach to history. The group developed their own approach in response. By 1844, however, Marx had broken with the Young Hegelians and had developed his own approach to the study of history. Exiled from Germany for his radical journalism, Marx spent time in France and Belgium (he again fell foul of the authorities in these countries for his radical views and activities), developing his ideas within the revolutionary context of working-class struggle that was breaking out amongst industrialised western Europe during this period. Marx finally settled in England in 1849. During his period of enforced exile Marx met Friedrich Engels (1820–1895) a fellow German radical with whom he was to develop a systematic critique of capitalist political economy. A prodigious writer, amongst Marx's key works are *The German Ideology* (Marx and Engels, 1846); *Poverty of Philosophy* (1847); *Theories of Surplus Value* (1862) and perhaps his most famous and influential texts, *Capital*, Vols 1–3 (1867). With Friedrich Engels he wrote the *Communist Manifesto* (Marx and Engels, 1848), the founding document for the Revolutionary communist movement which was beginning to establish itself across Europe at this time.

MARX'S SYSTEM OF IDEAS

Marx's system of ideas centres upon a materialistic understanding of social change, within which class, class conflict, labour and the organisation of production (the mode of production) play key conceptual roles.

Historical Materialism

Historical materialism relates to the approach to history that runs through Marx's ideas. Marx attacked the idea of naturalism that characterised the explanations of capitalist society put forward by liberal political economists such as Adam Smith (1723–1790) and David Ricardo (1772–1823). These theories, Marx suggested, only understood individuals as existing in isolation from the societies and environments in which they lived. Marx however suggested that human relationships are fundamentally social in essence, and are derived from the social nature of the capitalist mode of production. The social relations of production, in Marxist terms, determine the total social relations of a given social system in a given historical epoch or period (Jarvie and Maguire, 1994; Rigauer, 2002). Marx argued against the strongly held view that social relations (especially capitalist social relations) were fixed, and that their laws of development could be applied to every form of economic society. Marx emphasised the dialectically historical nature of the relations of production, and the specific forms these relations take in particular historical periods. For example, feudalism and the subsequent transition to capitalism are specific and transitory forms in the development of these relations.

Dialectical Materialism

Dialectical materialism underpins Marx's method, providing the philosophical grounding by which he approaches the analysis of society. Marx's dialectical materialism (developed from Hegel's notion of 'thesis, synthesis, antithesis') is a method of reasoning which argues that things (such as material objects and concepts) are situated within a system of relationships that are constantly changing. Marx's method differs from formal logic which suggests that the relationship between cause and effect is a relatively linear and straightforward relationship, that is, cause A results in effect B. Dialectical materialism, however, suggests the relation between cause and effect is only one aspect in the total network of relationships. The network of relationships, Marx suggests, is inherent with contradictions, oppositions and antagonisms, which must be included in the totality of analysis.

Marx's critique of capitalist society provides an explicit example of his method of dialectical materialism. As noted above, Marx provided both the political and philosophical grounding for the development of communism, and is closely associated with political expressions of anti-capitalism. However, it should be noted that Marx was not anti-capitalist in the sense that he viewed capitalism as a negative and destructive development in human history. As a dialectical materialist and humanist Marx considered the transition from feudalism to capitalism as an important progressive development of the social relations of production, overturning the traditional feudal order of subsistence, religious superstition, servitude and hereditary power. Utilising the dialectical method, Marx pinpoints that, on the one hand capitalism represents, for the first time, the moment in human history when the conscious social organisation of production provides the opportunity to benefit the whole of society. Yet, at the same time it contains a central contradiction which prevents the realisation of this potential – that is, that the product of social production is appropriated privately, by the capitalist in the form of profit. Through his method of dialectical materialism Marx illuminates the inherently social and creative nature of capitalist production. However, the drive for profit ulitimately prevents society from fully benefiting from this productive creativity. For society to totally transform itself into a truly social form of human organisation, this antagonism must first be overcome. That is, capitalism must be overthrown, thus establishing a new mode of social relations.

Labour

Human labour is a central aspect of the dialectical method. For Marx, human labour power is the source of value which in turn is transformed into and appropriated by the capitalist as surplus value in the form of profit. Labour is a social relationship unique to capitalism and is distinct from work, which is a recognised feature of all societies. Within capitalist social relations work is transformed into labour in that it produces value through exploitation. For example, Marxist theorists suggest that sport is a form of the capitalist labour process. As labourers, professional athletes are involved in the production of surplus value, and as such are exploited. Marx's conceptualisation of exploitation is not a measure of how much an individual is paid in the form of wages. Rather, exploitation relates to the relative relationship between the workers' productivity and the production of surplus value. The greater the surplus value produced the higher the rate of exploitation. The worker enjoys none of the surplus value they have produced as it is appropriated in the form of profit by the capitalist. It is in this specific sense of the concept that Marx would argue that a highly paid sportsman such as Tiger Woods, who earns millions of dollars in prize money and sponsorship, suffers a higher rate of exploitation than the low-paid and over-worked sweatshop workers who manufacture Nike sportswear, because the professional athlete's rate of productivity is far higher in relation to the production of surplus value, than that of the sweatshop worker, and as such suffers a higher rate of exploitation.

Alienation

Alienation is a concept developed by Marx which evolves out of his analysis of the dialectical antagonism that lies at the heart of capitalist society. Alienation is now commonly associated with a psychological or emotional sense of separation, and exclusion from society. However, Marx uses the term to describe the levels of separation that occur through the production and appropriation of surplus value (profit), that is that the social organisation of human creativity and productivity is appropriated privately as profit. Sport, a form of capitalist production, is therefore alienating. This is experienced as the workers' lack of control over the product of their labour – it does not belong to the worker, but he/she has to buy it back as a consumer in the market (Jarvie and Maguire, 1994: 93).

Ideology and Consciousness

The concept of ideology is very important to Marx's analysis of capitalist social relations. Ideology is understood as the socially determined systems of beliefs and ideas which inform the ways in which people perceive the social relations and forms of domination within which they live. For Marx, the beliefs and ideas which dominate human societies are necessarily flawed or distorted in specific ways, which mask the particular realities in which social relations and forms of domination operate. Marx refers to this as 'false consciousnesses'. Marxist sociologist, Ralph Miliband (1977) argued that working-class involvement in sport was a principal manifestation of 'false consciousness' (Jarvie and Maguire, 1994: 98), in that it detracted the working class from the task of confronting capitalism politically, and incorporated them into a system of pro-capitalist beliefs and values. Ideologically, sport appears as distinct and separate from capitalist productive relations, but is itself intrinsically linked to capitalist production and the creation of surplus value. For example, Marxist-inspired sports theorists argue that rather than being a break or escape from work, sport intrinsically prepares the worker, emotionally and physically, for work (see below).

MARXISM AND SPORT

Marx never wrote about sport, nor is their any evidence that he ever participated in or enjoyed sports during his life. However, since the 1970s the theoretical development of sport has been heavily influenced by Marxist ideas. Sports theorists such as Paul Hoch (USA), Jean-Marie Brohm (France) and Bero Rigauer (Germany), have

marxism

developed an understanding of sport heavily influenced by Marxist critiques of labour within capitalist social relations. For Brohm and Rigauer alienation is a central expression of sport. Sport is essentially a capitalist enterprise, and a form of industrial labour (Cashmore, 2000: 251). Brohm suggests that sport is dominated by the capitalist 'performance principle' premised upon normative and quantifiable forms of rationalised performance. Sport is specific to capitalist social relations reflecting the Marxist influenced idea that sport is a sub-section of a larger framework of capitalist industry. Whilst there are formal differences between a professional athlete and an office or factory worker, in Marxist terms, the relationship between the factory worker and the athlete is the same: they play the same function in the systematic accumulation of profit through the exploitation of human labour.

French Marxist Jean-Marie Brohm (1978) argues that the codified and organised structures of modern sport are produced by dominant capitalist interest groups. He suggests that sport is utilised as a means with which to contain and 'disarm' the working class. As noted above, sport is one of the few spaces within capitalist society which offers a semblance of physical and mental freedom. However, Brohm suggests this freedom is not only illusory but is actually an 'unfreedom', as the sports competitor is nothing more than what he terms a 'prisoner of time' – bounded by restrictive, heavily regulated and quantifiable relations of time and space. For Brohm these relations are exactly the same as the logic of capitalist production in that sport is judged only by its quantifiable outcomes and the efficiency with which these outcomes are produced (for example: How far? How high? How fast? How many?). The creative and more aesthetic impulses that sporting performances undeniably involve are excluded from consideration.

Similarly, Bero Rigauer (1981) suggests that the domination of sport by capital, and the subsequent routinisation of sporting performance, create a 'one dimensional' athlete. Rigauer draws upon German Marxist Herbert Marcuse's (1898–1979) text *One Dimensional Man* (1964) in which he suggests that advanced forms of industrial society incorporate its populations into systems of mass consumption, media and advertising, which bring about a 'one dimensional' form of thought and behaviour. Critical opposition is explicitly denied. As such, Rigauer suggests, sport and sports performers are appropriated into this 'one dimensional' universe whereby they are judged upon their productive efficiency rather than their creativity.

Drawing upon Marx's theory of value, Alan Ingham (2004: 19) provides a 'conceptual trilogy' through which he maps the processes of valorisation which characterise capitalism – how the capitalist mode of production transforms use values into first exchange values and then surplus values (2004: 13–19). Ingham suggests that the transition of play into games, and then games into sport reflect the capitalist value categories within this trilogy. Play is consistent with the value category 'use value'. Play has an immediate use value in the form of the pleasure and enjoyment of the player which he/she consumes immediately (2004: 15). Games are representative of 'exchange value'. Through the development of rules, 'habituation and reciprocal typification', simple play is transformed into games. Although games provide pleasure, they require inter-subject regulation – that is, agreed rules. In this respect games, unlike simple subjective play, are objective and sociable in nature, as they are dependent upon acts of social cooperation. In this respect Ingram suggests games embody (simple) social exchange value in that there is the expectation in game playing that 'In giving of oneself, one expects to receive in equal measure' (Ingham, 2004: 17). Sports, on the other hand, are undertaken purely as exchange values solely for the purpose of appropriating surplus value. As such, sports are representative of the domination of market values whereby the athlete's labour is directly appropriated by the capitalist to create profit in the form of surplus value (Ingham, 2004: 17).

THE NARCOTIC EFFECT AND FALSE CONSCIOUSNESS

In his 1972 text *Rip Off the Big Game: The Exploitation of Sports by the Power Elite*, Paul Hoch suggests there are important parallels between the function of modern sport and Marx's critique of religion. In 'Contribution to a Critique of Hegel's Philosophy of Right', published in 1843, Marx famously refers to religion as the 'opiate of the people' (often translated as 'opiate of the masses'), drawing attention to its ideological function as a 'social drug', distracting and absorbing the mental and physical energies of the working class. Hoch suggests that in seemingly offering temporary relief from the pressures of capitalism, sport can also be understood as a 'social narcotic' inducing a state of dependence amongst the working class (Cashmore, 2000: 94).

Drawing upon the work of John Hargreaves (1986), Cashmore (2000: 93) points to the four principle ideological functions of sport which work through this 'narcotic effect'. The first function is the role sport plays in training a 'docile labour force', promoting and inculcating within the working class the work discipline necessary for industrial capitalism. As already noted, there are many similarities between sport and industry. Both operate an institutionalised and increasingly sophisticated division of labour. Both rely upon the quantification of performance, and the increasing drive towards maximising efficiency and productivity. The second function of sport lies in its complete domination by the market, and the profit motive. This is seen most clearly through the trading and transfer of players, sponsorship, branding, media rights and the sale of merchandising. Thirdly, sport offers a clear expression of the ideological nature of capitalist society. For example Hargreaves notes the 'cult' of aggressive individualism, and the ruthless competition that dominate sport and wider capitalist society. Similarly, important capitalist ideologies, such as elitism, chauvinism, sexism, racism and nationalism are given explicit expression through the institutional and cultural structures of sport. As Cashmore (2000: 94) suggests these ideological attributes are often uncritically accepted as either necessary components, or unavoidable consequences of sport. Finally, Hargreaves notes the central importance of the state. In Marxist theory the state embodies the totality of the interests of capital. Principally the state works to safeguard the interests of the capitalist and to ensure that the conditions by which profit is produced – through the exploitation of the working class – are maintained as efficiently and effectively as possible. In this respect, state intervention in sport, through policy and sports promotion campaigns, for example, are consistent with the promotion and protection of the interests of capital (Cashmore, 2000: 94).

CONCLUDING REMARKS

Cashmore (2000: 251) suggests that the 'inescapable conclusion' of the application of 'classical Marxist' theory to sport is that sports seems little more than an expression of the repressive structures and forces employed to perpetuate the capitalist system through the appropriation of profit from human labour, and the inculcation of the working class with bourgeois beliefs. This somewhat 'pessimistic' view suggests that sport has little if any 'subversive' potential and can only serve the established structures of the capitalist order (Cashmore, 2000: 251). A more 'optimistic' reading of sport is provided by the development of the neo-Marxist theory associated with the Italian communist Antonio Gramsci's (1891–1937) theory of hegemony (see **Hegemony**). However, not withstanding the somewhat 'pessimistic' overtones, Marxist theory reveals very important aspects of sport and its relationship with wider capitalist society. It reveals that sport is not a separate and distinct domain or sphere, but represents a fundamental expression of social relations and the often contradictory and ideological nature that these relations take. For Marxists sport and leisure are not trivial or frivolous pusuits, but are an implicit product of the antagonisms and conflicts that lie at the heart of capitalist social relations.

REFERENCES

Brohm, J-M. (1978) *Sport: A Prison of Measured Time*. London: Ink Links.

Cashmore, E. (2000) *Sports Culture: An A–Z Guide*. London: Routledge.

Hargreaves, J. (1986) *Sport, Power and Culture: A Social and Historical Analysis of Popular Sports in Britain*. Cambridge: Polity Press.

Hoch, P. (1972) *Rip Off the Big Game: The Exploitation of Sports by the Power Elite*. New York: Anchor Doubleday.

Ingham, A.G. (2004) 'The Sportification Process: A Biographical Analysis Framed by the Work of Marx, Weber, Durkheim and Freud', in R. Giulianotti (ed.) *Sport and Modern Social Theorists*. Basingstoke: Palgrave Macmillan. pp. 11–32.

Jarvie, G. and Maguire, J. (1994) *Sport and Leisure in Social Thought*. London: Routledge.

Marcuse, H. (1964/2002) *One Dimensional Man: Studies in the Ideology of Advanced Industrial Society*. London: Routledge.

Marx, K. (1843/1975) 'Contribution to a Critique of Hegel's Philosophy of Right', in K. Marx and F. Engels *Collected Works, Vol.3: Marx and Engels 1843–44*. London: Lawrence and Wishart. pp. 3–129.

Marx, K. (1847/1995) *Poverty of Philosophy*. Loughton: Prometheus Books UK.

Marx, K. (1862/1987) *Theories of Surplus Value*. London: Lawrence & Wishart.

Marx, K (1867/1999) *Capital* (abridged edn). Oxford: Oxford University Press.

Marx, K. and Engles, F. (1846/1987) *The German Ideology: Introduction to a Critique of Political Economy* (student edn). London: Lawrence & Wishart Ltd.

Marx, K. and Engles, F. (1848/2008) *Communist Manifesto*. Oxford: Oxford University Press.

Miliband, R. (1977) *Marxism and Politics*. Oxford: Oxford University Press.

Rigauer, B. (1981) *Sport and Work*. New York: Columbia University Press.

Rigauer, B. (2002) 'Marxist Theories', in J. Coakley and E. Dunning (eds) *Handbook of Sports Studies*. London: Sage. pp. 28–47.

marxism

Methods are the systematic approaches and techniques employed in compiling a research data set, and how these approaches are operationalised in the field throughout the research process. 'Methodology' – effectively the theory of method – is a central subject area within the philosophy of knowledge and it asks critical questions about how social scientists (and scientists in general) collect and interpret evidence to support, or disprove, particular observations or claims. The question of how scientific claims are verified and attain the status of fact has itself become a prominent methodology in its own right, particularly within post-structuralist approaches to social enquiry (see Discourse and Post-Structuralism).

METHODOLOGY AND SPORTS STUDIES

According to Andrews et al. (2005: 1) the evolution of sports studies has comprised an 'eclectic mix of research ideologies', both methodologically and theoretically. They do not see this development as unduly negative, but rather they suggest, that, given the function of sports studies – 'Contextualizing sport within networks of political, economic and social linkages' – the range of research methodologies allows for a flexible approach. This flexible approach enables the employment of the methodological tools most 'suitable for the critical interrogation of the particular sporting phenomena under investigation' (2005: 1). However, the authors do note that this eclectic diversity has resulted in a tendency towards fragmentation and isolation within much of the research in the field, whereby research is often corralled into a particular 'school' of thought, or pigeon-holed as a representative of a particular ideological or theoretical outlook. As such, they suggest that sports studies often 'lack the unity of interests' that are otherwise found in other disciplines concerned with social investigation.

THE PRINCIPAL METHODOLOGICAL APPROACHES

The two principal methodological approaches are classified by their conceptualisation of the social phenomenon, by the subject they seek to investigate, the particular characteristics of the data collected, or the techniques employed in the collection of the data. They are: *quantitative* methods and *qualitative* methods.

A quantitative methodology or approach to data collection reflects in part the positivist assumption that social phenomena and behaviour can be measured numerically – and as such they are quantifiable in nature. For example, modern sporting competition is quantifiable in that it is dependent upon a form of numerical measurement to determine outcome – how many goals/points scored, how high, how far, how fast, how many touchdowns, home runs and so on. As an example of the possible application of quantitative methods in sporting research, Gratton and Jones (2004: 21) suggest that a researcher may be interested in the relationship between economic investment and success in sport. This, they suggest, may be approached by measuring the amount of money invested in a sport and measuring performance in that sport. An example might be the number of medals won by a particular country at a major event such as the Olympics, set against the funding provided by that country for the preparation of its athletes. This would produce a numerical data set which could then be analysed statistically to determine the strength or weakness of the relationship and test our initial hypothesis. Both variables in this example (economic investment and sporting performance) are directly measurable and can be converted into numerical values that are comparable and meaningful (Gratton and Jones, 2004: 21). The most common quantitative data collection methods include structured surveys and interviews with closed questions. Respondents are limited to pre-coded answers, (for example, Yes; No; Don't Know) which are assigned a value and can then be compared statistically.

Whilst quantitative research methods deal with numerical data, qualititative methods are concerned with analysing qualities that are not directly quantifiable, or reducible to numerical form (Gratton and Jones, 2004: 22). These include emotions, 'feelings, thoughts, experiences' (Gratton and Jones, 2004: 22). The qualitative researcher is not concerned with the question of 'how many' or 'how much' but rather with providing descriptions and understanding through non-quantitative data. In recent years qualitative research has undergone significant growth in sports studies, suggesting that sport sciences (and social sciences in general) reflect the increasing importance and scientific validity given to emotions, feelings and inductive forms of understanding. Qualitative approaches include field work, ethnographic accounts (see **Ethnography**) and observation, for example participant observation, whereby the researcher is placed in a research setting (the field), often as a participant themselves (for example, research into sporting cultures, such as windsurfing, or skateboarding is often carried out by researchers who are members or active in those cultures (see e.g. Beal and Weidman, 2003; Wheaton, 2004). Ethnographic forms of qualitative research involve important ethical questions concerning the relationship of the researcher to the subjects he/she are observing. Other forms of qualitative data collection include the unstructured interview and the semi-structured interview, wherein the respondent is asked specific questions on a topic but is not restricted in their answers.

However, whilst qualitative and quantitative approaches are underpinned by opposing philosophical and theoretical assumptions about the nature of the social world, that does not mean that these methodological approaches are necessarily exclusive of each other and incompatible. Nau (1995: 1) suggests that 'blending qualitative and quantitative methods of research can produce a final product which can highlight the significant contributions of both' (quoted in Gratton and Jones, 2004: 25). Indeed as Gratton and Jones (2004: 25) following Jayaratne (1993) suggest, qualitative data can be used to 'support and explicate the meaning of quantitative research' (Jayaratne 1993: 117). For a discussion of using a mixed approach to utilising both qualitative and quantitative methods in a combined approach to researching sporting fan cultures see Jones (1997). However, because of the divergent philosophical backgrounds of qualitative and quantitative methods, care should be taken when using both. Methods should be dictated by the research questions and the aims and objectives of the project, rather than the other way around. Just because a particular method seems 'easier' it does not mean it will be suitable to the object at hand. When choosing a methodological approach to data collection, one should bear in mind the implications of the time and cost involved in the project. A large survey might seem appropriate and produce the data required, but the time and cost taken to plan, pilot and then carry out the survey, might be highly restrictive. Time and cost are often the two biggest barriers faced by the researcher.

148

THE THEORETIC AND PHILOSOPHICAL UNDERPINNINGS OF RESEARCH METHODOLOGY

The development of methodological outlooks has in principle been shaped by the schematic opposition between *positivism* and *interpretivism*. Positivism (or, as it might otherwise be termed, empiricism) is a view that suggests that society is made up of self defining facts, and it is the role of the scientist to uncover and collect these facts using a range of suitable methodological tools. Positivist approaches make no distinction between the natural and social sciences – both are seen as determined by, and subject to, objective rules and laws, the only difference being the object of study (nature on the one hand, and society on the other). Facts have their own objective reality, independent of subjective interpretation, and can be tested empirically, free from moral, ethical and other value judgements. However, during the late eighteenth and nineteenth centuries a challenge to the positivist orthodoxy was mounted in the social sciences. This challenge was termed 'interpretivism', and it radically reformulated the role of science and the scientist and their relationship to society. Diametrically opposed to positivist approaches, interpretivism posits that the object of study – society – is fundamentally different from that of the natural sciences. As such it requires different approaches and methods of investigation, which recognise both the social and human nature of the object being studied and, equally importantly, the social and human nature of the research process itself. Consciousness and subjective meaning become central considerations for social scientists as it is recognised that social actors do not live or function within an objective given set of circumstances, but constantly interpret and reinterpret the world by constructing meaning.

The opposition between positivism and interpretivism represents a split between those that consider social reality as primarily objective and those that see it as subjective in character. The positivist tradition suggests that, like nature, society is subject to objective scientific laws which are observable through objective scientific enquiry. However, the interpretivist tradition understands society as being constructed through human interaction, and by the subjective meanings and interpretations human actors ascribe to their social environment. These meanings and interpretations are not fixed, but subject to change and fluctuation. Society is not subject to fixed objective laws as the positivists contend, but rather to specific and fluid rules which influence and shape patterns of behaviour in a particular social structure, context or environment. Interpretavism lays the theoretical premise for the development of social constructionism, a sociological theory of knowledge that considers how particular social contexts give rise to and develop particular practices and concepts, which, whilst appearing objective, natural and fixed are in fact constructed through specific social or cultural relations.

Despite their obvious differences in approach, both positivist and interpretive outlooks generally share an understanding that social research is

methods

essentially a rational scientific endeavour. However, developments in the study of knowledge in the last half of the twentieth century or so – particularly in the fields of post-structuralism and postmodernism – have brought further into question the perceived rationality and structure of scientific investigation and claims. This has had important implications for the social sciences (for detailed discussion of the challenges facing research into sport in the light of these developments see Andrews et al., 2005).

The theoretical approaches outlined above (positivism and interpretivism) are underpinned by particular philosophical traditions. There are principally two philosophical models that have held sway. They are: *inductivism* which was the dominant philosophical tradition from the seventeenth century to the nineteenth century; and *deduction* which begins to emerge in the late eighteenth century.

Inductivism is a philosophical approach that suggests that science begins with empirical observation and that through describing the correlation of the 'facts' observed it is possible to predict an outcome (the relationship between cause and effect). The process of observation is considered objectively independent of scientific theory.

By the late eighteenth century, leading social thinkers, such as David Hume (1711–1776) began to question the supposedly independent relationship between the process of observation, the object being observed, and the method employed in observing, suggesting that there is no pure scientifically objective observation independent of theory, or as Karl Marx was later to suggest, ideology (see **Marxism** and **Ideology**). The questioning of the relationship between object, observation and theory is premised upon a philosophical approach to knowledge known as deductive reasoning. This approach suggests that there is an implicit relationship between theory, the modes of observation and investigation, and the object/subject being observed. It is, the deductionists asserted, theories and hypothesis that provide the basis for observation, not the other way around.

By the mid-twentieth century, the deductionist approach had been fully embraced, but seemed to be being employed by many emerging theorists to support an all-out assault upon the nature and validity of scientific knowledge itself – post-structuralists such as Michel Foucault (1926–1984) argued that knowledge as a claim to truth was conditionally formed within discursive power relationships. Rather than being objectively true, bodies of knowledge were the product of relationships of power which either legitimised or de-legitimised particular statements as true or false.

Participants in this new attack upon knowledge were the theorists Karl Popper (1902–1994), Thomas Kuhn (1922–1996) and Paul Feyerabend (1924–1994), each of whom set about radically dismantling and reconstructing the way in which we think about and approach science and scientific enquiry.

Austrian born philosopher and academic Karl Popper (1934, 1963, 1972) suggested that the objective reality of scientific investigation was not to be found in its attempt to discover truth. Truth, he contented, could never be attained as it is specific rather than absolute. The goal of science, Popper concluded, was one of falsification. That is, the development of scientific theory involves rigorous and critical conjecture whereby previous theories and scientific knowledge are brought into question and proved false. For Popper scientific theories and claims cannot be proven as truth, they can only be falsified – that is, proven to be untrue, or false. Popper termed this process of falsification 'critical rationalism' and stated that it was this drive towards falsification that provided the unity of scientific method.

American physicist and philosopher of science Thomas Kuhn disagreed with Popper. For Kuhn, the dynamic shaping science was not the process of falsification whereby science progresses through the accumulation of new theories and knowledge. In his work *The Structure of Scientific Revolutions* (1962) Kuhn suggested that scientific knowledge, far from being critical, is marked by convention and conservatism. Science, he argued, develops within specific *paradigms*. Paradigms consist of a constellation of techniques, conventions, beliefs and values shared by a particular scientific community and a particular time. Kuhn's theory challenges the notion that scientists are involved in the objective pursuit of knowledge. Instead, he suggests scientists are the products of socialisation whereby they are incorporated into a particular community or system of beliefs and values. Science is not a 'heroic pursuit' but rather a mundane, everyday activity. As noted above, Popper believed that the unifying principle of scientific knowledge and theory was its focus upon falsification. Popper believed that scientific knowledge was commensurable – it could be measured against a common universal standard in order for theories and claims to be falsified. Scientific theories stood in relation to each other. However, Kuhn regarded science as non-commensurable. As specific scientific approaches and theories are the result of specific paradigms, scientific theories bear no relationship to each other; they cannot be measured, or compared, as they have different paradigmatic structures, values and viewpoints. For Kuhn there is no unity of scientific method.

This view was also shared by Austrian born radical philosopher Paul Feyerabend (1975, 1978) who suggested that science was an essentially anarchic enterprise – the result of accidental encounters, conjuncture, and 'curious juxtapositions' (1975, 1993: 9). Science and the philosophy of science, Feyerabend contended, were obsessed with their own mythology. Radically, Feyerabend argued that methodological rules were antithetical to, and hindered, the development of science. Science was not the product of paradigms, but ideology. Feyerabend conceptualised scientific knowledge as being both the result of, and a form of, ideology – a social construct run through with implicitly reactionary power relations, dogmas and sectional interests. As such, he suggested that democratically pluralist societies should take measures to protect themselves from science, just as it takes measures against other forms and expressions of ideologies – fascism, communism, racism, sexism and homophobia, for example. The title of Feyerabend's most celebrated work succinctly captures his analysis of the scientific – it is called *Against Method*. In *Against Method* (1975, 1993), and *Science in a Free Society*, first published in 1978, Feyerabend advances the notion of science as being an essentially anarchic activity. He suggests that there are in fact no rules and no unity of methodological approach. Methodology was an external imposition, intended to provide ideological rigidity and constraint. Methodology was for Feyerabend inherently anti-scientific and anti-humanitarian, functioning primarily as a means of establishing and maintaining the power of the 'expert' elites. Feyerabend's response was to demand that, as science was effectively an anarchic pursuit, scientists should reject the ideological constraint of method and embrace theoretical anarchism. For Feyerabend in science 'anything goes'. It is in this respect that Feyerabend holds similar views to those which characterise the development of post-war post-structuralism and postmodernism.

The work of Feyerabend and the post-structalists, such as Michel Foucault's discursive critique of knowledge and power, have had increasing influence within the social science of sport (see **Discourse and Post-structuralism** for detailed discussion).

REFERENCES

Andrews, D.L., Mason, D.S. and Silk, M.L. (2005) *Qualitative Methods in Sports Studies*. Oxford: Berg.

Beal, B. and Weidman, L. (2003) 'Authenticity in the Skateboarding World', in R.E. Rinehart and S. Sydnor (eds) (2003) *To the Extreme. Alternative Sports, Inside and Out*. New York: SUNY. pp. 337–52.

Feyerabend, P. (1975/1993) *Against Method*. London: Verso.
Feyerabend, P. (1978) *Science in a Free Society*. London: New Left Books.
Gratton, C. and Jones, I. (2004) *Research Methods for Sports Studies*. London: Routledge.
Jayaratne, T. (1993). 'Quantitative Methodology and Feminist Research', in M. Hammersley (ed.) *Social Research: Philosophy, Politics and Practice*. London: Sage. pp. 109–23.
Jones, I. (1997) 'Mixing Qualitative and Quantitative Methods in Sports Fan Research', *The Qualitative Report*, 3(4), http://www.nova.edu/ssss/QR/QR3-4/jones.html
Kuhn, T.S. (1962/1996) *The Structure of Scientific Revolutions*. Chicago: University of Chicago Press.
Nau, D. (1995) 'Mixing Methodologies: Can Bimodal Research be a Viable Post-Positivist Tool?', *The Qualitative Report* 2(3), http://www.nova.edu/ssss/QR/QR2-3/nau.html
Popper, K. (1934/2002) *The Logic of Scientific Discovery*. London: Routledge. (English translation 1959.)
Popper, K. (1963/2002) *Conjectures and Refutations: The Growth of Scientific Knowledge*. London: Routledge.
Popper, K. (1972) *Objective Knowledge: An Evolutionary Approach*. Oxford: Oxford University Press. (Revised 1979.)
Wheaton, B. (2004) '"New Lads"? Competing Masculinities in the Windsurfing Culture', in B. Wheaton (ed.) *Lifestyle Sport: Consumption, Identity and Difference*. London: Routledge. pp. 131–53.

Olympism

'Olympism' may be defined as the philosophy of the Olympic Games. This philosophy is, in essence, that the Olympic Games are contested in a timeless spirit of amateurism which values taking part above winning and pure sport above commercial gain. Thus, the Games mitigate aggressive nationalism and instead promote peace and international harmony. This, as the merest scrutiny of the history and contemporary practice of the Games reveals, is a myth. Indeed, it could be argued that no sports competition in human history has entailed so many myths as the Olympic Games.

The myth of the Olympics as a haven of international goodwill derives, in the first instance, from the expressed philosophy of the French nobleman Baron Pierre de Coubertin (1863–1937), the chief instigator of the modern Olympic movement. The philospophy and

olympism

153

public declarations of de Coubertin formed the template for modern Olympism. Here is a sample:

> May joy and good fellowship reign, and in this manner, may the Olympic Torch pursue its way through ages, increasing friendly understanding among nations, for the good of a humanity always more enthusiastic, more courageous and more pure.
>
> Olympism is a doctrine of the fraternity between the body and the soul.
>
> Olympism seeks to create a way of life based on the joy found in effort, the educational value of a good example and respect for universal fundamental ethical principles.
>
> Racial distinctions should not play a role in sport.
>
> The important thing in life is not victory but combat; it is not to have vanquished but to have fought well.
>
> The Olympic Spirit is neither the property of one race nor of one age.[1]

These aphorisms were uttered and reiterated principally between the 1890s and 1920s

Another key myth is that the modern Olympics were an authentic revival of the ancient Greek Olympics. This, too, is mistaken (see Cartledge, 2000; Kidd, 1984). *But* Olympic history does show that the International Olympic Committee (IOC), along with successive National Olympic Committees (NOCs) and International Federations (IFs) have continued to *invoke* the ideals of de Coubertin and the spirit of Olympism. You can see this for yourself, easily enough. Go to the official website of the Olympic Movement (http://www.olympic.org/uk/index_uk.asp) and click on 'Olympic Games'. This will very likely call up the following statements:

> The games have always brought people together in peace to respect universal moral principles
>
> The upcoming games will feature athletes from all over the world and help promote the Olympic spirit.

Sociologists and historians widely agree, however, that, in making these assertions, the Olympic Movement ignores its own history. To illustrate this, we can look at the three key, and linked, areas of *peace*, *commerce* and *competitiveness* in relation to the Olympic movement.

THE OLYMPICS, WAR AND PEACE

Here Olympic ideas are rooted in late Victorian interpretations of the ancient Greek Games. These Games were seen, by Coubertin and the other early modern Olympians, as a haven of tranquillity away from the frequent fighting that characterised Ancient Greece. It is now argued, however, firstly that the games were merely a truce and, secondly, that the early Olympic Games were themselves full of violence.

'The original Olympics', wrote Paul Cartledge, Professor of Greek History at Cambridge University recently, 'were desperately alien to what we understand by competitive sports today' (2000: 10). The games were held in Olympia in the Peloponnese, Greece's southernmost peninsula. There were nine main events, for males only, and these included track events, chariot racing and pankration (a mixture of boxing, wrestling and gouging in which no holds were barred). The games were punctuated by religious ritual and were held in tribute to the god Zeus, the overlord of Mount Olympus. Olympic victors were seen as touched by divinity and, in the context of the tournament, received only simple crowns of olive leaves (olive trees grew wild in the Altis – the sacred precinct of Zeus). But these athletes earned large sums elsewhere – and were therefore, to borrow a term much-used in British sport in the 1950s, 'shamateurs'.

Importantly, there was *no* gentlemanly spirit at the ancient Olympics: instead the games were characterised by 'martial pugnaciousness'. There was an Olympic truce (two months either side of the five-day festival) but this was not a symbol of amity. It was simply a ceasefire to ensure the safe passage of spectators and competitors. In Ancient Greece inter-state warfare was endemic. There is a final irony. The Greeks are seen to have invented competitive sport: the Greek word 'agon', meaning competition, is the origin of the English word 'agony' (Cartledge, 2000: 10–11).

What we can observe in the formation of the modern Olympic movement is de Coubertin interpreting the English Victorian fair play ethic, *itself* interpreting ancient Greek ideals. Step-by-step, we can see these peace-seeking/ fair-play interpretations being woven into the practice of the Olympic movement and into its own corporate history – the story that it tells of its own development. For example, the 1920 Games (the Games of 1916 had been scheduled for Berlin) were awarded to the Belgian city of Antwerp, in recognition of that country's suffering in the First World War. For the following Games, in Paris, a closing ceremony was instituted, in which the flags of the IOC and the host nation were hoisted. Four years

olympism

later, in Amsterdam, there was a new protocol for the opening procession, with the Greeks first, and the hosts last.

According to the IOC (and it is a popular view):

> The 1936 Olympics, held in Berlin, are best remembered for Adolf Hitler's failed attempt to use them to prove his theories of Aryan racial superiority. As it turned out the most popular hero of the games was the African American sprinter and long jumper Jesse Owens, who won four gold medals.[2]

These are often known as the 'Nazi Olympics'. There was a boycott campaign in the USA and Europe, which was resisted by the IOC. The IOC website sees these Games as a triumph over prejudice. Critics, however, argue that permitting the Games opened the way for further persecution of blacks, Jews and others in Nazi Germany. Nazi Germany was, in effect, de-politicised and was represented simply as a country that could stage a compelling sporting spectacle (Guttmann, 1984; Mandell, 1987).

At the Helsinki Olympics of 1952 the Soviet Union entered for the first time, making this the First 'Cold War' Olympiad. Again the IOC website puts an optimistic, internationalist slant on this: 'Although their [the Soviet Union's] athletes were housed in a separate "village", warnings that Cold War rivalries would lead to clashes proved unfounded'. However, it is widely accepted that at every Games between Helsinki and Seoul in 1988 an informal, ideological Cold War face-off took place between the USA and USSR/'Iron Curtain' countries. Each super power organised a boycott of the Games: the United States in 1980 and the USSR in 1984 (Wagg and Andrews, 2007). For the Olympics of 1956 in Melbourne it was resolved that, for the closing ceremony, athletes should enter the stadium together as a symbol of 'global unity'. Eight years later in 1964 the Games took place in Tokyo to mark Japan's post-war reconstruction. Yoshinori Sakai, the final bearer of the Olympic torch, was elected because he had been born on the day an atom bomb had been dropped on Hiroshima in August 1945.

The IOC website acknowledges controversy in the Games of 1968 in Mexico City – principally for Mexico City's high altitude, which created difficulties for athletes from colder countries. But other controversies are not mentioned – notably, the popular demonstrations in Mexico City against the expense of the games at which many protestors were shot dead by police, and the Black Power protest by US 200m runners Tommie Smith and John Carlos. Smith and Carlos were sent home in disgrace.

Political controversy continued to attend the Olympic Games: in 1972 in Munich nine Israeli athletes were killed by Palestinian hostage-takers. The Games were suspended for 34 hours. In Montreal in 1976 there was a boycott by African countries over the participation of New Zealand, whose rugby team had recently toured apartheid South Africa. In 1980 and in 1984 there were boycotts arising out of 'Cold War' disputes between the United States and the Soviet Union. In 1996 at Atlanta a terrorist bomb killed one person and injured 110. At the time of writing (Spring 2008) angry protests against China's continued subjugation of Tibet attended the passage of the Olympic torch on its way to the Olympiad of 2008 in Beijing. And so on.

Throughout these controversies the IOC has maintained the view that the Games must go on and that 'politics' must not intrude upon them. The 'Nazi Olympics' are a case study in the taking of such a stance (Guttmann, 1984; Mandell, 1987). But has the IOC promoted peace or simply turned a blind eye to war and discord? Scholars, it's fair to say, are doubtful of the IOC's claims and, since the boycott of the Moscow Games of 1980, instigated by US president Jimmy Carter and British prime minister Margaret Thatcher, the argument that politics and sport can be kept separate – the broader ideology from which Olympism derives – has been difficult to sustain. Most would accept the observation of the sociologist Garry Whannel (1983) who asks whether the people who say 'Keep politics out of sport' are not, in reality, saying 'Keep the politics of sport as they are'.

THE OLYMPICS AND COMMERCE: GOD OR MAMMON?

The modern Olympics were forged in the late nineteenth century, in part out of an admiration for ideals of amateurism widely perceived as British. The Games represented a strong opposition to professionalism and commodification in sport and an attempt to set sport symbolically apart from the cash nexus. When FIFA proposed 'broken time payments' for footballers in the 1932 Games (since only 17 teams had been eligible in 1928), they were turned down. Football was then dropped from the Olympics and in 1930 FIFA started its own tournament: the World Cup.

The Games still offer no cash prizes – only medals and the winners' crown of olive branches – but otherwise commercialism has been steadily accommodated at successive Olympiads. From the first modern Olympiad, in Athens in 1896, advertising was permitted in the official programme. (The Games were partly financed by George Averoff, a Greek trade magnate, who paid for the refurbishment of the main stadium.) In 1900 in Paris and again in 1904 in St Louis the games were part of trade fairs. In 1912 in Stockholm, 12 Swedish companies bought the rights to take photographs and sell memorabilia. At the Paris Games in 1924 advertising signage was permitted for the first time. Four years later in Amsterdam the IOC sold concessions, for instance for running restaurants within the stadium. Contrary to popular opinion, it was the Los Angeles Olympics of 1932, and not the subsequent one in 1984, that was the first Games to make a profit.

Much of the more recent commercialisation of the Olympic Games has gone hand in hand with the development of broadcasting. The IOC first sold the rights to broadcast the tournament in 1948 (in London), although the cheque, paid by the BBC, was never cashed – probably in the belief that the BBC could not afford to honour it.

The 1956 winter Games in Cortina D'Ampezzo were the first to be broadcast live on TV and two years later TV rights were incorporated into the Olympic Charter. The summer Games were now televised, beginning with Rome in 1960, and, by the time of the Tokyo Games in 1964, the IOC had 250 corporate relationships. A new cigarette brand called Olympia was developed and there were the first satellite broadcasts. The Olympic rivalry between sports goods companies dates from the 1960s, when Adidas and Puma fought it out at the summer Games, ski manufacturers at the winter ones. For the Munich Games of 1972 an advertising agency was employed by the IOC as a licensing agent. Among other things they devised the first official mascot for the Olympics.

The Olympics Games of 1984, in Los Angeles, are widely seen as a watershed in the commercialisation of the tournament: they have been called 'The Hamburger Olympics' (Gruneau, 1984). For this Olympiad, the matter of sponsorship (by now the IOC had over 600 sponsors and suppliers) was streamlined. There were now to be 34 Official Sponsors, along with companies purchasing 'supplier rights' and other licensees. Television rights to these Games were bought in 156 countries and the tournament was seen by an estimated 2.5 billion viewers. This clearly constituted a huge global market for sponsors, and, for the 1988 Games (in Seoul and Calgary) a worldwide marketing programme (known as TOP) was instituted, based on nine business categories covering goods and services marketable worldwide.

The major development of the 1990s was the incorporation of black Africa into the Olympic media market. The winter Games of 1994, in Lillehammer (Norway), were seen in 120 countries (as opposed to 86 for the previous ones in Albertville) and many of the newly involved countries were in black Africa. For the Atlanta Games of 1996, which were funded entirely from private sources, the IOC underwrote the cost of broadcasting to Africa. These Games were seen in 214 countries by around 3.2 billion viewers, 90% of the available audience.

The Sydney Olympics of 2000 were another milestone for the new marketing. The International Olympic Committee (IOC) and the Sydney Organising Committee for the Olympic Games (SOCOG) generated approximately US$3 billion during the period 1997–2000 from the marketing of the Sydney 2000 Olympic Games; mostly from the sale of collective broadcasting rights, sponsorships, tickets and licenses. The IOC generated approximately 63% of the overall revenue while SOCOG's unprecedented marketing success within the host country of Australia generated nearly 37% of the overall revenue. The Sydney 2000 Olympic Games now stand as the most watched sports event ever. More than 3.7 billion people tuned in to watch in 220 countries and territories, generating more than 36.1 billion television viewing hours. Spectators purchased more than 92% of Olympic Games tickets, far exceeding the previous record of 82.3% that had been set in Atlanta. The official website of Sydney 2000 was the most popular destination on the internet during the Games, experiencing more than 11.3 billion hits. As Richard Pound, Chairman of the IOC Marketing Commission for Sydney 2000, was to claim: 'The Sydney 2000 Olympic Games set a course for the future of the Olympic Movement – it stands now in our collective memory as a tribute to the most successful marketing effort the world has ever seen' (IOC, http://www.olympic.org/uk/organisation/facts/introduction/100years_uk.asp (accessed: 11 December 2008)).

The marketing triumph that had defined the Sydney Games to its organisers was paralleled by the next winter Games which established marketing-related records in the areas of broadcasting, ticketing and sponsorship. These included more than 1.525 million tickets sold, representing 95% of the available tickets, and a total of US$ 876 million in sponsorship revenue. At these Games, to quote the IOC web site: 'The balance between the commercial agenda and the Olympic image was achieved'. The IOC adds that 'Few ambush marketing incidents were encountered; all minor ambush incidents were effectively addressed' and that 'Olympic Market Research clearly shows passion for the Olympic Games, support for Olympic sponsors and enjoyment of the Olympic Games experience across constituencies and demographics'.

IT MATTERS NOT WHO WON OR LOST...?
THE OLYMPICS AND WINNING

The early Olympics were very relaxed affairs and there was no detailed preparation for events. As we have seen, the emphasis placed by de Coubertin, and other early modern Olympians, was on chivalry. Only at the sixth modern Olympics – 1924, in Paris – was the Olympic motto 'Citius, Altius, Fortius' – 'Swifter, Higher, Stronger' – adopted. Eight years on, in Los Angeles, there was still greater stress on victory: the victors' rostrum was introduced; the winner's national flag raised; a photo finish camera certified the results of races; and automatic timing devices confirmed records.

During the 1930s there were frequent disputes over who was, or was not, an amateur and complaints about the professionalised training routines of some nations, notably the United States and Germany. At the second London Olympics in 1948, Fanny Blankers-Koen (Netherlands) was world record holder in six events but only allowed to compete in four. But from the early 1950s new problems came into play – principally the emergent Cold War between the Soviet Union and the United States and the concurrent rise of rationalised (science-based, achievement-oriented) sport (Gruneau, 1984). This brought two principal problems: an accentuation of the controversy over amateurism – since many Soviet athletes had sinecures in the armed forces and many American competitors were on athletic scholarships at US universities – and the use of stimulants. In 1950s the use of drugs in athletics was already widely acknowledged (Dimeo, 2007), and, when Dutch cyclist Knud Jensen died competing in the Rome Olympics of 1960 he was found to have been using amphetamines. A series of IOC meetings on the drugs question followed and, after one such meeting, in Tehran in 1967, drug testing was introduced into the Olympics. Meanwhile, as Beamish and Ritchie (2004) point out, the time spent in training by Olympic athletes doubled between 1950 and 1970.

These developments seemed to bring a still greater realism to the IOC. For, whereas in 1972 its Eligibility Commission had disqualified Austrian skier Karl Schranz for endorsing ski equipment, two years later a new eligibility code was introduced, recognising, in effect, commercial interests, zeal for competition and *de facto* professional athletes. These things were now simply regulated, not rejected.

CONCLUSION

Where does all this leave the Olympic movement? Perhaps there is an assessment on which the IOC, its many business partners and political opponents might agree. As the German academic Arnd Kruger wrote in 1999, 'The Olympic Games have adapted well to the postmodern world' (see **Postmodernism/Postmodernity**) (Kruger, 1999: 24). This means, in effect, that the Games no longer have to practise fair play, an obliviousness to commerce or an amateur disdain for preparation (if, indeed, they ever did). They now provide an 'image' of these historic virtues. This image becomes a product sold on the global media market. The image is nurtured by the IOC's publicity machine which now stresses the heroic aspects of past tournaments. The IOC website, for example, tells the tale of Australian rower Henry Pearce, who, in the Amsterdam Olympics of 1928, stopped rowing in the quarter-final of the single sculls to let some ducks pass his boat. The same year, it is pointed out, Pearce was refused admission to Henley because he worked as a carpenter and at that time manual workers were deemed professionals under Amateur Rowing Association rules. Modern Olympic rowers, of course, will not be expected to make such gestures; they will simply be bearers of the apparently time-transcendent myths of the Olympic Games (Wagg, 2006).

Small wonder then that in the early years of the twenty-first century, a group of scholars assembled to explore the proposition that we had entered the era of 'post-Olympism'. One implication of this term is that the Olympics survive essentially as a spectacle: one of the most popular Olympic events among television viewers is the opening ceremony, which involves no sport at all (Bale and Christensen, 2004: 11).

NOTES

Unless otherwise stated, information for this chapter was taken from http://www.olympic.org/uk/organisation/facts/introduction/100years_uk.asp (accessed: 16th March 2005).
1. De Coubertin website: http://www.brainyquote.com/quotes/authors/p/pierre_de_coubertin.html
2. IOC website: http://www.olympic.org/uk/index_uk.asp

REFERENCES

Bale, John and Christensen, Mette, Krogh (eds) (2004) *Post-Olympism? Questioning Sport in the Twenty First Century*. Oxford: Berg.

Beamish, Rob and Ritchie, Ian (2004) 'From Chivalrous "Brothers-in-Arms" to the Eligible Athlete' *International Review of the Sociology of Sport*, 39(4): 355–71.

Cartledge, Paul (2000) 'Olympic Self Sacrifice', *History Today*, 50(10): 10–15.

Dimeo, Paul (2007) 'Good Versus Evil? Drugs, Sport and the Cold War', in Stephen Wagg and David L. Andrews (eds) *East Plays West: Sport and the Cold War*. London: Routledge. pp. 149–62.

Gruneau, Rick (1984) 'Commercialism and the Modern Olympics', in Alan Tomlinson and Garry Whannel (eds) *On the Ball*. London: Pluto Press. pp. 1–15.

Guttmann, Allen (1984) *The Games Must Go On: Avery Brundage and the Olympic Movement*. New York: Columbia University Press.

Kidd, Bruce (1984) 'The Myth of the Ancient Games' in Alan Tomlinson and Garry Whannel (eds) *On the Ball*. London: Pluto Press. pp. 71–83

Kruger, Arnd (1999) 'The Unfinished Symphony: A History of the Olympic Games from de Coubertin to Samaranch' in Jim Riordan and Arnd Kruger (eds) *The International Politics of Sport in the Twentieth Century*. London: E. and F.N. Spon. pp. 3–27.

Mandell, Richard D. (1987) *The Nazi Olympics*. Champaign: University of Illinois Press.

Wagg, Stephen (2006) '"Base Mechanic Arms": British Rowing, Some Ducks and the Shifting Politics of Amateurism', *Sport in History*, 26(3): 520–39.

Wagg, Stephen and Andrews, David L. (eds) (2007) *East Plays West: Sport and the Cold War*. London: Routledge.

Whannel, Garry (ed.) (1983) *Blowing the Whistle: The Politics of Sport*. London: Pluto Press.

FURTHER READING

Bale, John and Christensen, Mette Krogh (eds) (2004) *Post-Olympism? Questioning Sport in the Twenty First Century*. Oxford: Berg.

Guttmann, Allen (1984) *The Games Must Go On: Avery Brundage and the Olympic Movement*. New York: Columbia University Press.

Guttmann, Allen (2002) *The Olympics: A History of the Modern Games*. Champaign: University of Illinois Press.

Hill, Christopher (1992) *Olympic Politics*. Manchester: Manchester University Press.

Kruger, Arnd and Murray, William (eds) (2003) *The Nazi Olympics: Sport, Politics and Appeasement in the 1930s*. Urbana: University of Illinois Press.

MacAloon, John (1984) *This Great Symbol: Pierre de Coubertin and the Origins of the Modern Olympic Games*. Chicago: University of Chicago Press.

Mandell, Richard D. (1987) *The Nazi Olympics*. Champaign: University of Illinois Press.

Riordan, Jim and Kruger, Arnd (eds) (1999) *The International Politics of Sport in the Twentieth Century*. London: E. and F.N. Spon.

Tomlinson, Alan and Whannel, Garry (eds) (1984) *Five Ring Circus*. London: Pluto Press.

Wagg, Stephen and Andrews, David L. (eds) (2007) *East Plays West: Sport and the Cold War*. London: Routledge.

Politics/Policy/ Power

The term 'politics' derives from the ancient word 'polis', meaning a city state. There is no universally agreed meaning to the word today, but it is generally accepted to refer to the pursuit and exercise of power. This is invariably in relation to the formal practice of government, and the phrase 'going into politics', used to describe the embrace of politics as a profession, assumes its separateness from the rest of social life. (You cannot go into something without going out of something else.) A 'policy' is a plan of action and the word is used, ordinarily but not exclusively, in relation to formal political bodies, such as governments, ministries and political parties. Most modern governments now have a declared sports policy of some kind.

It should be added, however, that since the 1960s, 'politics' has come to have a more diffuse meaning, taking in what the radical psychiatrist R.D. Laing (1967) called 'the politics of experience'.[1] This has meant that many or most areas of social life – wherever power is sought or exercised – are now recognised as political. This is shown by the increased currency of such phrases as 'office politics', 'sexual politics' 'environmental politics', 'the personal is political' (see **Feminism**) and, of course, 'the politics of sport'. It also accords with longstanding definitions of power in sociological analysis: the German social theorist Max Weber's (widely accepted) definition, for example, has been summarised as 'the probability that a person in a social relationship will be able to carry out his or her own will in the pursuit of goals of action, regardless of resistance' (Abercrombie et al., 2000: 274). This definition applies equally to relationships between governments and people, between husbands and wives, doctors and patients, teachers and students … and so on. Similarly, power is wielded in the world of sport – by politicians, administrators, club proprietors, coaches and others – and their powers include: the power to dictate what sports will be played and according to which philosophies; the power to allocate lucrative tournaments to particular venues; the power to discriminate against, or in favour of, certain social groups; and the power to abuse the vulnerable. These powers, and the politics and policies that frame, or have framed, them, will be considered in this section.

POLITICS, SPORT AND GOVERNMENT

As has been made clear elsewhere in this book (see **State, Nation and Nationalism**) the British state took a growing interest in the bodies of its citizens, and their access to sport and exercise, from the late nineteenth century onward. But, beyond the promotion of drill, games and gymnastics in state schools and the nurturing of non-government bodies such as the National Playing Fields Association (founded 1925) and the Central Council for Physical Recreation (founded in 1935 as the Central Council of Physical Recreative Physical Training), it regarded sport as a private matter. This position was rooted in the nineteenth-century liberal notion that the role of the state should be minimal and in the prevailing amateur ethos of sport, which held, however hypocritically, that it should be unpolluted either by the cash nexus or by the intervention of government (see also **Olympism**).

As modern sport grew in popularity around the world, however, this ethos began to be threatened by the rise of mass sport. This was represented by the largely unfettered commercialisation of sport in the United States and by the overt politicisation of sport in 'totalitarian' countries: a description widely held to fit the Soviet Union, Nazi Germany and Fascist Italy.[2]

In the Soviet Union, sport was militarised and built into the government's GTO (Ready for Labour and Defence) programme, begun in 1931, and there were regular inter-republic *Spartakiads* to promote socialist unity (see Riordan, 1980). In Germany in the 1930s Nazi political strategists were similarly critical of 'unpolitical' or 'bourgeois' sport, and the Berlin Olympics of 1936, under the supervision of Hitler's propaganda chief Josef Goebbels, were the first to be staged as a media spectacle. In Italy, fascist leader Benito Mussolini promoted the building of several modernist, futurist stadia, including the Olympic Stadium in Rome, Berta Stadium in Florence and Stadio Dall'Ara in Bologna, all of which were used for the World Cup Finals of 1934 – an event ignored, like the previous (inaugural) finals in Uruguay, by the English FA.

While the British government distanced itself from the use of sport for propaganda purposes and from state exercise programmes, national fitness was nevertheless a concern in political circles during the 1930s, and, as Garry Whannel observes, 'The rise of fascism in Europe prompted British establishment figures to compare the nationalistic fervour of fascist youth movements with the supposed listless, apathetic state of Britain's youth' (1983: 89). This helps to illustrate a more general point, which is that the governments of modern industrial societies have invariably had the same political imperatives – health, fitness for work and/or military action, the discouraging of youthful disorder, the promoting of social cohesion, and so on – with regard to sport. The difference, historically, is that in fascist and communist societies these matters were the subject of detailed policy and planning, while in Western liberal democracies there was a piecemeal approach, biased towards the government funding of voluntary bodies, with the state itself formally only responsible for sport and exercise in schools.

Following the Second World War, the purported differences between capitalist and communist countries in the political disposition of sport were ideologically enhanced by the Cold War, with sportspeople from, say, the Soviet Union depicted in the West as state-regulated automata and Western athletes depicted in the Soviet Union as representatives of decadent societies where true sporting ideals were perverted (see Wagg and Andrews, 2007).

In societies such as Britain, the Cold War had several important linked effects on the politics of sport and sports policy. The notion of sport as a spectacle, and as an important vehicle for nations' presentation of themselves, grew in political importance, chiefly through the expansion and televising of the Olympic Games. In Britain, with growing anxiety about the country's international sport performance, the Minister for Sport, previously a wholly marginal political figure in the Department of Education and Science, was moved in 1969 to the Department of Housing and Local Government, meaning that funding for sport was no longer part of the government's education budget (Whannel, 1983). Moreover, the then occupant of the post, Denis Howell, politically more visible than any of his predecessors, called for detailed planning of Britain's campaign in the next Olympics, scheduled for Munich in 1972 (see Wagg, 2007: 118).

Furthermore, the burgeoning post-colonial politics of anti-racism and the growing importance of sport in international relations, combined to make the Western liberal ideology of un-politicised sport unviable. Two years after South Africa had declared independence from Britain in 1961, the South African Non-Racial Olympic Committee (SANROC) was formed and campaigned to have South Africa excluded from Olympic and other international sport until apartheid, the country's system of racial exclusion, had been abolished. Britain and other Western nations insisted that, while they did not condone racism, politics should not intrude on sport. However, in 1980, with the army of the Soviet Union occupying Afghanistan, the same governments called for a boycott of the Olympic Games in Moscow. In Britain, athletes in the civil service and police were forbidden to take leave to participate. This made the slogan 'Keep politics out of sport', a rallying cry principally of the political right, effectively redundant. As Whannel suggested, 'For "Keep politics out of sport" read "Keep the politics of sport the way they are"' (1983: 19). This did not mean, however, that in countries such as Britain the national policy for sport became any more sharply defined. Neil Macfarlane, sport minister in the Conservative government of Margaret Thatcher from 1981 to 1985 reflected later that:

> being Minister for Sport was rather like someone bicycling away on one of those keep fit machines; the pedals were going round at varying speeds, but not getting anywhere. Unlike the Minister for Housing, or the Minister for Social Services, for whom there is a straightforward legislative framework, there are no terms of reference for a minister with responsibility for sport, and, indeed there are no legislative guidelines. The job is what you make it. (Macfarlane, 1986: 64–5)

Despite this continuing vagueness, certain trends and tensions are discernible in British sport policy. The moving of the sport minister to the Department of Education within Harold Wilson's Labour government in 1969 was followed in 1971 by the establishment of the Sports Council by the incoming Conservative administration of Edward Heath. While the number of purpose-built sports centres grew greatly in the 1970s – from 30 in 1972 to 350 in 1978 (Whannel, 1983: 92) – by the early 1980s the policy emphasis had shifted from a 'Sport for All' notion of sport as a public benefit, to a greater concern with the targeting of sports funds (see Green, 2004). This was for several reasons. A series of riots in major English cities over 1980 and 1981 made it more likely that the government of Margaret Thatcher would put socially palliative money into 'those inner cities' for sports facilities (Whannel, 1983: 21).[3] Moreover, the Thatcher government was one of a growing number expressing neo-liberal philosophies and committed to privatisation and the rolling back of the state.

These factors should be added to the growing government recognition, beginning, as we've seen, from the late 1960s, of the importance of doing well in international sports competition. This has meant a further retreat from the ideal of 'Sport for All' – seen by some academics as no more than a slogan in any event (Green, 2004: 369) – and a greater resolve to find and nurture elite athletes. Some date this from the late 1970s when the Sports Council, with an eye on the Moscow Olympics, offered sport's governing bodies extra funds to employ top coaches for their most promising performers (Coghlan and Webb, 1990: 170). By the early 1990s sport had progressed towards the centre of the business of government. In 1992, the Conservative Prime Minister John Major instituted a Department of National Heritage (DNH), the political head of which would have cabinet rank and be responsible for sport. Two years later a National Lottery was introduced, with a significant slice of the revenue it generated being spent on sport via Sport England, the reconstituted Sports Council. In 1996 UK Sport was established and now bears specific responsibility for distributing Lottery money in the national pursuit of sporting excellence. It is accountable to parliament via the Department of Culture, Media and Sport, as the DNH became in 1997.

In 1997, after 18 years in Opposition, the Labour Party returned to office in Britain, its leadership now preferring to call the party 'New Labour'. This label was seen by the sociologist Stuart Hall as heralding 'entrepreneurial governance' wherein 'the role of the state "nowadays" is not to support the less fortunate or powerful but to help individuals themselves provide for all their social needs' (Hall, 2003). A clear corollary of this new perspective was that 'poverty' as a concept disappeared from the mainstream political vocabulary and was replaced by 'social exclusion' (see Collins and Kay, 2003: 1–23). This has had at least two important consequences: first, all sports governing bodies have been required to draw up strategies for promoting 'social inclusion' – a synonym in contemporary political discourse for 'equality of opportunity' and funding has more readily accrued to sports projects relating to this issue. Second, there has been a proliferation of private fitness clubs and of individual sport and/or exercise activities, such a walking, swimming, yoga and 'fun running' (Hutton, 1999). Popular marathons have often been sponsored by private health firms, reaffirming the new political imperative that health is a personal responsibility.[4]

The 'New Labour' administration of Tony Blair (1997–2007) was typical of governments of its time, with emphases in sports policy placed on social inclusion, elite athletes, privatisation and the pursuit of success in (and the right to stage) major international tournaments. Here 'New Labour' sought to decant old wine into new bottles, often marrying fresh rhetorics to state sport objectives which had long been cited by Marxist sociologists. For example, Chris Smith, the first Secretary of State for Culture, Media and Sport insisted that sport in schools must be competitive because 'We cannot escape the fact that life is competitive'[5] and Kate Hoey (Blair's second minister for sport) asserted that government spending on sport would improve the nation's health and diminish crime.[6] The thrust of *Game Plan*,[7] the Blair government's principal policy document on sport, links these time honoured objectives to the more contemporary aims of producing high performance athletes and attracting large sporting events to the United Kingdom. There has, however, been political and academic debate over whether the two strands of policy can be reconciled, there being no reliable evidence that a large sports event has ever promoted an increase in grassroots sports participation in the host country (see Conn, 2005; Taylor et al., 2004).

Looked at in the round, 'New Labour' policies, like policies in numerous other countries, can be seen, to an extent, as a consummation of the new political movements of the 1960s. Feminist and anti-racist struggles, along with post-war campaigns on the issue of disablement, are strongly reflected in the contemporary politics of equal opportunities and social inclusion. These politics have, in turn, carried over into the international arena. For example, as we've seen elsewhere in this book (see **Gender**) female athletes threatened to hold their own Olympics in the early 1920s before, gradually, being admitted to the 'official' Olympic tournament. Similarly the first Paralympics, growing out of the Stoke Mandeville Games for disabled war victims begun in 1948, was first held in parallel to the main summer Games in Rome in 1960.

Three years later post-colonial politics inspired the short-lived Games for the New Emergent Forces (GANEFO), wherein several emergent, mainly Asian and/or communist countries set up their own tournament, having been banned from the Olympics for excluding Taiwan and Israel from the previous year's Asian Games. (The Soviet Union supported GANEFO, but, with any participant now banned from the Olympics, boxed clever by sending a team of below Olympic standard.)

Similarly, the politics of sexuality were brought to bear on international sport with the inaugural Gay Games in San Francisco in 1982. The first four Gay Games were held in North America, where the gay movement has, arguably, been strongest politically; they moved to Europe (Amsterdam) for the first time in 1998 and are scheduled for Cologne in 2010.

SPORT AND THE EXERCISE OF POWER

The exercise of power can, of course, be considered on several levels. We have seen elsewhere in this book the intellectual influence of the French philosopher-historian Michel Foucault and noted, in particular, the increased currency given to Foucault's concepts of 'governmentality' and 'discourse' (see **State, Nation and Nationalism**). Adapting Foucault, we can say that one of the greatest powers in relation to sport is the power to define what sport is and is not and what it can and cannot be. As this section should have made clear, sport in most, though not all, modern societies is defined variously as a private matter, a context for the pursuit of high achievement and as a means to extremely lucrative media spectacles. It is seen far less as a matter of state provision or a tool for conviviality. These definitions of sport are established through discourse: that is, they become part of an established way of talking about sport to the extent that other definitions of sport become unrealistic, even unthinkable. This discursive power is impossible to trace to particular individuals or groups – it extends, as Foucault wrote, 'into the very grain of individuals ... their actions and attitudes, their discourses, learning processes and everyday life' (1980: 39, quoted in Cole et al., 2004: 211).

Other academics, of course, have adopted a more conventional view of power, assuming it to be the enacting of policies by state or similar organisations, possibly against the will of other interested parties. Here there has been much study of the nuts and bolts of sports policy – how sports policies are framed and carried through, which groups benefit by these policies and which perceive their interests to be undermined, and so on. Among the principal writers here are Barrie Houlihan and Ian Henry, both of whom have been identified as exponents of the 'pluralist' approach (Horne et al., 1999: 217 – see Henry, 1993: Houlihan, 1991, 2002). It might be thought that studies which focus on the various governing and statutory bodies and other 'players' that are party to, or recipients of, a policy decision would more readily lend itself to the pluralist perspective. In the case of Western capitalist societies, it would also reflect what is widely perceived as a fragmentation in the area of sports policy – what in the British case the sociologist Maurice Roche has termed a 'disorganised shambles' (quoted in Horne et al., 1999: 217), as distinct from the more centralised and coherent sports policies concocted by communist governments.

Houlihan is also the leading scholar on comparative sports policy and his research in the mid-1990s led him to conclude that this policy was becoming increasingly internationalised (Houlihan, 1997). Houlihan had already theorised the increased importance of sport in international politics – a development traceable, as we have seen, back to the 1930s. He proposes three perspectives through which the place of sport in international relations can be understood: *realism* (wherein the state is the principal focus – as in the use of sport as a tool of foreign policy), *pluralism* and *globalism*, the last acknowledging the growing power of transnational organisations in the making of sport policy (Houlihan, 1994). It's fair to say that this last perspective – or range of approaches – is the one which currently finds most favour among sport sociologists. A good example here is the body of work by John Sugden and Alan Tomlinson on FIFA, the international governing body of football (see e.g. Sugden and Tomlinson, 1998, 2003). This work is in turn a good example of the 'Brighton approach' to the exercise of power relations in international sport – a blend of sociology, history, politics and investigative reporting (see Sugden and Tomlinson, 2002: 10).

Finally, while it is true that, following Foucault, athletes – say, swimmers – may, under a coach's gaze, 'become agents who exercise power over them-selves' (Cole et al., 2004: 211), it is also true that coaches, and others, may seek to exercise a power over their charges which not only conforms to more conventional theories of power but is also wholly illegitimate. In this regard there is a growing scholarly literature on sexual harassment in sport, of which the principal exponent is Celia Brackenridge. As Brackenridge argues, sexual harassment is 'generally defined as unsolicited and unwanted sexual attention that a person in a position of power pays to someone in a subordinate posi-tion' (quoted in Volkwein-Caplan and Sankaran, 2002: 15). It is possible to suggest that, as the political emphasis on high performance sport has grown, bringing with it a growth in intensive coaching regimes, the likelihood of the sexual harassment of female athletes may have grown with it. Some victims of sexual abuse in sport, from Brackenridge's research, make clear that the abuse grew out of their emotional and professional dependence upon, and their admiration for, their coaches. 'I often needed calming down because I'd had a hard session', said one. 'He did rape me but I didn't know it was hap-pening. … I was infatuated with him ... He was in a way like a father. I was totally in love' '[It] was my fault', said another. 'I knew the sexual stuff was wrong ... I looked up to him. I respected him. I absolutely idolised him. [I thought] if that's the price, it's worth it' (Brackenridge, 2001: 97–8).

NOTES

1. Laing also coined the term 'the politics of the family' (1971).
2. See e.g. PBS television history documentary *People's Century, Episode 8: Sporting Fever*, 1995. Available at http://www.pbs.org/wgbh/peoplescentury/episodes/sportingfever/(accessed: 3 May 2007).
3. For discussion of urban disorder in Britain in the 1980s see Robson (1988) and Benyon and Solomos (1987).

4. E.g., in Britain, the popular annual Great North Run is sponsored by BUPA, a leading private health insurance firm.
5. Chris Smith in debate with Frank Eves, 'Should Labour Encourage Competitive Sport in Schools?', *Guardian* 26 June 1999.
6. Kate Hoey (2002) 'Spend on Sport and Save on Health and Crime' Posted on *Guardian* website 11 February 2002: http//www. guardian.co.uk/sport/2002/feb/11/katehoey#history-byline (accessed: 11 December 2008).
7. Published jointly by the Department of Culture, Media and Sport and the government's Social Exclusion Unit, December 2002.

REFERENCES

Abercrombie, Nicholas, Hill, Stephen and Turner, Bryan S. (2000) *Dictionary of Sociology.* London: Penguin.

Benyon, John and Solomos, John (eds) (1987) *The Roots of Urban Unrest.* Oxford: Pergammon Press.

Brackenridge, Celia H. (2001) *Spoilsports: Understanding and Preventing Sexual Exploitation in Sport.* London: Routledge.

Coghlan, John F. and Webb, Ida M. (1990) *Sport and British Politics Since 1960.* Basingstoke: The Falmer Press.

Cole, C.L., Giardina, Michael D. and Andrews, David L. (2004) 'Michel Foucault: Studies of Power and Sport', in Richard Giulianotti (ed.) *Sport and Modern Social Theorists.* Basingstoke: Palgrave Macmillan. pp. 207–223.

Collins, Michael F. and Kay, Tess (2003) *Sport and Social Exclusion.* London: Routledge.

Conn, David (2005) 'London 2012 Must Learn from Manchester's Mistakes: The Commonwealth Games Were a Hit But They Did Not Increase Local Participation in Sport', *Guardian*, 30 November, http://sport.guardian.co.uk/print/0, 3858, 5344590-112398,00.html (accessed: 30 November 2005).

Foucault, Michel (1980) *Power/Knowledge.* New York: Pantheon Books.

Green, Mick (2004) 'Changing Policy Priorities for Sport in England: The Emergence of Elite Sport Development as a Key Policy Concern', *Leisure Studies*, 23(4): 368–9.

Hall, Stuart (2003) 'New Labour has Picked Up Where Thatcherism Left Off,' *Guardian*, 6 August.

Henry, Ian (1993) *The Politics of Leisure Policy.* London: Macmillan.

Horne, John, Tomlinson, Alan and Whannel, Garry (1999) *Understanding Sport.* London: E. and F.N. Spon.

Houlihan, Barrie (1991) *The Government and Politics of Sport.* London: Routledge.

Houlihan, Barrie (1994) *Sport and International Politics.* Hemel Hempstead: Harvester Wheatsheaf.

Houlihan, Barrie (1997) *Sport, Policy and Politics: A Comparative Analysis.* London: Routledge.

Houlihan, Barrie (2002) 'Political Involvement in Sport, Physical Education and Recreation', in Anthony Laker (ed.) *The Sociology of Sport and Physical Education.* London: Routledge Falmer. pp. 190–210.

politics/policy/ power

Hutton, Will (1999) 'Sport is Back – and This Time it's Personal', *The Observer*, 20 June: 30.

Laing, R.D. (1967) *The Politics of Experience and the Bird of Paradise*. Harmondsworth: Penguin.

Laing, R.D. (1971) *The Politics of Family and other Essays*. London: Tavistock.

Macfarlane, Neil, with Michael Herd (1986) *Sport and Politics: A World Divided*. London: Willow Books.

Riordan, James (1980) *Sport in Soviet Society*. Cambridge: Cambridge University Press.

Robson, Brian (1988) *Those Inner Cities: Reconciling the Social and Economic Aims of Urban Policy*. Oxford: The Clarendon Press.

Sugden, John and Tomlinson, Alan (1998) *FIFA and the Contest for World Football*. Cambridge: Polity Press.

Sugden, John and Tomlinson, Alan (2002) 'Theory and Method for a Critical Sociology of Sport', in John Sugden and Alan Tomlinson (eds) (2002) *Power Games: A Critical Sociology of Sport*. London: Routledge. pp. 3–22.

Sugden, John and Tomlinson, Alan (2003) *Badfellas: FIFA Family at War*. London: Mainstream.

Taylor, Matthew, Chaudhury, Vivek, Kelso, Paul and Miller, Stuart (2004) '£2bn from Lottery Fails to Revive Sporting Life', *Guardian*, 21 August, http://www.guardian.co.uk/Print/0,3858, 4998575–103690,00 html (accessed: 23 March 2005).

Volkwein-Caplan, Karin A.E. and Sankaran, Gopal (2002) *Sexual Harassment in Sport: Impact, Issues and Challenges*. Aaachen: Meyer and Meyer.

Wagg, Stephen (2007) 'If You Want the Girl Next Door ...: Olympic Sport and the Popular Press in Early Cold War Britain', in Stephen Wagg and David L. Andrews (eds) *East Plays West: Sport and the Cold War*. London: Routledge. pp. 100–122.

Wagg, Stephen and Andrews, David L. (eds) (2007) *East Plays West: Sport and the Cold War*. London: Routledge.

Whannel, Garry (1983) *Blowing the Whistle: The Politics of Sport*. London: Pluto Press.

FURTHER READING

The best critical introduction to the relationship between sport and politics is Garry Whannel's (1983) *Blowing the Whistle* (London: Pluto Press), currently being re-written for a second edition.

John Hoberman's (1984) *Sport and Political Ideology* (Austin, TX: University of Texas Press) is a scholarly and exhaustive examination of the role of sport in specific political ideologies and systems. James Riordan's (1977) *Sport in Soviet Society* (Cambridge: Cambridge University Press) and Susan Brownell's (1995) *Training the Body for China* (London: University of Chicago Press) are among the leading texts on the conduct of sport in communist societies.

In the matter of the making of sports policy, the books of Barrie Houlihan, more muted and measured in their arguments than others in the field, are a good way in. See his three books cited above: Barrie Houlihan (1991) *The Government and Politics of Sport* (London: Routledge); Barrie Houlihan (1997) *Sport, Policy and Politics: A Comparative Analysis* (London: Routledge) and Barrie Houlihan (1994)

Sport and International Politics (Hemel Hempstead: Harvester Wheatsheaf). Other excellent summaries are Ian Henry's (2001) *The Politics of Leisure Policy* (Basingstoke: Palgrave) and Kevin Hylton and Peter Bramham (eds) (2008) *Sports Development: Policy, Process and Practice* (London: Routledge).
For the global politics of sport, James Riordan and Arnd Kruger (eds) (1999) *The International Politics of Sport in the Twentieth Century* (London: E. and F.N. Spon) and P. Arnaud and J. Riordan (eds) (1998) *Sport and International Politics: The Impact of Fascism and Communism* (London: E. and F.N. Spon) are good introductory texts, and so, for the period roughly 1945 to 1990, is Stephen Wagg and David L. Andrews (eds) (2007) *East Plays West: Sport and the Cold War* (London: Routledge). John Sugden and Alan Tomlinson's *FIFA and the Contest for World Football* is an excellent account of international football politics. For Olympic politics, a suitably critical and informative book is Alan Tomlinson and Garry Whannel (eds) (1984) *Five Ring Circus: Money, Power and Politics at the Olympic Games* (London: Pluto Press). Among more recent critical scholarship, two books by the Canadian sociologist Helen Jefferson Lenskyj stand out: *Inside the Olympic Industry: Power, Politics and Activism* (Albany, NY: SUNY Press, 2000) and *The Best Ever Olympics: Social Impacts of Sydney 2000* (Albany, NY: SUNY Press, 2002).
For the sexual abuse of power in sport, see Celia H. Brackenridge (2001) *Spoilsports: Understanding and Preventing Sexual Exploitation in Sport* (London: Routledge). Finally, Lincoln Allison has three edited collections which range over this topic: *The Politics of Sport* (Manchester University Press, 1986), *The Changing Politics of Sport* (Manchester University Press, 1993) and *The Global Politics of Sport* (London: Routledge, 2006).

Postmodernism/ Postmodernity

To begin, postmodernism and postmodernity are, in essence, two different concepts. Whilst obviously related it is important to note that the terms are used to define distinct historical, social and intellectual developments.

Postmodernism relates to the philosophical body of thought that attempts a theoretical understanding and analysis of the contemporary moment – notably capitalist development from the latter half of the twentieth century. Theoretically, postmodernism is predicated upon the intellectual refutation and rejection of modernist thought systems. Modernity represents the historical period that emerges with the advent of scientific, intellectual, technological and social revolution in eighteenth century Europe. This period is known as the Enlightenment and distinguishes the rational, secular modern world from the world that preceded it – the world of religion and superstition. Modernity, Sarup (1988) contends, implies 'the progressive economic and administrative rationalisation and differentiation of the social world', which becomes manifest in the capitalist state. As a term, postmodernism has its origins in the Western art movements of the 1930s. By the 1960s it became a term most especially associated with the American East Coast art movement. However, by the 1980s, postmodernism (or PoMo as it is often referred to in short hand) had successfully crossed over into other areas, such as design and architecture, and, perhaps most notably, literary theory. It is in the discipline of literary theory that postmodernism matures as a form of social investigation – for example in the work of Jacques Derrida (Rail, 1998: x–xi).

Postmodernity, on the other hand is a term that is widely used to describe the development of social and economic structures and relationships within a period of profound capitalist restructuring and reorganisation. Fredric Jameson suggests that postmodernity is the epoch of 'late capitalism' (see **Capitalism**) – the hitherto unsurpassed extension of the market into every aspect of social life. Noting these distinctions is important in that it is possible to recognise and theorise postmodernity, whilst maintaining a critical distance to the claims of postmodernism. American Marxist social theorist Fredric Jameson and Slovenian philosopher Slavoj Žižek are two prominent thinkers who have written widely on the nature and development of postmodern culture, but eschew the interpretative and theoretical claims of postmodernism.

CHARACTERISING POSTMODERNITY

To suggest that we now live in a postmodern society is to suggest that the social, political and economic forms of organisation that have dominated previous periods of capitalist development (modernity), have become inadequate. As Sarup (1988) notes, logically the terms means 'after modernity. It refers to the incipient or actual dissolution of those social forms associated with modernity'. The salient features of postmodern society are primarily the shift from mass and collectivised forms of society towards more individuated forms of social engagement, primarily through the sphere of consumption. Where modernism is defined in part by the premise that the dynamic sphere of society lies in production, postmodern society is characterised by its focus upon the realm of consumption as providing the dynamic and impetus behind new forms of capitalist development (see **Consumption**). As noted above, Sarup (1988) suggests that modernity is characterised by its tendency towards the 'differentiation' of the social world; postmodernity, on the other hand, is representative of a dissolving and/or collapse of these points of differentiation and of the bounded nature of the social world. For example, modernity makes a clear distinction, in terms both of space and of time, between work and our lives outside work. Traditionally, people physically travelled to a workplace that was distinct (in appearance and location) from the place they lived; many of us still do. We also, conventionally, have to attend work for a given number of hours (the working day) and for a set number of days (the working week). Indeed, this bounded, differential approach to space and time dominated every aspect of social life within modern capitalism. Not only do we work in specific times and places within modernity, but we consume in particular places and at particular times, usually collectively; we participate in sport and leisure in particular places and at particular times. Moreover, the way we relate to ourselves and others as members of society within modernist frames of reference reflects the bounded nature of modernity – members of society are identified by a collective set of characteristics which differentiate one group from another. As social scientists many of these social characteristics are familiar to us – class, gender, race, ethnicity, nationality, religious beliefs, political alliances, sexual orientation and disability are amongst the plethora of categories that have been employed under modernity.

However the postmodern nature of contemporary social and economic relations has dissolved the bounded, polarised and compartmentalised nature of social life. The impact of globalisation (see **Globalisation**) has seemingly altered the ways in which we understand and subsequently attempt to organise the relationship between time and space, which has become increasingly fluid and transient. The development of virtual technologies, the rapidity of global communications and the dominance of the mediated image have profoundly altered the way we now live our lives. The lives we build for ourselves and the social structures within which we live have become much more diverse, fragmented and fluid. The postmodern social experience is implicitly more individuated and personalised, and identities much more fluid, resembling a bricolage.

The most celebrated proponents of postmodernism are the three post- war French intellectuals, Jean-François Lyotard (1924–1998), Jean Baudrillard (1929–2007) and Jacques Derrida (1930–2004). Although these theorists of postmodernism are products of post-war continental (post-) structuralist philosophy (see **Discourse and Post-Structuralism**), it is in the United States of America that postmodernism is first legitimised as a system of ideas. It is, for example, at a conference at the Johns Hopkins University, Baltimore in 1966, that Jacques Derrida first comes to international recognition. Likewise, both Lyotard and Baudriallard were to have long and fruitful academic relationships with the USA.

Perhaps the most confounding and frustrating aspects of postmodern social theory is that those individuals who are readily identified as its leading exponents, nevertheless deny their status as postmodern theorists. Both Derrida and Baudrillard, throughout their lives, denied the validity of the label postmodernism. Baudrillard even went so far as to deny it had any meaning at all, dismissing it as 'a word which people use but which explains nothing' (Gane, 1993: 21). At one level Baudrillard's claim underlines the ironic, playful, almost contrary problematising of categorical concepts and bounded meanings that is so associated with postmodernism. Indeed, one of the essential elements of postmodernism is that it constitutes an attack on theory and methodology, which it sees as a limitation on the development of ideas. Scientific methods and the claim to universal objective truths, according to postmodernism, reflect modernism's now redundant approach to the social world – scientific knowledge is characterised as little more than the competing claims of particular interest groups engaged in struggles of power (see **Discourse**; **Methods**). Given its anti-method perspective, postmodernism is not a unified theory, unlike Marxist or Figurational sociology (see **Marxism**; **The Civilising Process**). Postmodernism is in itself a multifaceted grouping of theories and intellectual positions that rejects the modernist notion of unified theories. Postmodernism questions the claims of 'metanarratives' (or 'grand narratives') – theories that claim to explain everything and to posit universal truths. Lyotard (1984: xxiv–xxv) defined postmodernism as 'incredulity towards metanarratives'. The sports sociologist Genevieve Rail (1998) outlines how postmodernism offers a challenge to classical social thought, via its two central dynamics – 'a dismissal of

key concepts in sports studies

universal principles, totalising theories and the search for one "Truth", as well as a new celebration of difference and diversity [which] require new social theories, epistemologies, and ontologies', or new ways of thinking (Rail, 1998: ix).

POSTMODERNITY AND SPORT

The recognition of the postmodern has been one of the features of the development of the sociological analysis of sport over the last 10 to 15 years or so, and postmodern themes and problematics have become much more prevalent within the academic literature. Horne et al. (1999) suggest that within the context of postmodernity 'sporting exchange can be seen as another form of cultural playfulness'. The emergence of television programmes during the 1990s, such as the Gladiators game show, in which contestants were pitted in competitive 'combat' against a team of muscle bound athletes (Horne, et al., 1999: 280), and more recently reality/celebrity television programmes such as 'The Games' illustrate the postmodern nature of contemporary society, with their emphasis upon self-reflexive irony, parody and pastiche, and their emphasis upon the image as an object of consumption. Ellis Cashmore (2000) suggests that sport is a constitutive element of postmodernity. Although rooted in modernity, sport has taken an unmistakably postmodern turn. The emergence of new, 'alternative', often risked-based 'extreme' sports which eschew modernist notions of competition and collectivity and embrace the new cultural logics of individuality, style and consumption (see Reinhart and Sydnor, 2003) characterise the emergence of sporting forms that are postmodern in nature. However, sports that might formerly be characterised as modernist – for example, football (soccer), rugby and cricket – have also been transformed by the advent of postmodernism. The intensification of commercial and media interests in sport during the 1980s and 1990s has effectively transformed these sports into leading examples of the 'hyperreal' (see below). Cashmore suggests: 'Sport is a reality, or to use Baudrillard's word, hyperreality that is sustained, dramatized and presented by the electronic media and consumed by a fandom which implicitly confirms its reality' (2000: 280). Significant areas of research have included the relationship of sporting media and the production and consumption of sporting symbols, 'signs' and values (Cole and Andrews, 1996; Cole and Denny, 1995), the impact of virtual technologies and the internet (McDaniel and Sullivan, 1998), and the impact of the postmodernism in understanding the sporting body (Butyrn, and Masucci, 2003; Fernandez- Balboa, 1997; Markula, 1995).

POSTMODERNISM AND SPORT

Rojek (1993: 277) suggests that the development of postmodernist analysis within the study of sport and leisure has been hindered and misrepresented by the 'rhetoric of traditions of collectivist thought'. For Rojek, postmodernism is the third of three 'crucial moments' in the post-war development of the sociology of sport and leisure, which, at the time he was writing, was in its infancy and hence largely underdeveloped. The critical study of sport had largely been dominated by two preceding moments: *functionalism* (1945–early 1970s); and *politicisation* (early 1970s–mid-1980s), an approach dominated by leftist or Marxist perspectives (Rojek, 1993: 277–9), which were particularly concerned with the function and structuring of power relations through sport and leisure in capitalist society. However, the influence of postmodernist perspectives has become increasingly integral to the critical understanding of sport. Postmodernism's analytical emphases upon 'differentiation, discontinuity [and] fragmentation' (Rojek, 1993: 279) have become key themes within analysis of (post)modern sport.

Among the theorists generally identified as postmodernist, it is the work of Jean Baudrillard that has had most resonance within the analysis of contemporary sport. Work that has significantly drawn upon the theories of Baudrillard include: Andrews (1996, 1998, 2001) on the postmodern nature of the consumerisation of North American sport; Bale (1998) on the transformation of the relationship between sport, fandom and space; Redhead (1999) on the 'hyperreality' of the soccer World Cup; and Giulianotti (1991, 1999) and Giulianotti and Gerrard (2001) on the cultural identities of soccer players and spectators formed within increasingly consumerised and media simulated contexts. However, it is the work of Rail (1998) that has, according to Andrews (2000: 130), so far provided the 'most informed and instructive' Baudrillardian understanding of postmodern sport. Mapping the 'implosion of sport and aesthetic, corporal and media realms' (Andrews, 2000: 130), Rail provides a theoretical synthesis of the key developments in Baudrillard's writing, suggesting that sport functions as a key 'producer and reproducer of the cultural present in postmodern society, and as privileged object of overconsumption' (Rail, 1998: 156, quoted in Andrews, 2000: 130).

The most influential aspects of Baudrillard's work concern his development of the related concepts, 'hyperreality' and 'simulacrum'. 'Hyperreality' describes a condition wherein the divisions between reality and the imaginary implode and become indistinguishable. Rojek (1993) suggests that the 'hyperreal' is consistent with the development of mechanical and electronic forms of simulation (such as the internet and video games, for example), which undermine and call into question our relationship with reality and fiction. Under these conditions social experience becomes dominated by spectacle, sensation and simulation. Indeed, central to the notion of the 'hyperreal' is the recognition that simulations can be, and often are, experienced as more real than reality itself. This moment, at which the distinction between representation and reality – between the sign and what the sign represents – collapses is termed by Baudrillard the 'simulacrum'.

The way in which 'hyperreality' empties reality of meaning and significance (Appignanesi and Garratt, 2004: 55) is explored in Baudrillard's essay on the Heysel Stadium disaster of 1985, where rioting football fans at the European Cup final between England's Liverpool Football Club and Juventus of Italy resulted in the deaths of 39 people. These events were broadcast live across Europe as millions watched waiting for the game to kick off. Baudrillard (2002: 75) contends that the singular significance of these events lies not in 'violence per se but the way in which this violence was given worldwide currency by television', and how in this process 'turned into a travesty of itself'. Rather than simply an act of tragic violence, the Heysel Stadium disaster, is, for Baudrillard, a telling example of the 'hyperreal' condition of postmodern society, as the violence itself is transformed by its highly mediated nature into a 'simulacrum of violence' (Baudrillard, 2002: 75) – an event that 'occurs in a vacuum, stripped of its context and visible only afar, televisually' (Baudrillard, 2002: 79).

Other examples of the sporting 'simulacra' have included the analysis of the development and growth in sportswear manufacturing. Appignanesi and Garratt (2004: 132) suggest that the popular Nike Air Jordan sports shoe is a 'simulacra' in that it is produced and consumed explicitly as 'expensive street-cred ... sportswear with nothing to do with sport'. Indeed, as they suggest, the number of muggings and murders for items of desirable and expensive sportswear throughout the USA during the 1980s and 1990s (Appignanesi and Garrett, 2004: 132) is testament to the postmodern collapse of reality into 'hyperreality', which has produced a 'reality' in which sportswear fashion, such as Nike Air Jordan shoes, surpasses in desirability, the object or thing it is supposed to be a copy or reproduction of.

In his analysis of consumer capitalism, Baudrillard developed the concept of symbolic value or 'sign value' as a means of conceptualising the primacy of the commodity within postmodern culture, and the new forms of social relations that emerge from this development (1968, 1970, 1973), further underlining the postmodern nature of contemporary capitalism. Baudrillard suggests that under these new postmodern conditions, commodities are produced and consumed primarily because of the symbolic meanings they come to represent, rather than for their usefulness (use value) or price (exchange value). The emphasis upon the symbolic and the sign evident in Baudrillard's work has been very influential in the analysis of the celebrity culture that has seemingly engulfed all aspects of modern living, including sport. For example, the England and LA Galaxy soccer player, David Beckham, has been cited by a number of writers as an example of the simulacrum. Beckham's celebrity is no longer embedded in his ability as a professional athlete, but instead has completely transcended the sphere of sport. In this respect he has become a fully fledged postmodern 'sign' (Cashmore, 2002; Cashmore and Parker, 2003), or free 'floating signifier' (Whannel, 2001) – in essence a simulacrum of a football player, or perhaps even a simulacrum of a celebrity? Drawing upon the concept of sign value, David Andrews suggests that the black American basketball and cultural icon, Michael Jordan, functions primarily as an 'affectively orientated [post-] Reaganite commodity-sign'. Andrews suggests that Jordan has been transformed into a hyperreal identity, which for all its counter cultural and celebrated transgressiveness, sits quite comfortably within the postmodern cultural logic of late capitalism (Andrews, 1996).

Richard Giulianotti (2004) (see also Giulianotti and Gerrard, 2001) applies Baudrillard's work in his analysis of sporting celebrity, illustrating the playfully 'fatalistic' boredom and alienation that underpins contemporary celebrity life. In his analysis of consumer culture Baudrillard suggests that rather than providing a liberating pluralist sphere of originality and authenticity, consumerism is endemic of a 'hyperconformity' – a hyperconformity to playfully consume. Giulianotti suggests:

> sports celebrities and their fans appear to embrace this hyperconformity of consumption in self-parodic fashion. Particular stars like Dennis Rodman (basketball) and Paul Gascoigne (football) show a fatigued zeal and curious hyperconformity in stretching their public notoriety as 'bad boys' to new limits. (2004: 230)

CRITIQUES OF POSTMODERNISM

As shown above, postmodernism is not without its problems and inconsistencies and these difficulties have drawn frequent criticism of its value as a social theory. Perhaps the most consistent critique of postmodernism has concentrated on its inherently relativistic nature. Postmodernist theory concludes that claims to truth, knowledge and understanding are simply that – claims – and these claims have no internal consistency or validity, other than when they are placed against other statements of truth. In this sense, relativism suggests that all claims to truth (ideas, beliefs and value systems, for example) are in and of themselves equal – they have no internal content other than when compared or contrasted with other systems or claims. One of the most ardent critiques of postmodernism, Slavoj Žižek has drawn attention to the 'relativist' contradiction that lies at its heart. Postmodernism, Žižek contends, posits itself as an attempt to theorise social relations whilst rejecting attempts to understand social relations in their totality (mega narratives). Totalising narratives, such as belief systems and ideological frameworks, according to postmodern theory, are illegitimate forms of understanding. However, as Žižek sees it, postmodernity is actually the age of totalising beliefs in their most dogmatic and inflexible form. For example, Žižek counterpoises the 'appearance' of the postmodern – the collapse of totalising narratives and the elevation of subjective experience and choice as forms of reflexive freedom – with the claim that the freedom that the so-called reflexive postmodern subject enjoys is actually a compunction, an obligation to 'enjoy' rather than a 'freedom-to-enjoy' (1991: 237). In postmodernity, freedom is reversed into its opposite. It becomes non-freedom. For Žižek, freedom is conditional upon a framework of rules or laws, such as ideology. Using the example of language to illustrate his point, Žižek suggests one can only express oneself freely and creatively, once the rules of language, its syntax and grammar, have been mastered. Without the framework of these rules creativity becomes impossible, and is experienced as a burden. Thus the paradox of postmodernity is that the freedom afforded through the collapse of totalising frameworks and laws is actually experienced, not as a freedom, but as oppression, which manifests itself in a desire for discipline, or the continued search for frameworks of meaning and understanding.

Following Fredric Jameson, Žižek criticises the postmodernists (such as Lyotard) for succumbing to the cultural logic of late capitalism. Jameson suggests that postmodernism emerges as a result of culture's attempt to accommodate and respond to its own domination and colonisation by the commodity (see **Commodification**). Jameson offers a set of characteristics – which include the integration and mixing of styles and genres which were otherwise distinct; the loss of a sense of history, which has been replaced by a desire for nostalgia; and a euphoric celebration and attachment to the surface nature or depthlessness of culture (manifest largely in the predominance of the image) – which define the postmodern moment, and have been reified by postmodernist theorists.

Like Jameson, leftist critics, such as American cultural theorist Thomas Frank (2001; Frank and Weiland, 1997), have suggested that the celebration of difference, bricolage and identity which forms an integral expression of the postmodern age, are nothing more than the contemporary restructuring of the capitalist market, which employs an ever expanding and technologically sophisticated array of means by which to exploit a new global division of labour.

REFERENCES

Andrews, D. (1996) 'The Fact(s) of Michael Jordan's Blackness: Excavating a Floating Racial Signifier', *Sociology of Sport Journal*, 10(2): 148–67.

Andrews, D.L. (1998) 'Feminizing Olympic Reality: Preliminary Dispatches from Baudrillard's Atlanta', *International Review for the Sociology of Sport*, 33(1): 5–18.

Andrews, D. (2000) 'Posting Up. French Post-Structuralism and the Critical Analysis of Contemporary Sporting Culture', in J. Coakley and E. Dunning (eds) *Handbook of Sports Studies*. London: Sage. pp: 106–37.

Appignanesi, R. and Garratt, C. (2004) *Introducing Postmodernism*. London: Icon Books.

Bale, J. (1998) 'Virtual Fandoms: Futurescapes of Football', in A. Brown (ed.) *Fanatics!* London: Routledge. pp: 265–77.

Baudrillard, J. (1968) *The System of Objects*. London: Verso. Republished 1996.

Baudrillard, J. (1970) *The Consumer Society: Myths and Structures*. London: Sage. Republished 1998.

Baudrillard, J. (1973) *For a Critique of the Political Economy of the Sign*. St Louis: Telos Press. Reprinted 1981.

Baudrillard, J. (2002) *The Transparency of Evil: Essays on Extreme Phenomena*. London: Verso.

Butyrn, T.M. and Masucci, M.A. (2003) 'Posthuman Podiums: Cyborg Narratives of Elite Track and Field Athletics', *Sociology of Sport Journal*, 20: 17–39.

Cashmore, E. (2000) *Sports Culture: An A–Z Guide*. London: Routledge.

Cashmore, E. (2002) *Beckham*. Cambridge: Polity Press.

Cashmore, E. and Parker, A. (2003) 'One David Beckham? Celebrity, Masculinity and the Soccerati', *Sociology of Sport Journal* 20(3): 214–31.

Cole, C.L. and Andrews, D.L. (1996) '"Look – It's NBA *Showtime!*": Visions of Race in the Popular Imaginary', in N.K. Denzin (ed.) *Cultural Studies: A Research Volume*, Greenwich, CT: Vol. 1. JAI Press. pp. 141–81.

Cole, C.L. and Denny, H. (1995) 'Visualizing Deviance in Post-Reagan America: Magic Johnson, AIDS, and the Promiscuous World of Professional Sport', *Critical Sociology*, 20(3): 123–47.

Fernandez-Balboa, J. (1997) 'Physical Education Teacher Preparation in the Post-Modern Era: Toward a Critical Pedagogy', in J. M. Fernandez-Balboa (ed.) *Critical Postmodernism in Human Movement, Physical Education, and Sport*. Albany: State University of New York. pp. 121–38.

Frank, T. (2001) *One Market Under God: Extreme Capitalism, Market Populism and the End of Economic Democracy*. London: Secker and Warburg.

Frank, T and Weiland, M. (eds) (1997) *Commodify Your Dissent. Salvos from The Baffler.* New York: W.W. Norton.

Gane, M. (ed.) (1993) *Baudrillard Live: Selected Interviews*. London & New York: Routledge.

Giulianotti, R. (1991) 'Scotland's Tartan Army in Italy', *Sociological Review*, 39(3): 503–27.

Giulianotti, R. (1999) *Football: A Sociology of the Global Game*. Cambridge: Polity Press.

Giulianotti, R. and Gerrard, M. (2001) 'Evil Genie or Pure Genius? The (Im)moral Football and Public Career of Paul "Gazza" Gascoigne', in D.L. Andrews and S.J. Jackson (eds) *Sports Stars*. London: Routledge. pp. 124–37.

Giulianotti, R. (ed.) (2004) *Sport and Modern Social Theorists*. Basingstoke: Palgrave.

Horne, J., Tomlinson, A. and Whannel, G. (1999) *Understanding Sport: An Introduction to the Sociological and Cultural Analysis of Sport*. London: Routledge.

Jameson, F. (1991) *Postmodernism, or, The Cultural Logic of Late Capitalism*. London: Verso.

Lyotard, J-F. (1984) *The Postmodern Condition. A Report on Knowledge*. Manchester: Manchester University Press. Originally published 1979.

Markula, P. (1995) 'Firm but Shapely, Fit but Sexy, Strong but Thin: The Postmodern Aerobicizing Female Bodies', *Sociology of Sport Journal*, 12(14): 424–53.

McDaniel, S. R. and Sullivan, C. (1998) 'Extending the Sport Experience: Meditations in Cyberspace', in L. A. Wenner (ed.) *Media Sport*. London: Routledge. pp. 266–81.

Rail, G. (1998) 'Seismography of the Postmodern Condition: Three Theses on the Implosion of Sport', in G. Rail (ed.) *Sport and Postmodern Times*. New York: SUNY. pp. 143–62.

Redhead, S. (1999) *Post-Fandom and the Millennial Blues*. London: Routledge.

Reinhart, R.E. and Sydnor, S. (eds) (2003) *To the Extreme: Alternative Sports, Inside and Out*. New York: SUNY.

Rojek, C. (1993) 'After Popular Culture: Hyperreality and Leisure', *Leisure Studies*, 12(3): 277–89.

Sarup, M. (1988) *An Introductory Guide to Post-Structuralism and Postmodernism*. London: Harvester Wheatsheaf.

Whannel, G. (2001) *Media Sport Stars: Masculinities and Moralities*. London: Routledge.

Žižek, S. (1991) *For They Know Not What They Do. Enjoyment as a Political Factor.* London: Verso.

'Race' and Ethnicity

Contrary to popular supposition, these two words do *not* mean the same thing, although they are often, even in official documentation, used interchangeably. Many people, including most scientists, now doubt the usefulness of the word 'race' and when used in sociological literature it now usually appears in inverted commas (as above).

Furthermore, and again contrary to a widespread assumption, we *all* have an ethnicity. It's not something that only certain people(s) have access to.

The word 'race' first appeared in the English language in the sixteenth century. It was used then to mean a people with an identifiable culture and, therefore, a shared destiny – for example, the Saxons or the Celts. People were perceived to have fixed characteristics – as poets, dreamers, hard workers, militarists and so on.

In the eighteenth and nineteenth centuries, the word was adopted by scientists and Western societies thus witnessed the growth of 'race science'. This science drew on increasingly popular typifications derived from travel, trade and imperialism. These typifications were, in turn, invariably based on the early Western European, often Christian, attribution of colours – especially of black, which symbolised evil, death and ignorance, and of white, which stood for purity and goodness.

Different race scientists arranged the world's population into different 'hierarchies of colour', but 'white' people were always at the top of these hierarchies. Moreover, racial hierarchies were readily linked to social and political philosophies, such as imperialism, Social Darwinism (the belief that the most able social groups will always prosper at the expense of the less able ones) and eugenics (that is, controlled breeding, in pursuit of an intellectually of physically superior human population). These can be read as *racist ideologies* – interpretations of the world which render it 'only right' or to be expected that some social groups should govern and/or exploit others.

Race thinking dominated science into the early twentieth century and until, say, the 1950s, human behaviour was thought by most scientists to be largely genetic. Following the Second World War, however, there has been a trend away from 'scientific racism' in the West – possibly as a result of the destruction wrought in the name of 'race' by Hitler's Third Reich.

key concepts in sports studies

184

Today most biologists reject any link between *genotype* and *phenotype*. They argue that gene pools are widely distributed both within and between perceived 'racial' groups and that, besides, there is no necessary link between *genotype* (gene pool) and *phenotype* (physical characteristics, such as skin colour, bone structure and so on).

This, of course, doesn't stop people defining themselves and others in racial terms. But it means that 'race' is not a *biological* category, but a social one. It is simply a *discourse* – a way we have of talking about the social world (see **Discourse and Post-Structuralism**). This process sociologists call *'racialisation'*. Within this discourse, 'races' may be defined negatively (by racists – shouting 'Paki' in the street, perhaps, or claiming that some groups are inherently less intelligent than others) or positively, as part of dealing with racism – for example via the 1970s slogan 'Black is Beautiful' or the MOBO (Music of Black Origin) Awards.

ETHNICITY

'Ethnicity' means, simply, way of life or cultural tradition. It is usually linked to *nationality*, but is made up of numerous elements, including religion, food, music, costume, and so on. There is a misleading tendency to use the word 'ethnicity' as if it applied only to certain people or groups; in practice it is often – indeed usually – forgotten that 'whites' have ethnicity too.

It is a paradox that, in the age of globalisation, there has been an upsurge of nationalism and militant ethnicity (NB 'ethnic cleansing' in Balkans, the break-up of the Soviet Union …) (see **State, Nation and Nationalism**).

It was widely hoped that the placing of the word 'race' in inverted commas and a growing preference for the word 'ethnicity' would diminish racism and discrimination. But sociologists such as Paul Gilroy (1990) have pointed to the danger of 'ethnic absolutism' – the ascribing of fixed characteristics to members of a group now defined as ethnic. This is simply racism by other means and, indeed, those wedded to racial thinking have tended simply to move their assumptions away from *biology* and onto the terrain of *culture*. They now speak, therefore, of people with backward, dangerous or 'failed' ways of life, rather than of people who are genetically inferior (see e.g. Back, 2002: 9–10).[1] To address this difficulty, sociologists such as Stuart Hall (1996) have called for a subtler approach which recognises 'new ethnicities', based on a variety of identities, a hybridity of influences and the expectable fractures of class and gender (see **Identity and Difference**).

We can infer from this that the notion of 'race', while always divisive and misleading, has carried different meanings in different societies and at different times in history. Under slavery, for example, black people were ordinarily treated as chattels – especially in the southern states of America. In the time of empires established by European nations in what we now call 'the developing world', people of darker skins were seen as having a child-like mentality. In more recent, post-colonial, times the term 'race' often became synonymous with 'immigration'. Thus, while the anti-racist politics of the post-1960s era have outlawed much direct reference to the colour of people's skins, nevertheless a number of words and phrases – 'asylum seekers', 'economic migrants', 'terrorists', 'people who hate our values', 'those inner cities', and so on – appear to have become metaphors for 'race' in countries like Britain and the USA. As the Palestinian writer Edward Said (2003) has consistently argued, Western politicians and thinkers 'created' the East as mysterious and exotic, as less rational and inferior. Still today the terms 'East' and 'West' are usually seen as binary cultural opposites.

We can look for these metaphors, and binary opposites, in the cultures of sport. And we can begin with another paradox. Sport, as the sociologists Ben Carrington and Ian Macdonald have pointed out, is an area where the cultural racism prevalent since the Second World War can be most successfully challenged; but sport has also provided a platform for the expression of racist sentiments (Carrington and Macdonald, 2001: 2). We can see this from the following examples.

SPORT AND THE IDEA OF RACIAL SUPERIORITY

After the conclusion of the US Civil War in 1865, black people were widely perceived as 'animal-like'. In his book *Mortal Engines* (1992) the American academic John Hoberman quotes a surgeon in New Orleans to this effect (p. 44). Despite this, American slaves were freed and many male ex-slaves became boxers. They were not, however, allowed to fight white fighters.

This was because of racist notions that black boxers had excessive brute strength and an absence of human feeling. Later promoters sought black–white contests, commercially exploiting racism, although many white fighters, including one-time heavyweight champion Jack Dempsey, refused to take on black opponents. Similarly, when the white German boxer Max Schmeling fought black American Joe Louis for the heavyweight title in the 1930s, the boxing public tended to divide along 'colour', rather than national lines, with Schmeling carrying the hopes, not only of the Hitler regime in Nazi Germany but of many white Americans besides (Erenberg, 2006).

SPORT AND SEGREGATION

Baseball is generally regarded as America's 'national sport'. Until after the Second World War US baseball had separate 'black leagues'. This system did not begin to break up until after the Second World War: Jackie Robinson (born 1919 in the southern state of Georgia to a family of sharecroppers) became the first African American to play major league baseball in 1947 (for the Brooklyn Dodgers).

In South Africa under apartheid (which means 'separate development' and which lasted as a policy roughly from 1950 to 1990), sport was similarly segregated. Black Africans and white British and Dutch descended Africans played separately.

Sport played a part in establishing the different ethnic identities that characterise contemporary South African society: Afrikaners tend to play rugby, Africans 'soccer' (see e.g. Nauright, 1997).

SPORT, 'RACE' AND ACCESS

After the abandonment of the 'colour bar' in various countries, the degree of access to sport by previously excluded 'minorities' came to be scrutinised. Sociologists have looked at the access of these minorities to particular sports, then at access specifically to positions of responsibility and authority.

Some questions sociologists might ask about sport, 'race' and access include:

- Is sport an avenue of upward social mobility for racialised minorities?
- If black people feature strongly in sport, is that because they don't aspire to other careers?
- … Or is it, perhaps, as has been suggested by the sociologist Ellis Cashmore (1982) because there are more racial barriers in those other careers?
- Do ethnic minorities 'over-invest' in athletic pursuits, to the detriment of more intellectual activities, as John Hoberman (1997) has claimed of African Americans?
- How far can racialised minorities progress in sport?

Caribbean intellectual Tim Hector was fond in his writing of quoting American academic Michael Eric Dyson, who argued in 1993 that:

> the nature of oppression of blacks in the United States produced in African-American cultural practice the ability to flout widely understood boundaries through mesmerisation and alchemy, a subversion of common perceptions of the culturally or physically possible, through the creative and deceptive manipulation of appearance' The important thing was for blacks to go beyond the established limits. (Hector, 2005: 164)

But if African American basketball players, West Indian cricketers and boxers such as Muhammad Ali could produce this mesmerisation and alchemy, there's little doubt that ethnic minority sportspeople have faced obstacles that other groups did not face, and little doubt either that they faced a glass ceiling when it came to management. Al Campanis, an official of the Los Angeles Dodgers, said in 1987:

> I truly believe [African Americans] may not have some of the necessities to be … a field manager or perhaps a general manager … They are gifted with great musculature … They are fleet of foot … [But] as far as having the background to become club presidents or presidents of a bank … I don't know.[2]

Sociologists point to a similar problem in the United Kingdom. Colin King (2004), for example, recently suggested that black footballers who wish to become coaches or managers have to behave as if they were white, in order to gain the necessary acceptance.

There is, moreover, the problem of 'stacking'. This occurs when stereotypical thinking about ethnic minority sportspeople affects their distribution within a team. As the remarks of Al Campanis suggest, black sportspeople have often been assumed to lack the qualities of leadership and mental stamina that certain positions in team sports might demand. Research seems to indicate that ethnic minority players have been concentrated in particular positions – say, on the wing in association football, where skill, rather than organisational ability might be required.[3]

SPORT AND ETHNIC ABSOLUTISM

The history of sport is replete with examples of how it was claimed for different nations that their fixed characteristics were expressed through their sports – sports which invariably were adopted as 'national sports'. The Celtic myths which surrounded the rise of Welsh rugby (Andrews, 1991), for example, or Gaelic football (Sugden and Bairner, 1993) were steeped in racial assumptions about the inherent qualities of the people who played these games. Similarly, the late nineteenth century saw an upsurge in American nationalism in the United States, which brought the weaving of similar myths around certain sports now designated as 'all American', such as baseball, and the suppression of sports perceived as immigrant or colonial (i.e. British) (Pope, 1997).

Assumptions and campaigns such as these were common in the second half of the nineteenth century when modern sports and national identities were both in the process of being formed. More recently, with the growing acceptance of multi-cultural or multi-ethnic societies, there have been examples of how sport can counter ideas of ethnic absolutism. For example, when she won a gold medal at the Sydney Olympics of 2000 the black British athlete Denise Lewis draped herself in the Union Jack, thus neatly negating the rallying cry of extreme right-wing parties in the UK that there 'Ain't no black in the Union Jack'.

At the same time, sport can help point to tensions between 'race' and nation. One of the best examples of this came in 1966 when heavyweight boxing champion Muhammad Ali refused induction into the US army during the Vietnam War. He is widely quoted as saying: 'I ain't got no quarrel with them Vietcong'. Similarly, two years later at the Mexico Olympics, black US athletes Tommie Smith and John Carlos gave a clenched fist salute on the medal podium after the men's 200 metres. And when the Australian aborigine athlete Cathy Freeman won over the same distance in the 1994 Commonwealth Games in Victoria, Canada, she celebrated by carrying the aborigine flag alongside the Australian one. In each case, the sportspeople concerned were heavily criticised, but in each case they were stating, in effect, that they, and the ethnic groups they represented, were only fully embraced by the nation in some social contexts (army duty, sport ...) and not beyond these.

'RACE', IMMIGRATION AND CITIZENSHIP

But, in sport, while full social inclusion may have been withheld from ethnic groups born within the boundaries of nations, citizenship has, on occasion, been readily accorded to individuals born outside those boundaries. Consider the case of Zola Budd, a white South African runner, with a British grandfather. She applied for British citizenship in 1984. This was granted within days. She joined an athletic club in southern England and ran for Britain in the Los Angeles Olympics of the same year, coming seventh. She then returned to South Africa. Budd's temporary Britishness was possible under the British Nationality Act of 1981, which removed the guarantee of citizenship to those born on British soil, while opening it to those born abroad but with a British family connection. As critics pointed out this criterion, in practice, was likely to apply almost solely to white people.

In general, though, there has been a loosening of qualification criteria by national and supra-national sporting bodies. Post-war English cricket teams have almost always included at least one person born outside the UK. Likewise the Republic of Ireland football team has drawn heavily on the Irish diaspora (Irish-descended families spread across the world), and African and Caribbean teams on the black diaspora. FIFA's new 'lighter touch' regulations here reflect the global nature of the contemporary sports marketplace (Bale and Maguire, 1994). The footballer Owen Hargreaves, who made his England debut in 2001, is one of a large number of contemporary players who qualify for several countries – in his case six: the constituent nations of the UK, plus Canada and Germany.

Besides, the same processes of globalisation have made the old racial categories difficult to sustain. The golfer Tiger Woods, for instance, has described his heritage as 'Cablinasian', since he is descended from 'Caucasians', African Americans, American Indians and Asians. (The term 'Caucasian' was coined by racial scientists who believed that the 'white race' had originated in the Caucasus region of Eurasia. Despite its inappropriateness, the term is still in popular usage.)

WHITE MEN CAN'T JUMP? SPORT, 'RACE' AND SCIENCE

Nevertheless, race theory and logic are still used in relation to black sports people and black sporting bodies. Once again, stereotypes are very important – for instance, 'Asians don't like contact sports', 'Black players haven't got the bottle', 'White men can't jump' … . Some scientists still claim that black people have heavy bones and weak ankles (and therefore don't make good swimmers) or that white people are not anatomically or physiologically equipped for jumping. These notions are now, on the whole, seen as scientifically unsound and are treated with extreme scepticism by sociologists. Do Swiss have a skiing gene, we might ask? Or

Australians a cricketing one? Writers such as Marek Kohn, however, have argued that the validity of socio-biological analysis must at least be recognised. Kohn, who sees himself as a socialist[4] and progressive, wrote in 1995:

> it seems reasonable to suppose that human groups do vary in some physiological traits that are implicated in athletic ability, and that some of this variation is genetic in origin. But that does not warrant jumping to conclusions about the relationship between physiology and performance, since sport is a cultural phenomenon, not a biological one. (Kohn, 1995: 86)

It should be added that the human groups to which Kohn refers are population groups, and not 'races'. Thus, as the Danish physiologist Bengt Saltin has suggested, it may be that Norwegian fishermen living near the Arctic Circle have physiological differences from the inhabitants of a remote Kenyan village that are in part genetic. This might indeed help to explain Kenyan running prowess,[5] but Saltin does not rule out diet as a determining factor.

NOTES

1. The term 'cultural racism' is thought to have been coined by the French Caribbean writer Franz Fanon in the late 1960s.
2. From an interview with Ted Koppel on the late-night ABC news programme *Nightline*, 15 April 1987, the 40th anniversary of Jackie Robinson's Major League Baseball debut.
3. Pioneering work here was done by Grusky (1963) and Loy and McElvogue (1970).
4. http://www.readysteadybook.com/Article.aspx?page=marekkohn (accessed: 15 March 2007).
5. See e.g. http://www.kenya.com/runners.html

REFERENCES

Andrews, David L. (1991) 'Welsh Indigenous! And British Imperial? – Welsh Rugby, Culture and Society 1890–1914', *Journal of Sports History*, 18(3): 335–49.
Back, Les (2002) *New Ethnicities and Urban Culture*. London: Routledge.
Bale, John and Maguire, Joseph (eds) (1994) *The Global Sports Arena*. London: Frank Cass.
Carrington, Ben and Macdonald, Ian (eds) (2001) *'Race', Sport and British Society*. London: Routledge.
Cashmore, E. Ellis (1982) *Black Sportsmen and Society*. London: Routledge and Kegan Paul.
Erenberg, Lewis, A. (2006) *The Greatest Fight of Our Generation: Louis v. Schmeling*. New York: Oxford University Press.

Gilroy, Paul (1990) 'Nationalism, History and Ethnic Absolutism', *History Workshop*, 30, Autumn.

Grusky, Oscar (1963) 'The Effects of Formal Structure on Managerial Recruitment: A Study of Baseball Organization', *Sociometry*, 26: 345–53.

Hall, Stuart (1996) 'New Ethnicities', in David Morley and Kuan-Hsing Chen (eds) *Stuart Hall: Critical Dialogues in Cultural Studies*. London: Routledge. pp. 441–9.

Hector, Tim (2005) 'One Eye on the Ball, One Eye on the World: Cricket, West Indian Nationalism and the Spirit of C.L.R. James', in Stephen Wagg (ed.) *Cricket and National Identity in the Postcolonial Age*. London: Routledge. pp. 159–77.

Hoberman, John (1992) *Mortal Engines: The Science of Performance and Dehumanization of Sport*. New York: The Free Press.

Hoberman, John (1997) *Darwin's Athletes: How Sport Has Damaged Black America and Preserved the Myth of Race*. New York: Mariner Books.

King, Colin (2004) *Offside Racism: Playing the White Man*. Oxford: Berg.

Kohn, Marek (1995) *The Race Gallery: The Return of Racial Science*. London: Vintage.

Loy, J.W. and McElvogue, J.F. (1970) 'Racial segregation in American sport', *International Review of Sport Sociology*, 5: 5–24.

Nauright, John (1997) *Sport, Culture and Identities in South Africa*. London: Leicester University Press.

Pope, S.W. (1997) *Patriotic Games: Sporting Traditions in the American Imagination 1876–1926*. New York: Oxford University Press.

Said, Edward (2003) *Orientalism*. London: Penguin Books.

Sugden, John and Bairner, Alan (1993) *Sport, Sectarianism and Society in a Divided Ireland*. Leicester: Leicester University Press.

FURTHER READING

Carrington, Ben and Macdonald, Ian (eds) (2001) *'Race', Sport and British Society*. London: Routledge.

Coakley, Jay (2004) *Sport in Society: Issues and Controversies* (8th edn) (Chapter 9). New York: McGraw Hill.

Hoberman, John (1997) *Darwin's Athletes: How Sport Has Damaged Black America and Preserved the Myth of Race*. New York: Mariner Books.

Kohn, Marek (1995) *The Race Gallery: The Return of Racial Science* (Chapter 4, London: Vintage.

Marqusee, Mike (1999) *Redemption Song: Muhammad Ali and the Spirit of the Sixties*. London: Verso.

St Louis, Brett (2004) 'Sport and Common-Sense Racial Science', *Leisure Studies*, 23(1): 31–46.

Rationalisation

Rationalisation, as an idea and as a process, is at the heart of modernism, the values and assumptions that characterise life in an advanced, industrial (or post-industrial) and technologically sophisticated society. 'Rational' means literally 'based on reason', as opposed to untestable or 'faith-based' explanations of the world. Rationalisation is therefore the process which is said to have steadily transformed the societies of northern Europe and North America ('the West') after, and as a result of, the Enlightenment of the seventeenth and eighteenth centuries.

In this process – in effect, the transition from tradition to modernity – there are a number of important elements:

1. Scientific thinking supplants religion as the principal source of explanations of the world and what happens in it. People die, for instance, as the result of illness or human failing, rather than through God's will.
2. Similarly, laws founded on traditional authority are replaced by laws based on impersonal criteria. For example, under the traditional authority of monarchs, subjects could be punished – perhaps put to death – simply at the monarch's command. Under impersonal laws, people can be punished only if they are judged, usually by their peers, to have infringed some written code, not at the whim of some powerful individual. There is a corresponding growth in bureaucracy, the workings of which are increasingly governed by these impersonal rules.
3. We see the steady emergence of a strong central state, usually at the expense of a feudal nobility. Part of breaking the power of this nobility is to deprive them of their armies, giving the state the monopoly of the legitimate use of violence.
4. Science and the astute use of capital by a rising commercial middle class combine to foster industrialisation, and, in the twentieth century, work and industrial production become increasingly standardised. In sociological literature this can be known either as Taylorism – after the American writer Frederick Taylor, who wrote books about the scientific organisation of work and workers in the early 1900s (1911, 1915) – or Fordism – after the US automobile magnate Henry Ford, who pioneered mass production techniques in his factories and once famously pronounced: 'You can have any colour of car you want so long as it's black'.

5. Life, in this rationalised society is taken to be less *affective* (governed by emotion) and more *instrumental* (in pursuit of an end – that is, dis-passionate).

6. There is a correspondingly lower tolerance of fighting for its own sake and other emotionally driven behaviour, and, similarly, a growing discomfiture with the public exercising of bodily functions – along with state formation, a key element in what the German social theorist Norbert Elias (2000) called 'the civilising process' (see **The Civilising Process**). This, in turn, is linked to the growth of privacy – a manifestation, according to some writers, of the rise of capitalist individualism (Zaretsky, 1976).

It's fair to say that the history of sport is, in large part, the history of rationalisation. In the early nineteenth century, for example, we see the suppression of 'uncivilised', 'irrational' sports. The mob football and animal sports that had been the life blood of village culture in pre-industrial England became the subject of legal prohibition in early nineteenth-century England. These acts seem to have been driven by the perceived need for social discipline – as the poet Thomas Babington Macaulay famously noted: bear baiting was opposed historically, not because it gave pain to the bear, but because it gave pleasure to the spectators. Time for games of any kind was scarce in the opening decades of industrialisation, and, when the working week began to be shortened, early Victorian legislators and policy makers prescribed rational recreation for the masses in their still relatively sparse leisure time: visits to the library, walks in the park and other means to conventional self improvement. Games, in the first third of the nineteenth century, were still frowned on, even where they were widely practised: public school headmasters, for instance, generally abhorred games as an ongoing threat to good order. Samuel Butler, head of Shrewsbury school between 1798 and 1831 once described football as 'fit only for butcher boys'.

All this changed rapidly in the second half of the nineteenth century following the vital development of codification – a defining part of the process by which sport has been rationalised. Football's first written rules were committed to paper by senior pupils at Rugby school in the 1840s. Some 20 years later, in 1863, the Football Association was formed and, eight years after this, the Rugby Football Union appears. In these newly constituted modern sports, as in sports of aristocratic patronage which began to be regulated in the previous century, there were now *impersonal* and *universal* rules binding all players of these games. These rules would be upheld by match officials and, where necessary, by governing bodies. These bodies, in time, were constituted on an international basis: FIFA, the governing body of world football, was founded in 1904, the Imperial Cricket Conference in 1909, and so on.

Meanwhile, games were rapidly transformed, in the eyes of political and educational authority, from licensed mayhem into a rational means by which appropriate social values might be imparted and good citizens produced. Sport in the late nineteenth century became a valued part of the curriculum, first in the public schools (which begin to clear more pitches and recruit more games masters), then in the emergent state system (where there was a debate over whether children should be merely drilled or have ball games), and thereafter in British colonies. In each case, sports were now thought to furnish the necessary disciplines, of body and of mind, appropriate to a modern society.

Sociologists have, of course, theorised these developments in different ways. One influential analysis has been provided by Elias and other adherents to his theory of the civilising process. This process, though, is dealt with separately in this book so two other approaches will be considered briefly here.

Firstly, Marxism (see also **Marxism**). Marxist writers, of course, stress the importance of *economics* and *material life*, albeit with different emphases. Some, especially in the 1980s and 1990s, concentrated on the relationship between sport and hegemony (see also **Hegemony**). From this perspective, sport has been seen as a way in which the new industrial employing class built a cultural bridge to the (equally new) working class and used it to urge its values on them. Sport, it is argued, helped to establish moral and political leadership. John Hargreaves in *Sport, Power and Culture* (1987) and John Clarke and Chas Critcher in their equally ground-breaking *The Devil Makes Work* (1985) would be leading exemplars here.

Other perhaps more traditional Marxists have discussed crucial links between sport and the working of the advanced capitalist economy, arguing that sport, as an activity, is increasingly shaped by the dictates of such an economy. Modern sport, they would argue, is characterised by the same instrumental, ends-related mentality that centuries of post-enlightenment rationalisation have brought. It pursues maximum efficiency: athletes strive constantly for 'personal best' performances, football managers in most leagues seldom have more than a year to 'get results', and so on. During the course of this process, the human body becomes, in the memorable phrase of the American writer John Hoberman, a 'mortal engine' (1992). Moreover, sport creates, and drives, huge markets – for sports goods, merchandise, equipment. In addition, myriad industries are touched by sport through sponsorship or celebrity endorsement. Aside from being mortal engines, contemporary sportspeople are also, as the French Marxist writer Jean-Marie Brohm remarks, human sandwich boards (1989). Brohm's observation, made originally back in the 1970s, might now seem to some to be greatly understated: some sportspeople now seem to be part of huge global marketing operations: David Beckham, Tiger Woods, Michael Jordan ... (LaFeber, 2002) (see **Commmodification**).

Another persuasive approach has come from the inheritors of the intellectual tradition established by Max Weber, historically the leading critic of Marx. These writers, as Weber himself did, question the determinant power of economics in Marxist theory and, predictably, point up the importance of *non-economic factors* – religion, science, bureaucracy, and so on – in explaining social life. They see much in the fact that rationalisation characterised both capitalist and communist societies. The chief exponent of Weber's ideas on sport and rationalisation is another American academic, Allen Guttmann and his ideas are elaborated in his book in *From Ritual to Record* (2004). In this book, Guttman develops his thesis that there are seven characteristics of modern sport that define its transition from unstructured, traditional, often purposeless play. These are:

1. *Secularism*. Modern, rational games, unlike pre-industrial games, are separated from religion.
2. *Equality*. There is formal equality in modern sport. Even Manchester United, the wealthiest football club in the world, can only field 11 players at once – the same as every other club.
3. *Specialisation*. In modern sports people occupy increasingly specialist roles – quarterback, nutritionist, goalkeeping coach....
4. *Rationalisation*.
5. *Bureaucracy*.
6. *Quantification*.
7. *Records*.

There are some criticisms – besides the inevitable one from Marxists that such analysis under-emphasises material factors. It is, for example, argued that some of Guttmann's criteria, such as the keeping and breaking of records, pre-date industrialisation.

Lately, though, the argument has moved on and now encompasses McDonaldisation, a term coined by US sociologist George Ritzer in the early 1990s to refer to a process whereby the principles upon which the McDonalds burger chain has been run since its inception in the 1950s (effectively, a rationalised, Taylorised 'one best way' system) is now being adopted in institutions all over the world (Ritzer, 1993, 2002). This, of course, applies to the sport and leisure experiences of the world's population. Thus, traditional national sports are obliterated, paddy fields in the Far East are bulldozed to make way for golf courses (see **The Environment**) and a huge global TV audience of over 3 billion people sits down to watch one-size-fits-all sports events such as the Olympics and the football World Cup. Needless to say, this view of a rationalised global sport culture has its critics – see for example Alan Bairner's *Sport, Nationalism and Globalisation* (2001).

REFERENCES

Bairner, Alan (2001) *Sport, Nationalism and Globalisation*. New York: State University of New York Press.

Brohm, Jean-Marie (1989) *Sport: A Prison of Measured Time*. London: Pluto Press.

Clarke, John and Critcher, Chas (1985) *The Devil Makes Work: Leisure in Capitalist Britain*. London: Macmillan.

Elias, Norbert (2000) *The Civilising Process*. Oxford: Blackwell.

Guttmann, Allen (2004) *From Ritual to Record: The Nature of Modern Sports*. New York: Columbia University Press.

Hargreaves, John (1987) *Sport, Power and Culture: A Social and Historical Analysis of Popular Sports*. Cambridge: Polity Press.

Hoberman, John (1992) *Mortal Engines: The Science of Performance and Dehumanization of Sport*. New York: The Free Press.

LaFeber, Walter (2002) *Michael Johnson and the New Global Capitalism*. New York: W.W. Norton.

Ritzer, George (1993) *The McDonaldization of Society*. Thousand Oaks, CA: Pine Forge Press.

Ritzer, George (ed.) (2002) *McDonaldization: The Reader*. Thousand Oaks, CA: Pine Forge Press.

Taylor, Frederick (1911) *The Principles of Scientific Management*. New York: Harper.

Taylor, Frederick (1915) *Shop Management*. New York: Harper.

Zaretsky, Eli (1976) *Capitalism, the Family and Personal Life*. London: Pluto Press.

FURTHER READING

Bairner, Alan (2001) *Sport, Nationalism and Globalisation*. New York: State University of New York Press.

Brohm, Jean-Marie (1989) *Sport: A Prison of Measured Time*. London: Pluto Press.

Carter, J. Marshall and Kruger, A. (eds) (1990) *Ritual and Record: Sports Records and Quantification in Pre-Modern Societies*. Westport, CT: Greenwood Press.

rationalisation

Clarke, John and Critcher, Chas (1985) *The Devil Makes Work: Leisure in Capitalist Britain*. London: Macmillan.

Guttmann, Allen (2004) *From Ritual to Record: The Nature of Modern Sports*. New York: Columbia University Press.

Hargreaves, John (1987) *Sport, Power and Culture: A Social and Historical Analysis of Popular Sports*. Cambridge: Polity Press.

Hoberman, John (1992) *Mortal Engines: The Science of Performance and Dehumanization of Sport*. New York: The Free Press.

Holt, Richard (1989) *Sport and the British*. Oxford: Oxford University Press.

LaFeber, Walter (2002) *Michael Johnson and the New Global Capitalism*. New York: W.W. Norton.

Overman, S. (1997) *The Influence of the Protestant Ethic on Sport and Recreation*. Aldershot: Avebury.

Rigauer, B. (1993) 'Sport and the Economy: A Developmental Perspective', in E. Dunning, J.A. Maguire and R.E. Pearton (eds) *The Sports Process*. Champaign, IL: Human Kinetics. pp. 281–306.

Ritzer, George (1993) *The McDonaldization of Society*. Thousand Oaks, CA: Pine Forge Press.

Ritzer, George (ed.) (2002) *McDonaldization: The Reader*. Thousand Oaks, CA: Pine Forge Press.

Semiotics

(see also Discourse and Post-Structuralism; Postmodernism/Postmodernity)

Semiotics (or semiology) is the study of the construction of meaning through signs and symbols encoded in processes of signification and communication. Contemporary sociological analysis is frequently framed within, or influenced by, the study of semiotics. Consumer culture and the prevalence of the image and the symbolic – such as brands, logos, film and style subcultures – suggest that the everyday has become dominated by the *linguistic sign* – the object of semiotic analysis.

Swiss linguist Ferdinand de Saussure (1857–1913) is generally considered as the founder of modern structural linguists, or semiotics ('a science which studies the life of signs at the heart of social life' (Saussure, 1971: 33)). Saussure's influence and reputation was established after his death, with the publication of his series of lectures at the University of Geneva, *Course in General Linguistics*, in 1916. In this book Saussure formulates a set of general rules whereby language is analysed as a structured formal system subject to general rules.

STRUCTURAL SEMIOTICS

Saussure's approach to studying linguistics provided the framework which was to influence the study of language for much of the twentieth century. Saussure's principal influence is provided through his conceptualisation and analysis of the *linguistic sign*.

The *linguistic sign* is a two-sided concept. The first side comprises the *signifier*, or the material nature of the sign. This might be the sound of a voice (a verbal *signifier*) or the physicality of an object – a rose, for example. The second side of the sign, the *signified*, is made up of the mental or emotional meanings that are read into, or signified by, an object. When giving a rose to a loved one, whilst offering a physical material object (in the form of the flower), what is actually being communicated is a range of 'abstract' non-material emotions or meanings, such as in this case, love. In this communicative exchange, the rose represents the *signifier* and love is what is *signified*.

Structural semiotics stresses the arbitrary nature of the *linguistic sign*. There is, according to Saussure, no natural or essential reason why a *signifier* should produce a particular *signified* meaning. A rose is generally given as a token of love, but there is nothing materially about or within a rose that it should 'naturally' represent love – a lump of coal could also play the same function. Rather, Saussure concludes, the relationship between the *signifier* and *signified* is shaped by the social context within which language and processes of communication are formed. The *linguistic sign* is defined by the social structure. Whilst *linguistic signs* are arbitrary, their meanings are not. Meanings are given by the cultural and social contexts within which the sign is constructed.

The principles and methods set out by Saussure's structuralist approach were adopted by scholars and literary critics, such as Roland Barthes (1915–1980), Jacques Lacan (1901–1981) and Claude Lévi-Strauss (1908–), who began to employ them in areas of enquiry other than linguistics. These areas include psychoanalysis, philosophy, anthropology and

semiotics

199

sociology. However, structuralist approaches to semiotics eventually gave way to the development of post-structuralism and postmodern approaches to studying language and social systems of meaning.

POST-STRUCTURALIST SEMIOTICS

Although it represents a move away from structuralist approaches, the development of post-structuralist semiotics is not, in and of itself, a rejection of the work of Saussure. Nevertheless, Saussure's idea that semiotics is both systematic and scientific, is refuted by post-structuralist and postmodern approaches. Post-structuralists, such as Jacques Derrida (1930–2004), Michel Foucault (1926–1984), Julia Kristeva (1941–) and Roland Barthes (1915–1980), extended and developed the work of Saussure, particularly in relation to his argument that the relationship between *signifier* and *signified* is arbitrary in its nature. Many post-structuralists have taken this idea further, arguing that there is a total disconnection between the *signifier* and the *signified*. In other words there is no deep structural underpinning or framework within which meaning is embodied or conveyed. The *signifier* is quite literally empty.

In *Mythologies* (1973), a collection of essays first published in 1957, French literary theorist and philosopher Roland Barthes extended Saussure's mode of analysis to include images and practices, and extended semiology to the understanding of popular culture. Particularly interested in the ideological nature of 'truth', and the power relations embedded in the construction and signification of signs, Barthes suggests that popular cultural institutions and practices, such as wrestling, striptease, fashion, food and advertising, are mythologised through systems of signification which work to naturalise and conceal their ideological nature. For example, Barthes describes wrestling as a complex spectacle of signs which involves the bodies of the participants themselves, and the excessive gestures and facial expressions employed by the wrestlers. Barthes argues that wrestling is a myth in that it comprises a system which obscures its inherently social nature. Colby and Jansz (2004: 45) suggest that, although we generally agree that wrestling is 'fixed' – winners and losers, heroes and villains, are all ascribed their particular roles before the bout begins and the match, rather than a competitive sporting affair, is itself a playing out of these particular roles – the wrestling fan generally suspends this realisation and willingly allows him/herself to be subsumed by the system of signs. The wrestling fan 'believes' the myth, despite being fully aware of its 'mythologised' nature. Barthes believed, as did Saussure, that semiotics could be formalised, however he didn't share Saussure's notion that it could become a formally structured endeavour, subject to scientific processes of investigation. In this sense Barthes' work is a forerunner to the development of a fully fledged post-structuralist semiotics, developed in the 1960s through the work of literary and social theorists such as Jacques Derrida.

Derrida developed an approach to semiotics known as *deconstructionism*. Saussure suggests that words have no inherent meaning. Meaning is conveyed only by a relationship to something else, that is, through their 'difference'. Derrida developed this idea through the notion of *différance*, whereby meaning is always unstable and unfixed. In this sense texts never 'mean what the say', rather contradictions can be identified (such as footnotes, casual allusions and paradoxical phrases, for example) which defer the actual moment of signification. Meanings within texts are dependent upon unstated oppositional relationships to '*absent signifiers*' – that which is excluded through signification.

SPORT AND SEMIOTICS

Horne et al. (1999) suggest sport has no natural, essentialist pre-given definition. This is reflected in the very fact that sport, or what might be considered sport, lacks a stable formal definition. For example, are darts, synchronised swimming or ballroom dancing sports? Sport has no fixed meaning, but is encoded in wider cultural and social structures of meaning. As such, semiotics provides a valuable tool in decoding sport as a function of meaning and language. A semiotically influenced analysis of sport suggests sport/sports are 'symbolic practices' – constructed through systems of meanings, symbols, signs and texts.

Notable contributions to the semiotic study of sport have come in the form of the analysis of media narratives (Boyle and Haynes, 2000; Whannel, 1992), the construction of sporting celebrity (Armstrong, 1996; Cashmore, 2005; Cashmore and Parker, 2003; Whannel, 2001), the construction and de-coding of the (multiple) messages of sports branding (Bishop, 2001; King, 2004), and the processes of *representation* within sporting naratives (Cole and Andrews, 2001; Denison and Markula, 2005; Farred, 2004; Jackson and Andrews; 2005; McDonald and Andrews, 2001).

SPORT AND REPRESENTATION

As an analytical concept, *representation* refers to the ways in which particular aspects of 'reality' are constructed through social mediums (such as, for example, the mass media) and language. Identity is a key area in the study of representations (see e.g. Dyer, 1993; Hall, 1997; hooks, 1992; Macdonald,1995). The key markers of identity – class, age, gender and ethnicity – are understood not simply as representations, or textual constructions, but are constructed and produced through the processes of reception – how they are received and understood by individuals and groups whose identities are also constructed through and marked by the same key factors. For example, the notion of 'the gaze' is frequently used in the semiotic analysis of representations, as a means to understanding the constructed nature by which particular subject positions or identities look upon, or see other particular identities or objects. John Urry (2002) has used the notion of 'the gaze' to analyse the historical and cultural contexts of tourism and the constructed nature of 'the tourist'. Drawing upon the work of Urry, Richard Giulianotti deploys 'the gaze' (1999) in his analysis of the nature of contemporay football fandom and its interaction with the physical space of the postmodern football stadium.

An important area of sports social science, based upon semiotic approaches to representation, concerns the interactions of sporting celebrity, race and ethnicity. For example, in their studies of the 'black' global sporting icons, Tiger Woods (golf) and Michael Jordan (basketball), Cole and Andrews (2001), and McDonald and Andrews (2001), respectively, suggest that both these sports stars represent signs which sit at the centre of the interactions between American cultural politics and the politics of race, celebrity and global consumer culture. Both highly recognisable sportsmen, who are paid vast sums of money to endorse and promote sporting equipment by Nike, the authors' suggest that Woods and Jordan operate as semiotic signs within:

> a context defined by the regular fanning of apprehensions about and celebrations of America's multi-cultural racial future: racially coded celebrations which deny social problems and promote the idea that America has achieved its multicultural ideal. (Cole and Andrews, 2001: 70)

Not only are these sportsmen associated with the brand Nike, but through the actual process of branding – the conscious manipulation of Woods and Jordan as signs – both become associated with a representation of a particularly racially loaded ideological narrative about nationhood and social cohesion. For Cole and Andrews (2001), through processes of signification, Tiger Woods becomes embedded in narratives concerned with promoting a racially cohesive, but mythologised, version of contemporary America. Via the depiction of Woods as 'America's *multicultural* son' (Cole and Andrews, 2001: 83, original emphasis) consumers are not only invited to celebrate the golfer's own sporting and personal achievements but 'America's accomplished abolition of golf's elitism' (Cole and Andrews, 2001: 83).

A similar process plays itself out through the representation of Michael Jordan, who, according to McDonald and Andrews, adopts the function within popular narratives of a '"free floating" *racial* signifier representing a complex and fluid process that both engages with and disengages from an economy of signifiers related to stereotypical and ideological depictions of Black masculinity' (2001: 25, original emphasis). Through the highly mediated and commodified nature of Michael Jordan and the valorisation of his body and sporting ability, the authors suggest he 'serves as a highly visible signifier of racial otherness' (McDonald and Andrews, 2001: 25). Indeed, as they suggest, the dominant representation of Jordan presents a 'hyperreal image' of a 'preferred vision of Black masculinity', within which concerns with the realities of American (and global) racial and gender inequalities are obscured, nullified and naturalised through processes of mythologisation (McDonald and Andrews, 2001: 33).

REFERENCES

Armstrong, E.G. (1996) 'The Commodified 23, or, Michael Jordan as Text', *Sociology of Sport Journal*, 13: 325–43.

Barthes, R. (1973) *Mythologies*. London: Paladin. Originally published 1957.

Bishop, R. (2001) 'Stealing the Signs: A Semiotic Analysis of the Changing Nature of Professional Sports Logos', *Social Semiotics*, 11(1): 23–41.

Boyle, R. and Haynes, R. (2000) *Power Play: Sport, Media and Popular Culture*. Harlow: Longman.

Cashmore, E. (2002) *Beckham*. Cambridge: Polity.

Cashmore, E. (2005) *Tyson: Nature of the Beast*. Cambridge: Polity Press.

Cashmore, E. and Parker, A. (2003) 'One David Beckham? Celebrity, Masculinity and the Soccerati', *Sociology of Sport Journal*, 20(3): 214–31.

Colby, P. and Jansz, L. (2004) *Introducing Semiotics*. Royston: Icon Books.

Cole, C.L. and Andrews, D.L. (2001) 'America's New Son: Tiger Woods and America's Multiculturalism', in David, L. Andrews and Steven J. Jackson (eds) *Sport Stars. The Cultural Politics of Sporting Celebrity*. London: Routledge. pp. 70–86.

Denison, J. and Markula, P. (2005) 'The Press Conference as Performance: Representing Haile Gebreselassie' *Sociology of Sport Journal*, 22: 311–35.

Dyer, R. (1993) *The Matter of Images: Essays on Representation*. London: Routledge.

Farred, G. (2004) 'Fiaca and Veron-ismo: Race and Silence in Argentinian Football', *Leisure Studies*, 23 (1): 47–61.

Giulianotti, R. (1999) *Football. A Sociology of the Global Game*. Cambridge: Polity.

Hall, S. (1997) *Representation: Cultural Representations and Signifying Practices*. London: Sage.

hooks, bell (1992) *Black Looks: Race and Representation*. London: Turnaround.

Horne, J., Tomlinson, A. and Whannel, G. (1999) *Understanding Sport: An Introduction to the Sociological and Cultural Analysis of Sport*. London: E & FN Spon.

Jackson, S.J. and Andrews D.L. (eds) (2005) *Sport, Culture and Advertising: Identities, Commodities and the Politics of Representation*. London: Routledge.

King, A. (2004) 'The New Symbols of European Football', *International Review for the Sociology of Sport*, 39(3): 323–36.

Macdonald, M. (1995) *Representing Women*. London: Arnold.

McDonald, M.G. and Andrews, D.L. (2001) 'Michael Jordan: Corporate Sport and Postmodern Celebrityhood', in David, L. Andrews and Steven J. Jackson (eds) *Sport Stars. The Cultural Politics of Sporting Celebrity*. London: Routledge. pp. 20–35.

Saussure, F. de (1971) *Course in General Linguistics*. Paris: Payot. Originally published 1916.

Urry, J. (2002) *The Tourist Gaze* (2nd edn). London: Sage.

Whannel, G. (1992) *Fields of Vision: Television, Sport and Cultural Transformation*. London: Routledge.

Whannel, G. (2001) *Media Sports Stars. Masculinities and Moralities*. London: Routledge.

Sexuality

Sexuality can be understood in many different ways. It can be considered in relation to sexual activity and sexual identity, and debated in relation to social construction theory, to social control, or to political, economic and social practices. The study of sexuality and sport developed recently, and, interestingly, tends to highlight the experiences of heterosexual women, lesbians and gay men. For example, sports feminists have revealed the ways heterosexual women's sexuality is represented in sport practices and texts, such as the media, and lesbian and gay experiences in sport have been used to expose discriminatory practices evident in hegemonic sports such as football (both the British and USA versions). In addition to these existing accounts, transsexuality and transgender are emerging as an important focus of study. Transsexuality tends to indicate surgery and transgender involves adopting new gendered ways of being. Consideration of heterosexual men's sexuality tends to reside in the broader critical analysis of men and masculinity.

Sexuality can be described in essentialist terms – that is, as fixed and as a result of genetics/instinct, or it can be understood as shaped, controlled and regulated by social, political and economic factors. Those advocating the first interpretation view sexuality as 'natural' and promote heterosexuality as 'normal'. Writers from a social construction perspective (see e.g. Foucault, 1990; Seidman, 2003; Weeks et al., 2003) identify the church and medical profession during the nineteenth century as significant in shaping our understanding of 'modern' sexuality. Some time ago now, Diana Fuss (1989) challenged the conventional essentialist/constructionist dualism. She argued that constructionism 'when pushed to its extremes, risks collapsing into its opposite – essentialism' (1989: 40) and vice versa. In this way she contests the dualism and makes visible the slippages in the opposing views.

We can now talk about degrees of social construction and 'kinds of essentialism', and, more specifically, 'strategic essentialism' (Fuss, 1989: 4). Strategic essentialism has helped inform a politics of sexual identity. Identity politics underpinned the human rights movements of the 1960s, for example the lesbian and gay movement and the right to sexual equality campaigns (see **Identity and Difference**). We must not forget that in the UK it was not until 1967, only 40 years ago, when men were granted the legal right to have sex with each other, albeit in private, and not be criminalised for doing so. Similarly, the legal age of consent for young gay men was reduced from 21 years, to 18 years only in 1994, and is now the same as the heterosexual age of consent, which has always been 16 years. Sexual identity politics have often been used by sexual minorities to build resistance and challenge to sexual hierarchies. A more recent example is queer activism, which celebrates, often visually, multiple sexual (and gendered) identities in order to contest heterosexuality as inherently 'natural' and 'normal'. At this juncture, it is worth considering that naming the sexual self can be an affirmative act, whereas, categorisation is an act by those in power aimed at those with less power.

The complexities of sexual identity in relation to essentialism, social constructionism and strategic essentialism are clearly present within the study of sexuality and sport. Writers have successfully exposed the social construction of sexuality through physical activity, physical education and sport. For example, Helen Lenskyj, in 1986, shows how heteropatriarchal sporting institutions and ideologies, initially informed by the medical profession, contained women's sporting participation, produced women's sporting sexualities and regulated women's sporting bodies.

sexuality

205

Heterosexual femininity was viewed as fragile and weak and women's bodies were understood as frail. Consequently, women were permitted to take part in some sports but not others. Women who persisted in so-called men's sports and displayed a masculine style were consigned to an abhorred lesbianism.

Writers, such as Lenskyj, Pat Griffin and Brian Pronger worked hard to expose the ways sporting practice marginalises lesbian and gay sexuality. Underpinning their writing is the right lesbians and gay men have to be treated equally. Although it is not the focus, implicit to this work is a critique of men, masculinity and heterosexuality. We have gained a critical understanding of heterosexual men's sexuality via an interrogation of hegemonic masculinity. We are familiar with particular heterosexual practices, including sexual acts, which men adopt to objectify women and vilify gay men. In many ways the focus on hegemonic masculinity has meant we still know comparatively little about men, heterosexuality, sensuality and desire in sport. The existing accounts of men and masculinity do not fully explore different heterosexual men's experiences of sexuality and sport, especially in relation to ethnicity. Similarly, the accounts of female heterosexual femininity centre on the experiences of white Western women, references to ethnicity, sexuality and sport are sparse.

To reiterate, the study of sexuality and sport developed from a concern to dispel myths (such as the 'frailty' myth) about the consequences of women's active involvement in sport and was largely driven by a feminist agenda. Liberal concerns about opportunity and equal treatment were accompanied by a radical feminist focus on how women's bodies and sexuality were controlled and exploited by male sporting practices. For example, Mariah Burton Nelson (1996) exposes important empirical evidence on sex crimes committed by sportsmen against women and Celia Brackenridge (2004) details sexual abuse perpetrated by men in positions of power in sport (see also **Politics/Policy/Power**). These findings are a chilling reminder of sexual hierarchies and the need to remain mindful that sexuality, like gender and 'race', has a social arrangement, which is based on social power, control and exploitation.

To return to the heterosexual–homosexual relation, an interesting point is that sexuality, as a term of expression, sometimes stands for 'non-heterosexual' in a similar way as 'race' is often coded as a 'non-white' referent. As a result of collapsing the concept of sexuality to mean non-normative sexual activity/identity the term heteronormative developed to address the un-marked, un-named status of heterosexuality. Such a shift is not dissimilar to the interrogation of 'whiteness'. In addition, heteronormativty tends to index sexuality and gender. Those keen to criticise the gendering of sexuality and normative ordering of sex-gender-desire (e.g. woman-feminine-heterosexual) often associate with the idea of queer. 'Queer', in relation to sexuality, seeks to dislocate the privileging of heterosexuality and disturb heteronormative assumptions and practices. People who identify as queer, promote sexual and gendered identities that are non-normative and/or anti-normative.

Recent contributions to the study of sport and sexuality that rely on a notion of queer not only make visible the experiential diversity of sexuality and gender, they often adopt theory laid down by Michel Foucault (1990) and/or Judith Bulter (1990, 1993, 1998). For example, Heidi Eng (2006) makes use of Foucault's work on silence and space. She shows how, at international level, elite lesbian and gay athletes experience sport spaces and sport love-scripts (discourses) that deny them sexual identity and sexual activity. Butler's work has been deployed to help explain the difficulties transsexual and transgender people face in their pursuit of competitive sport. Butler's refusal to accept a fixed two-sexed binary gender system offers a potent challenge to the arrangement of competitive sport. Recently, writers (such as Symons and Hemphill, 2006; Travers, 2006) present cases of how transsexual and transgender inclusive policy challenges normative gender binaries and the two-sex system. It seems that the transsexual and transgender liberation movement is having an influence on how sport is organised, and previously excluded groups are beginning to be heard by those who organise events, tournaments and leagues.

The study of sexuality and sport is a relatively new field of inquiry (Caudwell, 2006). It incorporates existing analysis evident within feminist and pro-feminist critical discussion on sport, and includes emerging theoretical debates surrounding the body, queer, transsexuality and transgender. Sports social scientists tend to work from a predominantly social constructionist perspective; however it is evident that strategic essentialism has helped propel a human rights agenda. Generally, there has been a shift from accepting heterosexuality as foundational and a move to celebrating sexual diversity. Throughout, those writing on sexuality and sport have concentrated on the lived experiences of the marginalised, in this way documenting sexuality in sport is considered a political issue.

sexuality

REFERENCES

Brackenridge, C. (2001) *Spoilsports. Understanding and Preventing Sexual Exploitation in Sport*. London: Routledge.

Burton Nelson, M. (1996) *The Stronger Women Get, the More Men Love Football*. London: The Women's Press.

Butler, J. (1990) *Gender Trouble*. London: Routledge.

Butler, J. (1993) London: Routledge.

Butler, J. (1998) 'Athletic Genders: Hyperbole Instance and/or the Overcoming of Sexual Binarism', *Stanford Humanities Review*, 6(2): 103–11.

Caudwell, J. (ed.) (2006) *Sport, Sexualities and Queer/Theory*. London: Routledge.

Eng, H. (2006) 'Queer Athletes and Queering Sport', in J. Caudwell (ed.) *Sport, Sexualities and Queer/Theory*. London: Routledge. pp. 49–61.

Foucault, M. (1990) *The History of Sexuality, Vol. 1: An Introduction*. New York: Vintage Books. Originally published in French in 1976.

Fuss, D. (1989) *Essentially Speaking*. London: Routledge.

Lenskyj, H. (1986) *Out of Bounds. Women, Sport and Sexuality*. Ontario: The Women's Press.

Seidman, S. (2003) *The Social Construction of Sexuality*. London: W.W. Norton and Company.

Symons, C. and Hemphill, D. (2006) 'Transgendering Sex and Sport in the Gay Games', in J. Caudwell (ed.) *Sport, Sexualities and Queer/Theory*. London: Routledge. pp. 109–28.

Travers, A. (2006) 'Queering Sport', *International Review for the Sociology of Sport*, 41(3–4): 431–46.

Weeks, J., Holland, J. and Waites, M. (2003) *Sexualities and Society: A Reader*. Cambridge: Polity.

FURTHER READING

Bhattacharyya, G. (2002) *Sexuality and Society: An Introduction*. London: Routledge.
Miller, T. (2001) *Sportsex*. Philadelphia: Temple University Press.
Pronger, B. (1990) *The Arena of Masculinity*. London: GMP Publishers.

key concepts in
sports studies

208

Social Class

'The history of all hitherto existing society', as Karl Marx and Friedrich Engels wrote in their *Manifesto of the Communist Party* of 1848, 'is the history of class struggles' (1965: 39). This is a useful starting point for discussing the concept of social class, for three reasons. First, for many of the sociologists and historians who have analysed sport, class is a *given* – a central and crucial fact of life in all but the earliest human societies. Class, that's to say, could not be escaped or dismissed as a matter of, say, snobbery or the 'politics of envy'; it was *there*, as a decisive factor – for Marx, *the* decisive factor – in history and in the lives of individuals. Second, again following Marx, class has most commonly been seen by Western sociologists as a matter of *economics* – the class position of a person or a family has been defined by their place in the economy, or, as Marx phrased it, their relationship to the means of production. The history and sociology of sport have therefore, to a degree, been bound up with analysis of this class struggle – alongside, as witnessed elsewhere in this book, the historic struggles between gendered and racialised groups. Third, it's important to recognise that, in the words of the eminent social historian E.P. Thompson, 'the notion of class entails the notion of historical relationship' (1976: 9). That is, the classes were not simply large aggregates of people; they *related* to each other in important ways. Sport emerged out of, and has been contingent upon, this historical relationship *between* the social classes, as the following examples will show.

Until the nineteenth century European societies were governed and dominated by landowning aristocracies. Aristocrats were often lovers of sport – indeed, the word 'sport' was probably first used to describe their favoured leisure pursuits, summarised in England by the popular phrase 'huntin', shootin' and fishin''. The lower social classes of pre-industrial society – tenant farmers, peasants, landless labourers and their families – generally engaged in rowdier sports, which usually took place in or between villages on public holidays, 'holidays' being a corruption of 'holy days' or important dates in the religious calendar. A popular interpretation of these events is that they were carnivalesque – part of a brief period in the life of an otherwise highly stratified society which was given over to general mayhem and the pleasures of the flesh. There was little movement from one social class to another and relationships between the classes were governed by patterns of deference and obligation; riotous bouts of football, bottle kicking or cheese rolling on some saint's day acted, it is thought, as a social safety valve in an otherwise highly regulated social world. The historian Anthony Delves, for example, has described the rowdy football match that still took place between parishes in Derby in the early nineteenth century every Shrove Tuesday and Ash Wednesday (1981: 89).

What we call 'modern' sport also originated among sport loving aristocratic gentlemen, known to historians as 'the fancy'. One of the defining characteristics of a modern sport is that it has a set of written rules or laws and the first sports to acquire these were those played and/or patronised by the fancy: boxing, cricket, horseracing and rowing. Rules were invariably committed to paper in order to establish the terms of a wager (see Holt, 1992: 12–28).[1] However, it is the rising capitalist or *bourgeois* class of merchants, entrepreneurs, financiers and professionals that seems to have had the greatest influence on the emergence of sport as we know it. Often described in historical literature as 'people of the middling sort', these middle classes brought their values of hard work, sobriety, individual self improvement and the virtues of competition increasingly to bear on the leading institutions of European society. In Britain, in the eighteenth and nineteenth centuries, this process can be seen in the rise of Nonconformist religions, such as Methodism, in the extension of the vote to 'the men of property' and in important curricular changes in the country's most prestigious, or 'public', schools. Previously wild places for undisciplined young gentlemen, these schools gradually embraced scholarship and good order and began to modify their often brutal in-house games. Out of this crucible emerged the modern codes of association football ('soccer') and rugby football (see e.g. Dunning and Sheard, 1979: 46–129).

The late eighteenth and early nineteenth centuries saw the rise in Europe of the urban proletariat or working class – a huge agglomeration of propertyless manual workers and their families who migrated to the industrial towns and cities with only their labour power to sell. A brief examination of the relationship between this class and their *bourgeois* employers helps to clarify other issues in the social analysis of sport.

Firstly, the industrial capitalism supervised by the bourgeois class entailed new disciplines, including, crucially, time discipline. For rural workers the cock had been nature's timepiece; in urban industrial life, as Thompson observed, time became currency – it was 'not passed, but spent' (1991: 359). Secondly, in the context of these new imperatives, recreation became a political issue which divided society broadly along class lines: the upper-class 'fancy' enjoyed their hunting, prizefighting and horseracing and the new working classes retained their sporting pursuits – cock fighting, mob football and the like – whereas the leading spokespeople for the rising middle class were initially opposed to sport. Instead, during the first half of the nineteenth century, largely middle-class organisations such as the Temperance Movement counselled 'rational recreation' – the use of parks, playgrounds, libraries and the like – and early Victorian governments legislated against traditional lower-class – particularly animal – sports. Thirdly, discussion of these developments (and others) helped to provoke a debate among historians and sociologists about *social control*, with academics from different standpoints being uncomfortable with the implication that the early Victorian working class were passive recipients of these new disciplines, simply relinquishing their customary pleasures and marching meekly into the factories. (For a good summary see Bailey, 1987: 8–46.) More generally, they wished to see the working class as agents in the making of their own history and not simply as 'determined' by structural changes such as the rise of industrial capitalism. This led some scholars to make a 'linguistic turn' in their analysis – that is, they now saw culture simply as a kind of language, made up of signs and symbols, complex and largely independent of social structures (see e.g. Kirk, 1996). Class, in this view, becomes simply what people make it.

Arguments of this nature – about social control, cultural resistance and the degree to which working-class life can be understood in these terms – carry over, naturally enough, into discussion about the working class in the later nineteenth and twentieth centuries. Certainly, the British working class, and its menfolk in particular, took readily to some of the modern sports which had emerged from the nation's elite schools and universities in the latter half of the nineteenth century and were later evangelised in the working-class districts by priests, teachers, employers and others. Association football, in particular, became a vital element in working-class life. Originating in the most prestigious schools of Eton, Harrow and Westminster, 'soccer' gave rise to a range of local works', church and boys' teams and by the 1920s had become seen as 'the people's game'.

Was this, however, no more than a process of indoctrination whereby the working class learned respect for rules, authority and the notion that life was competitive? Much sociological writing about the British working class in the second half of the twentieth century was organised around the concept of *community* – a culture of mutual assistance, built around ideas of 'us and them' and mitigating the ravages of life under industrial capitalism. Key texts of the post Second World War period such as Willmott and Young's (1954/1975) *Family and Kinship in East London*, sought to describe this community; later literature, for example analysing working-class youth cultures, suggested that these communities were breaking up (e.g. Hall and Jefferson, 1976). More recently, following the 'linguistic turn', scholarly doubt has been raised as to whether there was ever such a thing as working-class culture at all. Sport historians and sociologists, for the most part, are reasonably certain that there was and that sport has played an important part in it. This is shown by Stephen G. Jones' (1988) *Sport, Politics and the Working Class* and Richard Holt's (1999) *Sport and the Working Class in Modern Britain*. Sport, these books suggest, gave working-class people some of their greatest pleasures and many of their heroes (Babe Ruth, Stanley Matthews, George Best ...) and helped to form their identity. Nowadays, however, there are revisionist, less starry-eyed appraisals of working-class communities and their sport. Karl Spracklen, for example, has suggested that rugby league, traditionally a working-class game, helped historically to define an 'imaginary community' that was exclusively male and 'implicitly white' (2001: 70).

SOCIAL CLASS, SPORT AND CONTEMPORARY SOCIETY

Two initial observations must be made about class in contemporary society before it can be related to sport. First, most societies have undergone a process of deindustrialisation: an ever greater proportion of workers in these societies are engaged in producing services, rather than goods or raw materials. This has had clear implications for the understanding of class since the people traditionally defined as working class – waged manual workers and their kindred – have apparently decreased in number, while formally non-manual workers have multiplied. The contemporary class structure, therefore, is seen by many now to be diamond- rather than pyramid-shaped. Second, analysis of class tends more than ever toward the subjective. The principal findings of *Middle Britain*, a research report by the Future Foundation in 2006 were that a large and rising number of people (44%) considered themselves 'middle class' and that a huge number of the richest Britons placed themselves in the 'working class'.[2] Writer and commentator Rod Liddle was sceptical:

> The fashion is that you can be whatever you want to be and nobody has a right to tell you any different, regardless of the evidence. If a plumber in Plumstead [south London] with a melanine topped cocktail bar in his front room and a mantelpiece full of porcelain cats and darts trophies insists that he is upper class, [William] Nelson [co-author of the report] brooks no objection. Similarly, if the Duke of Westminster wishes to insist he is a worker, it's fair game. (2006)

Many sociologists are still inclined to agree with Liddle and to examine the evidence for class. Leading leisure analyst Chas Critcher, for example, recently presented a powerful argument for the continued existence of class, suggesting that all the previously established quantitative criteria (income, mortality rates, educational achievement …) and qualitative criteria (culture, typical activities and attitudes …) still applied in the twenty-first century. Part of his case was that sport was still a factor in defining class difference: yachting, rowing, showjumping and the like remained upper-class sports; snooker, darts and rugby league working-class, and so on (Critcher, 2006). Clear social class differences in sport participation were shown in *The Development of Sporting Talent 1997*, a study of elite athletes published by the English Sports Council in 1998 (quoted in Horne, 2006: 146–7).

Indeed, it could be argued that sport defines class in another important way in contemporary societies, through its implicit associations with achievement and *social mobility*. Successful professional sportspeople are assumed, almost by definition, to have 'bettered themselves' and, thus, to have moved from one social class to another. A telling illustration of this is the consternation that greeted the declaration in 2006 that Zara Phillips, granddaughter of the British queen, was BBC Sports Personality of the Year, in succession to the athlete Kelly Holmes and the cricketer Andrew Flintoff, both of whom were from working-class homes. 'I'm not a Royalist', wrote one columnist,

> but neither am I one of those people who believes a British Republic can't come quickly enough. However, there's nothing more painful than seeing the Queen's prancing granddaughter voted Sports Personality of the Year for being the best of a few hundred mega-rich participants in one of the planet's most exclusive sports. (Gee, 2006)

Linked to the proliferation of *subjective* notions of class are the equally important notions of privatisation and consumption. Post-war debates about the English working class were dominated by the argument that manual workers were increasingly concerned only with the private realm of home, family and pay packet and were turning away from the public sphere of politics and trade union activity. This thesis was tested most notably in the influential 'Affluent Worker' study of the late 1960s (Goldthrope et al., 1968a, 1968b 1971). Despite the inconclusiveness of the 'affluent worker' arguments, the feeling has grown in Western societies that class should be defined through *consumption*, rather than *production* (see **Commodification; Consumption; Postmodernism/Postmodernity**). People are increasingly seen as having *identities* – a more personal term – than class positions and these identities are more likely to be conferred by what people buy and like than by what they do for a living (see **Identity and Difference**). Sport, of course, has a central place in the contemporary politics of identity and consumption, as does class. Garry Crawford has pointed out that working-class people are often excluded from live sporting events because they can't afford tickets: a good example here would be the cricket World Cup in 2007 in the West Indies, where ticket prices for most games equalled a month's wages for most people living on the Caribbean islands involved and TV cameras revealed many empty seats at most of the matches. Crawford (2004: 57–60) also suggests, following the influential sociologist Zygmunt Bauman, that sport has helped to maintain the sense of belonging previously felt in the now-extinct working-class communities: fans of a football team, for instance, constitute a 'neo-tribe' celebrating its common identity by wearing replica shirts, going to matches, conversing on internet message boards, and so on. Indeed, Anthony King's (1998: 155) research among Manchester United supporters found that the replica shirt was for many a proletarian credential, distinguishing 'real' working-class fans from the middle-class Johnny Come Lately consumers in their designer gear.

Finally, however, it is important to remember that, subjective analyses notwithstanding, the working class has not disappeared. On the contrary, as the journalist Paul Mason wrote recently:

> Today, in place of a static workforce working in the factories and drinking in the pubs their grandfathers worked and drank in, a truly global working class is being created ... since the collapse of communism the whole world's workforce has shared the experience of working in a market economy. (2007: xi)

Millions of jobs previously done in Europe or the United States are now done in the low wage economies of Asia and the Far East and many of these supply the sports consumption markets of the West. 'I've met Indian garment workers', writes Mason, 'who recognise the labels on the sportswear they are finishing but have no idea who their employer is, or when they're getting paid' (2007: xii). The emergence of a global labour market has led in turn to the formation of international organisations for the defence of labour. And, in a palpable refutation of the popular view that class is a thing of the past, these organisations have found themselves fighting that most Victorian of class battles: the campaign against child labour. In 2007 the global sportswear firm Nike reviewed the manufacture of footballs in Pakistan after it was revealed that they were being made by children and the Playfair Alliance, a coalition incorporating the Internationational Trade Union Confederation and the International Textile, Garment and Leather Workers' Federation claimed that 12-year-old children were being paid 14 English pence an hour to make goods licensed for the Beijing Olympic Games the following year (Taylor, 2007).

NOTES

1. For studies of these individual sports see Sugden (1996: 12–21), Brookes (1978: 34–44), Vamplew (1976) and Wigglesworth (1992: 58–60).
2. Summary of findings at http://www.futurefoundation,net/ffinthenews. php?disp=226 (accessed: 14 June 2007). See also http://news.bbc.co.uk/1/hi/uk/4974460.stm (accessed: 14 June 2007).

REFERENCES

Bailey, Peter (1987) *Leisure and Class in Victorian England*. London: Methuen.
Brookes, Christopher (1978) *English Cricket*. London: Weidenfeld and Nicolson.
Crawford, Garry (2004) *Consuming Sport: Fans, Sport and Culture*. London: Routledge.
Critcher, Chas (2006) 'A Touch of Class' in Chris Rojek, Susan M. Shaw and A.J. Veal (eds) *A Handbook of Leisure Studies*. Basingstoke: Palgrave Macmillan. pp. 279–87.
Delves, Anthony (1981) 'Popular Recreation and Social Conflict in Derby 1800–1850' in Eileen Yeo and Stephen Yeo (eds) *Popular Culture and Class Conflict 1590–1914*. Hassocks: Harvester. pp. 89–127.
Dunning, Eric and Sheard, Kenneth (1979) *Barbarians, Gentlemen and Players*. Oxford: Martin Robertson.
Gee, Donna (2006) 'Zara Phillips: After Kelly Holmes and Andrew Flintoff, a Right Royal Joke', http://www.sportingo.com/more-sports/zara-phillips:-after-kelly-holmes-and-andrew-flintoff-a-right-royal-joke/1001,1154 (posted: 13 December, accessed: 14 June 2007).
Goldthorpe, John H., Lockwood, D., Bechnofer, F. and Platt, J. (1968a) *The Affluent Worker: Industrial Attitudes and Behaviour*. Cambridge: Cambridge University Press.
Goldthrope, John H., Lockwood, D., Bechnofer, F. and Platt, J. (1968b) *The Affluent Worker: Political Attitudes and Behaviour*. Cambridge: Cambrdige University Press.
Goldthorpe, John H., Lockwood, D., Bechnofer, F. and Platt, J. (1971) *The Affluent Worker in the Class Structure*. Cambridge: Cambridge University Press.
Hall, Stuart and Jefferson, Tony (eds) (1976) *Resistance Through Rituals: Youth Subcultures in Post-War Britain*. London: Hutchinson.
Holt, Richard (ed.) (1999) *Sport and the Working Class in Modern Britain*. Manchester: Manchester University Press.
Holt, Richard (1992) *Sport and the British*. Oxford: Clarendon Press.

social class

Horne, John (2006) *Sport in Consumer Culture*. Basingstoke: Palgrave Macmillan.

Jones, Stephen G. (1988) *Sport, Politics and the Working Class*. Manchester: Manchester University Press.

King, Anthony (1998) *The End of the Terraces*. London: Leicester University Press.

Kirk, Neville (1996) 'Class and the "Linguistic Turn" in Chartist and Post-Chartist Historiography' in Neville Kirk (ed.) *Social Class and Marxism: Defences and Challenges*. Aldershot: Scolar Press. pp. 87–134.

Liddle, Rod (2006) 'We're All Working Class Now', *The Sunday Times*, 7 May, http://www.timesonline.co.uk/tol/comment/columnists/rod_liddle/article714062.ece (accessed: 14 June 2007).

Marx, Karl and Engels, Friedrich (1965) *Manifesto of the Communist Party*. Moscow: Progress Publishers.

Mason, Paul (2007) *Live Working or Die Fighting: How the Working Class Went Global*. London: Harvill Secker.

Spracklen, Karl (2001) 'Black Pearl, Black Diamonds. Exploring Racial Identities in Rugby' in Ben Carrington and Ian McDonald (eds) (2001) *'Race', Sport and British Society*. London: Routledge. pp. 77–82.

Sugden, John (1996) *Boxing and Society*. Manchester: Manchester University Press.

Taylor, Andrew (2007) 'Child Labour Caution for China Olympics', *Financial Times*, 10 June, http:/www.ft.com/cms/s/5eaa339a-177a-11dc-86d1-000b5df10621.html (accessed: 14 June 2007).

Thompson, E.P. (1976) *The Making of the English Working Class*. Harmondsworth: Penguin.

Thompson, E.P. (1991) 'Time, Work-Discipline and Industrial Capitalism', in *Customs in Common*. London: The Merlin Press. pp. 352–403.

Vamplew, Wray (1976) *The Turf: A Social and Economic History of Horse Racing*. London: Allen Lane.

Wigglesworth, Neil (1992) *The Social History of English Rowing*. London: Frank Cass. pp. 58–60.

Willmott, Peter and Young, Michael (1954/1975) *Family and Kinship in East London*. Harmondsworth: Penguin.

FURTHER READING

One of the principal arguments of this section has been that class is inherent in so much of the social analysis of sport written over the last 40 years. It is difficult, therefore, to point to literature which is not, in some way, about class. Eric Dunning and Kenneth Sheard's (1979) *Barbarians, Gentlemen and Players* (Oxford: Martin Robertson) and Tony Collins' (1998) *Rugby's Great Split: Class, Culture and the Origins of Rugby League Football* (London: Routledge), however, are just two examples of E.P. Thompson's 'historical relationship' between the classes being played out through sport. Chas Critcher's essay 'A Touch of Class' in Chris Rojek et al. (eds) (2006) *A Handbook of Leisure Studies* (Basingstoke: Palgrave Macmillan) is a good introduction to contemporary debates.

State, Nation, Nationalism

The *Dictionary of Sociology* defines the state thus:

> a set of institutions governing a particular territory, with a capacity to make laws regulating the conduct of the people within that territory, and supported by revenue deriving from taxation. The capacity to make and enforce law is dependent on the state's enjoyment of a monopoly of legitimate force. (Abercrombie et al., 2000: 343–4)

It's fair to say that, among sociologists, this definition has wide, but perhaps not universal acceptance.

States are *historical* phenomena: that's to say they have not always existed. Indeed many societies have, or have had, no state. Tribal societies, for example, typically have no written laws or separate institutions for dealing with, say, education, illness, crime or political decision making: typically these matters are handled within families or by elders. The earliest 'city states' can be traced back to southern Mesopotamia (what is now Saudi Arabia and Kuwait) in 3,000 BC.[1] But the modern state emerged in Europe in the sixteenth century and represents a distinct form of public power, separate from both ruler(s) and ruled. As such it marks the transition, in Max Weber's terms, from traditional to rational or legal authority and, thus, to modernity. The state is distinct from *civil society*, that is, the state (the apparatus of government) stands on the one side and the rest of societal life – domestic, economic, cultural and so on – stands on the other. It's as well, though, to note that influential recent writers such as the French philosopher-historian Michel Foucault (1926–1984) have not accepted this distinction: Foucault speaks of 'governmentality' – ways of managing human populations that transcend the political state (a point made, for example, by Pierson, 1996: 6). The emphasis placed by Foucault on management and control is a useful corrective to the notion that states have been inevitably democratic instruments. For the most part, they haven't. On the contrary, 'the state' has, historically, encompassed absolutist monarchies and totalitarian governments of both left and right. This might easily be forgotten, given the persistent reference in the early twenty-first century to 'failed states' – a concept promulgated by 'neo-conservative' academics in the United States, such as Francis Fukuyama (2004), who argues that some, invariably non-Western, states have failed to provide for their people. Critics of Fukuyama, and of the governments such as those of the United States and the United Kingdom who have endorsed the concept of 'failed state', have seen it simply as a pretext for intervening in the affairs of these countries. This feeds into a wider argument about the state: given globalisation and, thus, the decreasing importance of national boundaries, can we speak any longer of independent 'states'?

David Held (1992) has described the emergence of the modern state in Europe. After the fall of the Roman Empire in the mid-fifth century, most of what is today called Europe was dominated – one might say ruled, even menaced, rather than governed – by military conquerors exacting tribute. These were emperors, kings and princes enacting a pattern of plunder, for instance of harvests. There were no heads of state and no clearly demarcated territories. A similar system obtained in China.

The feudal system, which characterised the medieval period, entailed a pattern of ties and obligations between rulers and servants, and between lords and tribal warriors and involved the paying of dues by lower orders to higher. The feudal period also saw the growth of the power of towns and cities, which often had charters. With this urban development came, from around 1300, the growth of social groups, such as the nobility, the clergy, leading townsmen, etc., claiming political privileges. This, in turn, led to the establishment of political assemblies: diets, parliaments and councils. Between the fifteenth century and the eighteenth, these groups found themselves politically pitted against absolutist states, that is, those governed by monarchs claiming absolute power and asserting that this power was sanctioned by God. In some countries – France, Prussia, Spain and Russia for instance – these absolutist monarchies endured longer than in others: England had a 'constitutional monarchy' (one which shared power with an elected parliament) following the Civil War of the mid-seventeenth century.

Thereafter, we can see across Europe the development of key aspects of the modern state: the coincidence of boundaries and uniform rule; new (usually parliamentary) mechanisms of lawmaking; centralised bureaucracy; the extension of fiscal management; a standing army; the increased surveillance of subjects; and the growth of formal relations among states. States now claimed, and conceded to each other, right of jurisdiction in respective territories.

SPORT AND THE STATE

The state, it's fair to say, did not concern itself unduly with sport or games until the late nineteenth century. Before that, state intervention was confined to the occasional royal pronouncement about the lack of archers or the danger to public order posed by rowdy mob football. A good example here was the 'Declaration of Sportes' made by James I of England in 1618. In the seventeenth century, the political mouthpiece of the rising, urban middle class was often the Puritan priesthood, who condemned games as ungodly. James responded with a proclamation, re-issued by his son Charles I in 1633, instructing his subjects to ignore these strictures and have fun. He drew the line, though, at rougher sports:

> and as for our good people's lawful recreation, our pleasure likewise is, that after the end of divine service our good people be not disturbed, letted or discouraged from any lawful recreation, such as dancing, either men or women; archery for men, leaping, vaulting, or any other such harmless recreation, nor from having of May-games, Whitsun-ales, and Morris-dances; and the setting up of May-poles and other sports therewith used: so as the same be had in due and convenient time, without impediment or neglect of divine service: and that women shall have leave to carry rushes to the church for the decorating of it, according to their old custom; but withal we do here account still as prohibited all unlawful games to be used upon Sundays only, as bear and bull-baitings, interludes, and at all times in the meaner sort of people by law prohibited, bowling.[2]

Before considering the various dispositions of sport by modern states, though, it's necessary to consider the various theories of power in the modern state. Discussion here, in recent decades, has not strayed too far from three, comparatively well-worn, paths. Most analysts see power as a 'constant sum' concept – that is, in order for some people to have it, other people have to lack it. In all complex societies there are different interests and these interests may, or may not, be reconcilable. One view of this, popular in American sociology (and among politicians of many countries), is the *pluralist* perspective which sees the state as an 'honest broker' mediating between interest groups, those groups (and corresponding social divisions) being represented by political parties and pressure groups. The theory is most closely associated with the American political academic Robert Dahl and his book *Who Governs?* (2005), but the idea is strongly propagated within the political system of the United States, 'pluralism' being cited today on the State Department website as a fundament of American democracy.[3]

A second perspective, attractive with different inflections to theorists of either the left or the right, is *elite* theory, which sees an elite using the state to dominate a comparatively powerless populace. This idea has a long history in political theory, dating back to the Florentine writer Niccolo Machiavelli (1569–1527) and beyond, but is most closely associated in recent decades with the American radical C. Wright Mills (see **The Sociological Imagination**). The third approach is rooted in Marxism and sees the state either as the political instrument of a ruling or dominant class, or as inextricably bound up with the workings of the capitalist system.

It is some version of this third approach that has tended to influence most sociological writing on sport and the state in Western societies, and an essay by the Canadian sociologist Richard Gruneau in the early 1980s acts as template. Rejecting the liberal pluralist view that sport was a largely voluntary activity and that the state's relationship to it was largely neutral, Gruneau nevertheless also argued against the cruder, more deterministic Marxist readings of this link. Sport, he wrote, could not be seen simply as an ideological state apparatus (see **Ideology**), through which workers were socialised into the attitudes necessary to form a compliant, productive workforce. Class power and state power were not the same thing and sport should be seen as 'historically constituted and contested' and capable of taking on 'oppositional meanings' (Gruneau, 1982: 26–8).

We can apply Gruneau's argument to the historic relationship between sport and the British state. In the nineteenth century the state was not directly involved with sport, although sport was recognised at an official level – in the Clarendon Report (1864) on elite schooling, for instance – as a vital ingredient in the training of young upper-class males. Following the landmark Education (or 'Forster') Act of 1870, under which the state assumed responsibility for primary education, concern grew in official circles about the preparation of young, working-class bodies for work and, following the Boer War of 1899–1902, for military service. This concern led, among other things, to the introduction of Swedish gymnastics into the nascent state education system. Government concern for adult fitness developed in the 1920s and 1930s when the state supported voluntary bodies such as the National Playing Fields Association and the Central Council for Physical Recreation. In 1962 the British (Conservative) government for the first time designated a minister (Lord Hailsham) to be responsible for sport and through the 1960s there grew in Britain, and in the United States and Europe, a drive to promote mass participation in sport – a policy generally labelled 'Sport for All' (see Coghlan and Webb, 1990: 116–23).

Since the mid-1970s, with the trend towards the neo-liberal policy of 'rolling back the state', there has been a retreat from the commitment to public sport provision and a greater preoccupation with the 'national interest', with 'raising the national profile', and so on. This has led to a greater stress on the producing of elite athletes, to the welcoming of commercial sponsorship and to the establishment of national academies for various sports. It also led to the publication in 1995 of *Sport: Raising the Game* (Kamenka, 1976: 6–7). Probably the most prescriptive document in the history of state–sport relations in Britain, *Sport: Raising the Game* calls for sport to be placed near the heart of the school curriculum and for a national renewal in the British search for trophies in world sport.

The evidence from this very brief historical résumé might seem to support the view of Gruneau, and the majority of academic writers on this theme, that the state in a capitalist society does not act in any straightforward way to promote capitalist interests through sport. But, in relation to sport, it has certainly been attentive to the needs of commercial and military employers. Equally, there have been times when the state has promoted wider access to sport as a public benefit. Furthermore, as we have seen in other sections, people have sought successfully to play sport on terms specifically opposed to those prescribed by the state or dominant institutions in society such as the IOC. This appears to bear out Gruneau's point about the historical contestation and potentially oppositional nature of sport. It should be added that these writers were, in general, disposed to regard the USSR and other 'Iron Curtain' societies of the pre-1990 era as 'state capitalist', and not 'socialist' as these states preferred to style themselves.

THE STATE: SPORT, NATION AND NATIONALISM

All modern states are nation states. However, it is important to be clear that nations and nation states are not always the same thing. Nation states are defined, as we have seen, by territoriality, by their monopoly of the legitimate use of violence and by an impersonal structure of power. But nation states emerged only in the eighteenth and nineteenth centuries and the words 'nation' and 'nationalism' – the sense of loyalty to a nation – precede nation states by several centuries (Kamenka, 1976: 6–7). A nation, in this pre-state form, may have been based on many factors – language, geography and religion among them. But take the most cursory glance across the range of contemporary nation states – and there are, at the time of writing, 192 member states registered at the United Nations[4] – and it is clear that few are united around a common language or religion: the most popular first language in the United States, for example, is not English but Spanish; Belgium and Canada similarly have different language communities; countries such as Northern Ireland have religious divisions of longstanding; Spain and Sri Lanka are two among a number of countries which have separatist movements based on regional ethnicities; and so on. This tells us two important things: first, that nation states often face difficulties in gaining their necessary legitimacy – the loyalty of their citizens – 'The history of any country, presented as the history of a family, conceals fierce conflicts of interest', writes the radical American historian Howard Zinn (1996: 9); second, that there are numerous nationalisms which have no official nation to attach themselves to.

Sport has been a central factor in the forging of many nationalisms: if nations, as many accept, are, in Benedict Anderson's phrase, 'imagined communities' (1983) sport has often been a means to that sense of shared identity. Nationalism, after all, invariably involves uniting people in various contexts around stories, constructed national mythologies and invented traditions. For example, Steven Pope (1997) has shown the role of sport in the formation of American national identity – a process that entailed the creation of a myth around the 'invention' of baseball – David Andrews (1991) has written about the importance of rugby in the weaving of myths that attended the emergence of Welsh nationalism, John Hargreaves (2000) has described the tensions between Spanish nationalism and Catalan nationalism which were heightened by the Barcelona Olympics of 1992 and Hilary Beckles (1998) has analysed the importance of cricket in the forming of West Indian nationalism – another nationalism that has survived in the absence of a formal nation. There's little doubt either that sport has continued to be a key – probably, in the absence of war, *the* key – element in the sustaining of nationalist sentiment: as the British historian Eric Hobsbawm once famously observed: 'The imagined community of millions seems more real as a team of eleven named people' (1990: 143). This, of course, can apply equally to nations which enjoy a degree of political and ethnic coherence – as with Brazilian football, for example – as to nations which have historically been divided: in apartheid South Africa, for instance, rugby was the sport of Afrikaner nationalists and association football the sport of disenfranchised black South Africans. We may distinguish here between *ethnic* and *civic* nationalism: these ethnic nationalisms persist in South Africa, despite the dismantling of apartheid and subsequent attempts to build a new civic nationalism based on universal suffrage and the idea of a 'rainbow nation' (see Nauright, 1997).

SPORT, NATIONAL IDENTITY AND GLOBALISATION

'Globalisation' is a vogue term in academic and political circles (see **Globalisation**), but globalising tendencies are not new; they have been happening since before the beginning of the modern era. They began with the empires of the fifteenth century (Miller et al., 2001: 9). The globalisation of sport dates from the late nineteenth century with the first test cricket matches, the founding of the modern Olympic movement, and so on. Globalisation raises two questions about nation states and their sport cultures. First, given the growth of multi- and trans-national corporations and of supranational bodies such as the UN and the World Bank, do nation states any longer matter? And, second, are national sports cultures being washed away in a sea of global sport?

It is certainly the case that multi- and trans-national corporations now rival nation states in terms of annual income. The Gross Domestic Product of a reasonably prosperous nation state, such as Spain, Greece or New Zealand can now be matched by the yearly turnover of Microsoft, Hewlett-Packard and American Express respectively (Miller et al., 2001: 23). But, despite the fact that most of these companies are based in the United States, the US has not been especially successful in exporting its favoured sports to the rest of the world – partly, no doubt, because of its own strong (and strongly contested) national sporting identity and its attendant notions of 'American exceptionalism'. Moreover, within the more obviously globalised sports such as association football, there are signs that longstanding ethnicities can deal with, and absorb, change. For example, when Glasgow Celtic Football Club, historically a flagship for expatriate Irish nationalism, signed the Japanese player Shunsuke Nakamura, the club's supporters assimilated him with the playfully bi-cultural chant: 'He eats chow mein. He votes Sinn Fein' (Campbell, 2006).

The question remains, however, of whether national bodies and teams might be diminishing in importance, relative to inter- or supra-national ones. It is, for example, widely asserted that the Italian, Brazilian and Nigerian football teams are 'owned' by, or at least heavily obligated by the sponsorship of, the sportswear firm Nike; there were, moreover, persistent rumours that Nike had insisted that the Brazilian player Ronaldo, who had suffered a fit the night before, play in the World Cup Final in

Paris in July of 1998.[5] Indeed a recent book in the sociology of sport employs the term 'corporate nationalism' (Silk et al., 2005). Similarly, the International Olympic Committee is perceived in many quarters to be both corrupt and beyond democratic global governance: its annual income, like that of FIFA, exceeds that of a number of nation states and its last President, Juan Antonio Samaranch suggested that the IOC functioned 'as a state' (Miller et al., 2001: 12). Despite this, 'sportive nationalism', as a number of writers assert, and have demonstrated, is still strong, and local 'ethnic' sports survive (Bairner, 2001).

The link between sport and the nation state, then, seems unlikely to be broken any time soon. Certainly it is not threatened by any developments emanating from another specific nation state – as in the case of the widely invoked, and feared, process of 'Americanisation'. There seems little escape, however, from the incursions of global corporate capitalism, which is often mistaken for Americanisation. As has been made clear in other sections, however, there is always resistance (see **Culture; Imperialism/The Post-Colonial**) as manifested in such movements as the Global Anti-Golf Movement (see **The Environment**) and anti-Olympic campaigns.

NOTES

1. See, e.g. http://www.wsu.edu/~dee/MESO/SUMER.HTM (accessed: 26 April 2007).
2. http://history.hanover.edu/texts/ENGref/er93.html (accessed: 26 April 2007).
3. http://usinfo.state.gov/products/pubs/whatsdem/whatdm8.htm (accessed: 26 April 2007).
4. http://www.un.org/members/list.shtml (accessed: 27 April 2007).
5. 'The Great World Cup Final Mystery', BBC Sport Website, 2 April 2002, http://news.bbc.co.uk/sport3/worldcup2002/hi/history/newsid_1749000/1749324.stm (accessed: 2 May 2007).

REFERENCES

Abercrombie, Nicholas, Hill, Stephen and Turner, Bryan, S. (2000) *Dictionary of Sociology.* London: Penguin.

Anderson, Benedict (1983) *Imagined Communities.* London: Verso.

Andrews, David L. (1991) 'Welsh Indigenous! And British Imperial? – Rugby, Culture and Society 1890–1914', *Journal of Sport History*, 18 (3): 335–49.

Bairner, Alan (2001) *Sport, Nationalism and Globalization: European and North American Perspectives.* New York: SUNY Press.

Beckles, Hilary McD. (1998) *The Development of West Indies Cricket.* London: Pluto Press.

Campbell, Nicky (2006) 'Our Fans' Chants are Subversive, Surreal and Very, Very Funny', *The Guardian*, 7 December 2006, http://football.guardian.co.uk/Columnists/Column/ 0,,1966109,00.html (accessed: 28 April 2007).

Coghlan, John F. and Webb, Ida M. (1990) *Sport and British Politics Since 1960*. London: The Falmer Press.

Dahl, Robert (2005) *Who Governs? Democracy and Power in an American City*. New Haven, CT: Yale University 2005. Originally published 1961.

Department of National Heritage (1995) Sport: Raising the Game. London: Department of National Heritage.

Fukuyama, Francis (2004) *State Building: Governance and World Order in the Twenty-First Century*. London: Profile Books.

Gruneau, Richard (1982) 'Sport and the Debate on the State' in Hart Cantelon and Richard Gruneau (eds) *Sport, Culture and the Modern State*. Toronto: University of Toronto Press. pp. 1–38.

Hargreaves, John (2000) *Freedom for Catalonia? Catalan Nationalism, Spanish Identity and the Barcelona Olympic Games*. Cambridge: Cambridge University Press.

Held, David (1992) 'The Development of the Modern State' in Stuart Hall and Bram Gieben (eds) *Formations of Modernity*. Cambridge: Polity Press. pp. 71–125.

Hobsbawm, Eric (1990) *Nations and Nationalism Since 1780: Programme, Myth, Reality*. Cambridge: Cambridge University Press.

Kamenka, Eugene (1976) *Nationalism: The Nature and Evolution of an Idea*. London: Edward Arnold.

Miller, Toby, Lawrence, Geoffrey A., McKay, Jim and Rowe, David (2001) *Globalization and Sport: Playing the World*. London: Sage.

Nauright, John (1997) *Sport, Cultures and Identities in South Africa*. London: Leicester University Press.

Pierson, Christopher (1996) *The Modern State*. London: Routledge.

Pope, S.W. (1997) *Patriot Games: Sporting Traditions in the American Imagination 1876–1926*. New York: Oxford University Press.

Silk, Michael L., Andrews, David L. and Cole, C.L. (eds) (2005) *Sport and Corporate Nationalisms*. Oxford: Berg.

Zinn, Howard (1996) *A People's History of the United States: From 1492 to the Present*. London: Longman.

FURTHER READING

Bairner, Alan (2001) *Sport, Nationalism and Globalization: European and North American Perspectives*. New York: SUNY Press.

Cronin, Mike and Mayall, David (eds) (1998) *Sporting Nationalisms*. London: Frank Cass.

Held, David (1992) 'The Development of the Modern State' in Stuart Hall and Bram Gieben (eds) *Formations of Modernity*. Cambridge: Polity Press. pp. 71–125.

Miller, Toby, Lawrence, Geoffrey A., McKay, Jim and Rowe, David (2001) *Globalization and Sport: Playing the World*. London: Sage.

The Body/Embodiment (Health and Exercise)

BODIES MATTER

The body is fundamental to all forms of sporting practice. Yet in sport, as in many other spheres, practically and theoretically the body has been confined to the sphere of the natural sciences, especially biology and medicine (and the 'mind' to philosophy and psychology). This annexation reflects the 'rationalist bias in Western culture' (Hargreaves, 1987: 139) which entails a dualism in which the body and mind are separated, with the mind representing civilisation and the body representing nature. It is therefore hard, in Western thought, to imagine the body as anything other than a 'natural phenomenon'. Thus it is only very recently that the sociology of sport – mirroring sociology more widely – has taken the body seriously as a topic of enquiry. Brian Turner's *The Body and Society* (1984) marked the first 'genuine sociology of the body', although sport historians and sociologists had started to write about the sporting body from the 1970s (Hargreaves and Vertinsky, 2007: 1).

This omission, as Booth and Nauright note, is a 'double paradox'. 'First, by definition sport is a corporeal practice; second, power, inequality, and oppression are embodied' (Booth and Nauright, 2003: 1). How bodies function, appear and are treated is of central importance. John Hargreaves has argued that the body represents a major site of social struggle and that in 'the battle for control over the body' important power relationships, such as over class, gender, age, and 'race', are constituted and structured (Hargreaves, 1987: 140). Over the past 20 years there has been a proliferation of writing on all aspects of the body, recognising the cultural and social significance of embodiment in all areas of life and revealing a consensus that the 'body matters' (Hargreaves and Vertinsky, 2007: 1).

EMBODIMENT AND THE SOCIAL CONSTRUCTION OF BODIES

To use the term *embodiment* is to challenge the idea of the body being a 'natural' biological thing, and to recognise that our bodies are not just

key concepts in sports studies

226

biological, but that our physicality is moulded by social and cultural as well as physical processes (Shilling, 1997: 65). Human beings are *embodied subjects* and the material body is the site in which differences of gender, sexuality, race, ethnicity and class are constituted and made visible (Benson, 1997: 128) (see **Identity and Difference**). The body does more than provide the means by which to live, it 'shapes our identities and structures our interventions in, and classifications of, the world' (Shilling, 1997: 65). That is to say, our bodies are socially constructed; society has invaded, shaped, classified, and reproduced the body, and that unequal power relation underpins these processes.

In returning the body to the realm of sociology the kinds of questions and issues sociologists have taken up include: examining images of the sporting body; exploring how the body is constructed by social forces; and highlighting the ways in which body classifications and differences shape our identities and contribute to social inequalities such as gender and 'race'. Such bodily differences have been used to justify a range of oppressive practices, ranging, for example, from the use of racial classi-fications to segregate and exclude participants under apartheid in South Africa, to the exclusion of women from sport based on sex differences. We therefore need to challenge the 'common sense' views of the body as a natural, biological entity, and to examine the ways in which differ-ence is inscribed in and through bodies in ways that can contribute to 'social inequalities' (Shilling, 1997: 66).

In this section I focus on three (of the many) issues in understanding the social construction of bodies and embodiment.

1. Developing an understanding of the links between the body and identity, exploring some of the ways in which identity can be 'enacted, negotiated and subverted through bodily practices' (Benson, 1997: 124).
2. Exploring the significance of the body in consumer culture.
3. Highlighting some of the ways in which the sporting body has been theorised, focusing on the appropriation of the ideas of the French post-structuralist Michel Foucault.

CONSUMER CULTURE AND IMAGES OF THE BODY

Contemporary consumer culture is 'fuelled by a hedonistic fascination with the body' (Turner, 1984: 112). Bodies are everywhere; on television, in advertising, in magazines and newspapers, images of beautiful, sculpted and flawless bodies circulate and dominate. 'Consumer culture permits the unashamed display of the human body' (Featherstone, 1991: 179). However, the closer the body is to the 'idealised images of youth, health, fitness, and beauty, the higher its exchange value' (Featherstone, 1991: 179). Features on bodies, and how to keep them looking slim, fit and sexy, dominate magazines for women and, increasingly, men. Weight loss, plastic surgery and keep-fit regimes have become multi-million pound industries. People spend increasing amounts of time and money trying to hone and change the shape and appearance of their bodies. Thus, for Featherstone, the body is a site of continual maintenance, with programmes of body-work being organised around consumerist images of, and aspirations towards, fitness, health, lifestyle, appearance and so on. As Featherstone contends, consumer culture:

> latches onto the prevalent self-preservationist conception of the body, which encourages the individual to adopt instrumental strategies to combat deterioration and decay ... and combines it with the notion that the body is a vehicle of pleasure and self-expression. Images of the body beautiful, openly sexual and associated with hedonism, leisure and display, emphasise the importance of appearance and the 'look'. (Featherstone, 1991: 170)

Here the importance of the relationship between sport and the body is clear. As John Hargreaves argues, 'what links up consumer culture with sports culture so economically is their common concern with and capacity to accommodate the body' as a means of expression; 'to be sportive is to be desirable, fit, young and happy' (Hargreaves, 1987: 151).

Garry Whannel describes this relationship as 'fitness chic', that is, how fitness became fashionable in contemporary consumer culture (Whannel, 1992: 183). New images of physically active females emerged that challenged earlier images of female frailty, but that were articulated with sexual attractiveness (Whannel, 1992: 183), concealing new forms of domination and exploitation (Theberge, 1991: 125). Whannel outlines how in the 1980s and 1990s fitness in the UK became a 'serious business', demanding hard work, commitment and self sacrifice. Sport and fitness shifted from being done for 'fun' to becoming a way to success and self improvement; as Featherstone suggests, discipline and hedonism now come together (1991: 171). Whannel sees this cultural shift as reflective of the rise of competitive individualism in 1980s and 1990s Britain under the neo-liberal economics and laissez-faire philosophy espoused by Margaret

Thatcher. That is, this focus on *individual* responsibility, the discipline and self-management of our bodies, can be seen as an example of the intensification in the 'body politics' associated with the individualistic neo-liberal agenda and ideologies of contemporary capitalist Western societies (see also King (2003) on health and the neo-liberal body).

BODIES AND IDENTITY: BODY PROJECTS

For many commentators, one important consequence of this increasing visibility, malleability and commodification of the body in contemporary consumer culture, is that the body has become an increasingly mobile site of re-invention, and self-expression. In the affluent West, we increasingly see the body as a 'project' which should be worked at and completed as 'part of an individual's self identity' (Shilling, 1997: 69). Shilling outlines that while bodies were clearly worked on and altered in pre-modern societies – for example, in practices such as body decoration often linked with religious or communal ceremonies – body projects today involve a more 'individualised engagement' (Shilling, 1997). That is, bodies become important personal resources and symbols of identity. For example, as noted above, health has become a key concept in the fashioning of identity for the contemporary middle classes (Benson, 1997). While some body projects become full-time concerns, and/or involve whole scale transformations (such as in the case of plastic surgery), for most people, treating the body as a project relates to the ways in which we are increasingly concerned with the appearance, maintenance and management of our bodies as symbols of identity (Shilling, 1997). Examples of body projects include tattoos and body piercing; a wealth of self-care regimens to keep the body healthy; and exercise practices such as bodybuilding. There are also more radical body reconstructions, from liposuction to penis extensions. These reconstructions of the body, like body building, challenge notions of the 'natural' body, as well as the social construction of masculinity and femininity (see Shilling, 1997):

> You don't really see a muscle as a part of you … You see it as a thing and you say, well this thing has to be built a little longer, the biceps has to be longer; or the triceps has to be thicker … And you look at it and it doesn't even seem to belong to you. Like a sculpture … You form it. Just like a sculpture. (Arnold Schwarzenegger, cited in Benson, 1997: 122)

the body/ embodiment

Here we see the body as a 'thing' that can be literally 'shaped' as the will of the 'self' (Benson, 1997: 122). As well as providing a means of self expression, these body projects allow the individual exerciser some control over 'their flesh' in the context of a more disorganised and complex world. These examples also illustrate the separation of the *body–self* within Western corporeality: that is, how in Western cultures, there is seen to be an important distinction between body and mind/ the material and ethereal/ flesh and spirit (Benson, 1997). The body is therefore seen as a thing that can 'be shaped 'by the will of the "self"'(conceived as the "true me") – a project literally, and the medium through which messages about identity are transmitted' (Benson, 1997: 123).

Take for example, the prevalent (but historically variable) belief that 'good' bodies are sleek, thin and toned, and that the fat slack body is a 'bad body'. Fat bodies have become constructed not just as a matter of aesthetics but as uncared for, demonstrating a lazy and undisciplined 'self'. To be slim and toned is to be 'morally as well as physically in shape' (Benson, 1997: 123). Such discourses about good bodies have important implications for the ways in which we view 'impaired' bodies, such as through disability or illness (Benson, 1997). Writing on disability has stressed the ways in which those with bodily impairments are categorised as 'other' (Benson, 1997: 151); likewise, discourses around the moral panic generated by AIDS are often underpinned by (and reproduce) stereotypes of race and sexuality. Thus, as Shilling (1997) warns, investing in the body also has disadvantages; how do we deal with and negotiate the faulty or failing body such as experienced in ageing, illness and death? These body 'failures' clearly signal the limitations of identity being centred on the body, that our ability to 'master our bodily processes and produce our preferred selves is limited' (Benson, 1997: 125).

THEORISING THE SPORTING BODY

There are numerous social and cultural theorists whose ideas have been influential in understanding the contemporary sporting body. Important figures include Elias (1978) who discussed the historical processes involved in the development of 'civilized bodies'; Marcel Mauss (1979) who outlined ways in which our bodies are trained to become social bodies though various 'techniques of the body'; and Bourdieu (1978, 1984, 1988) who explores how in sport the body becomes a form of 'physical capital', that is, a possessor of power, status and distinction (see **Habitus**). Scholars of sport who have adopted Bourdieu's ideas include

Laberge (1995), Laberge and Sankoff (1988), Shilling (2005), Wacquant (1995) and Brown (2006).

Feminist analyses have, in contrast to much 'mainstream' sociological work, taken the body as a central focus of interest for some time (Hall, 1996; Theberge, 1991) and have remained extremely influential in progressing debate in the study of sporting bodies (Cole, 2000). Here I will highlight the feminist work on bodies inspired by the post-structuralist Michel Foucault. (For a more comprehensive coverage of Foucault's *oeuvre* and sport see Andrews, 1993; Cole et al., 2004; Hargreaves, 1987; Markula and Pringle, 2006; Rail and Harvey, 1995; Smith Maguire, 2002). I will briefly outline Foucault's understanding of the relationship between power and the body, and give some examples of the ways this has been adopted to understand the physically active body.

Foucault's work has had a profound influence in challenging traditional ways of thinking about power, about how power is inscribed on the body and how physical bodies are made (Benson, 1997). In the sporting context, his work reveals connections between bodies, sport and other networks of power (Smith Maguire, 2002):

> Broadly speaking a Foucauldian analysis of sport is concerned with how relations of power target and shape the body through different types of practices, forms of knowledge, and sets of norms in order to produce specific bodily capacities and particular attitudes towards the body and self. (Smith Maguire, 2002: 293)

Power for Foucault is not a thing that some people or groups have, instead he describes the ways it works in everyday interactions and institutions (Smith Maguire, 2002). He used the image of the Panopticon to illustrate how power functions, seeing the characteristic form of power in modern prisons – and other institutions such as school, hospitals, factories – as discipline and surveillance. 'Discipline shapes and produces individuals through techniques of surveillance that reverberate through the social and individual's bodies' (Cole et al., 2004: 212).

Foucault further argues in what has been termed the 'docile bodies' thesis (Hall, 1996: 54) that in these contexts bodies are developed to become compliant and useful, and that a range of technologies help to produce 'normal ' bodies:

> power is incorporated or invested in the body through meticulous, insistent work on people's bodies – on children in families and schools; on soldiers,

prisoners and hospital patients; in the gym, at the dinner table, and in the bathroom (Foucault, 1976, cited in Hargreaves, 1987: 140)

Foucault was interested not just in the ways in which the body was represented, but in *who* had the power to order those representations. He argued that bodies are constructed through discourses (see **Discourse**), and that 'discourses' of the body are developed in specific institutional contexts such as armies, prison, schools and hospitals.

Despite paying little attention to gender power and women's experiences, Foucault's theories have also been widely appropriated by (sporting) feminists (Cole, 2000) and 'infused with a feminist agenda' (Theberge, 1991: 125). Theberge (in an early but still pertinent contribution to this debate) suggests four key areas of convergence (Theberge, 1991: 126):

1. The 'body as a site of power or the locus of domination'.
2. The 'focus on local and intimate operations of power rather than on larger institutional formulations' (such as the state).
3. The 'emphasis on the crucial role of discourse in producing and reproducing power'.
4. A 'critique of Western humanism's privileging the experience and accounts of a Western masculine elite.'

Susan Bordo is one of many prominent feminist theorists who uses Foucauldian concepts to help understand the cult of health discussed above, particularly our preoccupation with fat, diet and slenderness, and the 'normalizing' functions of the technologies of 'diet and body management' (Bordo, 1990: 167). She argues these preoccupations are among the most 'powerful normalizing mechanisms of our century, ensuring the production of self-monitoring and self-disciplining "docile bodies" ... Habituated to self-improvement and self-transformation in the service of these norms' (Bordo, 1990: 167).

However, as Sandra Bartky outlines (1988), the gendering of experience is particularly significant; while both male and female bodies experience and are subject to these disciplinary processes, the meaning and aims of these health and fitness activities – which she calls 'technologies of femininity' – are different for women. For example, practices like aerobics focus on appearance and feminisation; they are important statements not just of sexual difference but of the ways femininity is constructed (Theberge, 1991: 125). As sports feminist C.L. Cole (1993) has argued, 'surveillance dominated capitalism' obscures the ways in which 'the body and exercise have become commodified in ways which manages gender relations' (Hall, 1996: 55).

Foucault's work on docile bodies has been criticised for presenting a monolithic understanding of power, leaving little space for understanding how people can challenge or resist this disciplinary power (see Hall, 1996). Foucault's later work – on concepts such as 'technologies of the self' – facilitates a more complex understanding of power that allows for the agency of individuals (see Markula and Pringle, 2006; Smith Maguire, 2002). Over the past decades a plethora of studies of embodiment in exercise and sporting practices from aerobics to bodybuilding have emerged that are influenced by Foucault's ideas (e.g. Markula, 1995). These studies illustrate the complex ways in which women and men both conform to and resist dominant discourses about bodies, sport and exercise (e.g. Bolin and Granskog, 2003; Heywood and Dworkin, 2003).

FURTHER READING

Andrews, D. (1993) 'Desperately Seeking Michel; Foucault's Genealogy, the Body, and Critical Sport Sociology', *Sociology of Sport Journal*, 10: 148–67.

Bartky, S. (1988) 'Foucault, Feminism and the Modernization of Patriarchal Power', in I. Diamond and L. Quinby (eds) *Feminism and Foucault: Reflections on Resistance*. Boston: Northeastern University Press. pp. 61–86.

Benson, S. (1997) 'The Body, Health and Eating Disorders', in K. Woodward (ed.) *Identity and Difference*. London: Sage, in association with the Open University. pp. 122–66.

Bolin, A. and Granskog, J. (eds) (2003) *Athletic Intruders: Ethnographic Research on Women, Culture and Exercise*. Albany, NY: SUNY Press.

Booth, D. and Nauright, J. (2003) 'Embodied Identities: Sport and Race in South Africa', *Contours: A Journal of the African Diaspora*: 1–26.

Bordo, S. (1990) 'Reading the Slender Body', in K. Woodward (ed.) *Identity and Difference*. London: Sage, in association with the Open University. pp. 167–81.

Bourdieu, P. (1978) 'Sport and Social Class', *Social Science Information*, 17(6): 819–40.

Bourdieu, R. (1984) *Distinction: A Social Critique of the Judgement of Taste*. London: Routledge & Kegan Paul Ltd.

Bourdieu, P. (1988) 'Program for a Sociology of Sport', *Sociology of Sport Journal*, 5(2): 153–61.

Brown, D. (2006) 'Pierre Bourdieu's "Masculine Domination" Thesis and the Gendered Body in Sport and Physical Culture', *Sociology of Sport Journal*, 23: 162–88.

Cole, C.L. (1993) 'Resisting the canon: Feminist Cultural Studies, Sport, and Technologies of the Body', *Journal of Sport and Social Issues*, 17: 77–9.

Cole, C.L. (2000) 'Body Studies in the Sociology of Sport: A Review of the Field', in J. Coakley and E. Dunning (eds) *Handbook of Sport Studies*. London: Sage. pp. 439–60.

Cole, C.L., Giardina, M.D. and Andrews, D.L. (2004) 'Michel Foucault: Studies of Power and Sport' in R. Giulianotti (ed.) *Sport and Modern Social Theorists*. Basingstoke: Palgrave. pp. 207–23.

Elias, N. (1978) *The Civilizing Process, Vol. 1: The History of Manners*. New York: Pantheon Books.

Featherstone, M. (1991) 'The Body in Consumer Culture', M. Featherstone, M. Hepworth and B. Turner (eds) in *The Body: Social Process and Cultural Theory*. London: Sage. pp. 170–96.

Foucault, M. (1976) *Discipline and Punish*. London: Allen Lane.

Hall, A. (1996) *Feminism and Sporting Bodies: Essays on Theory and Practice*. Champaign, IL: Human Kinetics.

Hargreaves, J. (1987) 'The Body, Sport and Power Relations,' in J. Horne, D. Jary and A. Tomlinson (eds) *Sport, Leisure and Social Relations*. London: Routledge & Kegan Paul. pp. 139–59.

Hargreaves, J. and Vertinsky, P. (2007) 'Introduction', in J. Hargreaves and P. Vertinsky (eds) *Physical Culture, Power, and the Body*. Abingdon: Routledge. pp. 1–24.

Heywood, L. and Dworkin, S. (2003) *Built to Win: the Female Athlete as Cultural Icon*. Minneapolis: University of Minnesota Press.

King, S.J. (2003) 'Doing Good by Running Well', in J.Z. Bratich, J. Packer and C. McCarthy (eds) *Foucault, Cultural Studies and Governmentality*. Albany, NY: SUNY Press. pp. 295–316.

Laberge, S. (1995) 'Towards an Integration of Gender into Bourdieu's Concept of Cultural Capital', *Sociology of Sport Journal*, 12: 132–46.

Laberge, S. and Sankoff, D. (1988) 'Physical Activities, Body Habitus and Lifestyles: Towards an Integration of Gender into Bourdieu's Concept of Cultural Capital', in J. Harvey and H. Cantelon (eds) *Not Just a Game: Essays in Canadian Sport Sociology*. Ottawa: University of Ottowa Press. pp. 267–88.

Markula, P. (1995) 'Firm but Shapely, Fit but Sexy, Strong but Thin: The Postmodern Aerobicizing Female Bodies', *Sociology of Sport Journal*, 12: 242–53.

Markula, P. and Pringle, R. (2006) *Foucault, Sport and Exercise*. London: Routledge.

Mauss, M. (1979) *The Phenomenology of Perception*. London: Routledge.

Rail, G. and Harvey, J. (1995) 'Body at Work', *Sociology of Sport Journal*, 12: 164–79.

Shilling, C. (1997) 'The Body and Difference', in K. Woodward. (ed.) *Identity and Difference*. London: Sage, in association with the Open University. pp. 63–120.

Shilling, C. (2005) *The Body in Culture, Technology and Society*. London: Sage.

Smith Maguire, J. (2002) 'Michel Foucault: Sport, Power, Technologies and Governmentality', in J. Maguire and K. Young. (eds) *Theory, Sport and Society*. Oxford: JAI. pp. 293–314.

Theberge, N. (1991) 'Reflections on the Body in the Sociology of Sport', *Quest* 43: 123–34.

Turner, B. (1984) *The Body and Society: Explorations in Social Theory*. New York: Blackwell.

Wacquant, L.J.D. (1995) 'Pugs at Work: Bodily Capital and the Bodily Labour Amoung Professional Boxers', *Body and Society*, 1: 65–94.

Whannel, G. (1992) *Fields in Vision: Television Sport and Cultural Transformation*. New York: Routledge.

The Civilising Process

The Civilising Process is the title of a book first published in two volumes in 1939 by the German social philosopher Norbert Elias. The book ranges over a number of themes – none of which, as it happens, is sport, which is mentioned only in passing – and, taken together, these themes describe a process which roughly equates to the development of modernity and the nation state in Western Europe. The first volume of the book was originally called *The History of Manners* and is concerned with growing restraint in society, from the late Middle Ages onward, with regard to the human body. This covers bodily functions and also damage to the body by spontaneous violence, such violence having been seen by many historians as the common coin of medieval life. The second volume was entitled *State Formation and Civilization* and is concerned, as the title implies, with the emergence of the modern state, the monopolisation by that state of the legitimate use of violence (via the army and the police) and the relation of this state formation to forms of behaviour that are either more temperate or more calculating.

Part of the 'civilising process' is a progress, according to Elias, from a society based on 'segmental bonding' – broadly speaking, a tribalism, with strong ties within a group and taken-for-granted antagonism between groups – to one based upon 'functional interdependence'[1] – that is, as the term implies, a growing acceptance among social groups that in a complex society they depend on each other. Human societies are thus understood in terms of changing configurations – hence the term 'figurational sociologist', often taken by, or ascribed to, the writers who have adopted the Elias approach. These writers include Eric Dunning, who has taught sociology at Leicester University in the United Kingdom since the late 1960s and Joseph Maguire of nearby Loughborough University. The influence of the Elias mode of analysis was, arguably, at its highest in the 1980s and early 1990s when social science scholars across the world addressed themselves to the problem of football spectator violence and the so-called 'Leicester School' often led the debate.

The term 'civilisation' is, of course, a term in popular usage and it is undoubtedly a judgmental and emotive word. Which of us, for example, would be content to be described as 'uncivilised'? Elias uses the term in a way that is more specific than this but which is, at the same time, wide-ranging – some might say all-encompassing. 'The concept of "civilization" refers to a wide variety of facts', says Elias at the beginning of the book,

> to the level of technology, to the type of manners, to the development of scientific knowledge, to religious ideas and customs. It can refer to the type of dwelling or the manner in which men and women live together, to the form of judicial punishment, or the way in which food is prepared. (Elias, 2000: 5)

According to this definition, the process toward 'civilisation' encompasses: the growth of the modern state, based on democratic principles, and a bureaucracy governed by impersonal rules, rather than the whim of individuals (monarchs, perhaps, or despots); the advancement of science, at the expense of religion, as a way of explaining the world; industrialisation and standardisation; the growth of privacy (and thus of the distinction between public and private life/space); an enhanced sensitivity towards bodily functions; and a tendency for actions to become less passionate or *affective*.

Through the civilising process, life, it is claimed, becomes more 'efficient', rational or 'civilised'. It should be noted that, for figurationist theory, no value judgment is implied in the word 'civilised'. Action is said to become more *instrumental*, that is, carried out in the pursuit of an end.

True to its title, the first volume is full of fascinating examples, culled from the period between the thirteenth and the nineteenth centuries, from books of everyday etiquette exhorting folk to behave in a more inhibited fashion. 'It is not polite to drink from the dish', says one from the thirteenth century, 'although some who approve of this rude habit insolently pick up the dish and pour it down as if they were mad' (Elias, 2000: 73). And the Brunswick Court Regulations of 1589 say: 'Let no one, whoever he may be, before, at, or after meals, early or late, foul the staircases, corridors with urine or other filth, but go to suitable, prescribed places for such relief' (Elias, 2000: 111–12). And, earlier in the same century, the scholar Erasmus counselled: 'Turn away when spitting, lest your saliva fall upon someone' (Elias, 2000: 130).

Thus, *The Civilizing Process* stresses the growth of inhibition. This inhibition originates in the courtly society of the Middle Ages, but grows with the rise of the middle classes and the modern nation state. This begins with the growth of the power of monarchy. Successive kings moved to weaken feudal nobility (e.g. in England King Henry VII instituted the Court of Star Chamber, which often sentenced noblemen to death). These nobles had to abandon their armies and, as we've seen, legitimate use of violence became the monopoly of the state: the armed forces and, from the early nineteenth century, the police.

There was a corresponding decline of violence for enjoyment and of the public exercise of bodily functions. In England, parliament was increasingly the place for the settling of political conflicts (especially after the English Civil War (1642–51)).

This, once again, is linked to the growth in society of 'functional interdependence' – the increased recognition on the part of social groups (classes, gender groups …) that they depend upon each other.

All this, so the argument runs, is due to, and constitutes, a *civilising process*.

It is, of course, not difficult to find examples from the field of sport and leisure that are fully in accord with the concept of a civilising process: the progressive suppression of 'uncivilised', 'irrational' sports, for example, in the eighteenth and nineteenth centuries; the urging on the populace of 'rational recreation' in early Victorian Britain; the codification of major sports such as cricket and boxing in the eighteenth century, and rugby and association football in the nineteenth; the evangelising of organised games, in schools and elsewhere, as a means to disciplining the body; and the setting up of governing bodies (i.e. bureaucracies) for individual sports and events such as the Olympics, all spring to mind.

Applying these observations more systematically to sport, we can note, first of all, that pre-modern sports were violent, with no written rules or restrictions on the number of participants. They were subject to local lore and not to universal regulation. The violence that characterised these games invariably gave pleasure to the participants. Together these games are typical of a society based on tribal or *segmental* bonding and examples of such games include pankration (an often lethal combat sport practised in Ancient Greece), rough and tumble, a similarly unregulated form of fighting in post-revolutionary America, mob football, pugilism, fox hunting and a number of other sports based on the baiting or otherwise tormenting of animals. With the 'civilising process' come more civilised restraints on the practice and enjoyment of sport: rules, governing bodies, universalism, sanctions/punishments, referees and so on. We see this in the founding, for instance, of the Football Association and the Rugby Football Union and an examination of these historic developments shows frequent tussles between traditionalists and civiliser-modernisers – as, for example, in the controversy in the early years of the RFU over whether hacking (kicking an opponent on the shins) should be permitted.

Sport comes to provide excitement in increasingly unexciting (i.e. civilised) societies. This overall process is called 'sportisation'.

Over the last 40 years or so, there has, of course, been increased public concern in many societies over violence in sport and, more especially, at sporting encounters. As we noted, figurationist sociologists have engaged with this concern and, in this context, it is important first of all to say that figurationists do *not* say sport is getting less violent. Eric Dunning, Elias' leading interpreter, distinguishes between different *kinds* of violence. He asks specific questions about the violence, such as:

- Is it actual or symbolic – as, for example, with the *haka* performed by the All Blacks rugby team?
- Is it legitimate or illegitimate?
- Is it rational – that is, a deliberate attempt to intimidate or injure an opponent – or affective, as with the spontaneous loss of temper? (Scambler, 2005: 94–5)

Figurationist sociologists argue that violence in sport may actually have *increased*, but that much of it is now *rational*, designed to achieve an end.

Their theory is more specifically about the *social construction* of violence – how it's handled by society. They argue that in modern, 'civilised' society there is a low tolerance of unsanctioned violence. This is reflected in the media rendition of issues such as football spectator violence and the comparative ease with which public indignation is mobilised in moral panics.

As has been suggested, this debate – in parliaments, police stations and university seminar rooms – as to the origins of 'football hooliganism' was a feature of public life in the 1980s and 1990s and it often seemed to revolve around the (figurationist) 'Leicester School' of writers. Various other explanations were in play, some suggesting that mayhem at matches was largely symbolic violence (the 'Oxford School' of academics, such as Peter Marsh (Marsh et al., 1978)), others that it was a response to the theft of the people's game (Taylor, 1971), still others that it derived from the break-up of working-class communities (John Clarke, (1973, see also 1978), for example, and others at the now-defunct Centre for Contemporary Cultural Studies at Birmingham University).

The 'Leicester argument', in its essence, is that football hooliganism is largely the work of the 'rough working class' (or, occasionally, the 'rough middle class') indulging in the ancient rite of fighting for fun. Such an attitude to hooliganism seems to be evidenced in the testimony of young men convicted of football violence and is apparently celebrated in the 'Steaming In' sub-genre of football literature (see books such as John King's (1997) *The Football Factory* and other books of this ilk, such as the works of the Brimson brothers).[1]

These, often self-professed, 'hooligans' can thus be seen as unassimilated to the 'civilising process'. As remedies, the Leicester team call for:

- more surveillance
- restrictions on the use of alcohol
- more involvement of women.

Pleasurable violence is seen as more likely to survive among men and/or the lower working class.

There have, inevitably, been some criticisms of figurational sociology:

Firstly, some sociologists argue that, surely, all sociology is 'figurational'. Critics also say that this account doesn't really explain anything – it's really description masquerading as explanation.

So, secondly, why did this civilising process happen? Many sociologists will see here a neglect of power and economic factors (certainly those working in a Marxist framework) and of theories of rationalisation (see, for example, Allen Guttmann, writing in the tradition of Weber).

Thirdly, outside of sport and the issue of spectator violence, the Elias perspective has had little impact on wider sociological debates. If the theory holds good for this spectator violence, why not, some might argue, for other social issues and phenomena?

Fourthly, the theory is seen as ethnocentric. The 'civilising process' seems applicable perhaps only to Europe, where the huge bulk of Elias's data is taken from. Fifthly, the idea of the civilising process is seen by some as untestable, a catch-all. Everything, it seems, is down either to the civilising process or to 'decivilising spurts', which occasionally interrupt it.

NOTE

1. See http:\\www.brimson.net/

REFERENCES

Clarke, John (1973) 'Football Hooliganism and the Skinheads', University of Birmingham, Centre for Contemporary Cultural Studies Stencilled Occasional Paper.

Clarke, John (1978) 'Football and Working Class Fans: Tradition and Change', in Roger Ingham (ed.) *Football Hooliganism: The Wider Context*. London: Inter-Action. pp. 37–60.

Elias, Norbert (2000) *The Civilizing Process: Sociogenetic and Psychogenetic Investigations* (revised edition edited by Eric Dunning, Johan Goudsblom and Stephen Mennell). Oxford: Blackwell Publishers.

King, John (1997) *The Football Factory*. London: Vintage.

Marsh, Peter, Rosser, Elizabeth and Harré, Rom (1978) *The Rules of Disorder*. London: Routledge and Kegan Paul.

Scambler, Graham (2005) 'Sport and Violence: A De-Civilizing Spurt', in *Sport and Society: History, Power and Culture*. Maidenhead: Open University Press. pp. 93–115.

Taylor, Ian (1971) 'Soccer Consciousness and Soccer Hooliganism', in Stanley Cohen (ed.) *Images of Deviance*. Harmondsworth: Penguin. pp. 134–64.

FURTHER READING

Dunning, Eric and Sheard, Kenneth (2004) *Barbarians, Gentlemen and Players: A Sociological Study of the Development of Rugby Football*. London: Routledge.

Dunning, Eric, Murphy, Patrick and Williams, John (1988) *The Roots of Football Hooliganism*. London: Routledge and Kegan Paul.

Elias, Norbert (1994) *The Civilising Process* (2 Vols: *The History of Manners, 1978; State Formation and Civilisation 1994*), Oxford: Blackwell. Originally Published 1939. (See also 2000 edition above.)

Elias, Norbert and Dunning, Eric (1986) *Quest for Excitement: Sport and Leisure in the Civilising Process*. Oxford: Blackwell.

Giulianotti, Richard (2004) 'Civilising Games: Norbert Elias and the Sociology of Sport', in R. Giulianotti (ed.) *Sport and Modern Social Theories*. Basingstoke: Palgrave Macmillan. pp. 145–60.

Guttman, Allen (2004) *From Ritual to Record: The Nature of Modern Sports*. New York: Columbia University Press.

Jarvie, Grant and Maguire, Joseph (1994) *Sport and Leisure in Social Thought*. London: Routledge. pp. 130–60.

Maguire, Joseph (1999) *Global Sport: Identities, Societies, Civilizations*. Oxford: Policy Press.

Rigauer, B. (1993) 'Sport and the Economy: A Developmental Perspective', in E. Dunning, J. Maguire and R. Pearton (eds) *The Sports Process*. Leeds: Human Kinetics. pp. 281–306.

Scambler, Graham (2005) 'Sport and Violence: A De-Civilizing Spurt?', in *Sport and Society: History, Power and Culture*. Maidenhead: Open University Press. pp. 93–115.

Williams, John, Dunning, Eric and Murphy, Patrick (1989) *Hooligans Abroad*. London: Routledge.

key concepts in
sports studies

The Environment

'The environment' is defined by the current *Concise Oxford Dictionary* as, among other things, 'the totality of the physical conditions on the earth or a part of it, esp[ecially] as affected by human activity' (Thompson, 1995: 452). The term 'the environment' has an ambiguous place in the political culture of many contemporary societies. It first appeared in the discourse of parliamentary politics in Britain when it was mentioned in the Queen's Speech of July 1970. The incoming Conservative government of Edward Heath created a Department of the Environment, but, in practice, this new ministry had administrative responsibility for housing and local government, public building and works and transport. There remained, for example, a separate Department of Energy, and until 'the appointment of Chris Patten as environment secretary in 1989, no environment secretary had shown any particular interest in the environment' and the issue remained 'a relatively minor issue on the British political agenda' (McCormick, 1991: 16–17, 7). That said, party politics are not always a good guide to the political significance of an issue. There are, for example, no specifically feminist political parties but few people would deny the importance of feminism. Similarly environmental issues have an acknowledged importance across the world and 'green movements' are, effectively, engaged in every country in struggles and debates over the disposition of the physical environment.

Although 'the environment' is a comparatively modern term, disputes about sport and the use of land are centuries old. The best examples here would include the growing opposition to folk football, especially in the eighteenth century, and historic disputes – still being conducted in the twenty-first century – over hunting. In the case of folk football, concern over these rowdy pleasures of the people was linked to changing class relations on the land – to enclosures, to property rights and to more temperate notions of public order. With the rise of capitalist agriculture, landlords increasingly challenged the concept of common land and the rights of the common people to rampage up hill and down dale pursuing their traditional holiday pastimes.

Hunting has similarly been a political issue in many societies. In Britain it dates back to Anglo Saxon times. Clearly hunting originates in the quest for food, but, as a sport, it has generally been the province of the elite: the poor lacked time and horses and access to the necessary land. Under the Norman kings of England (1066–1154) forest or game laws took precedence over common law (Thomas, 1993: 179). Poachers could still be hanged in early 1800s (Thompson, 1985). The political scientist Lincoln Allison, one of the few academics to comment on the relationship between sport and the environment, points out that in 1831 one-sixth of all convictions were for offences against the game laws (Allison, 1993: 218). Country estates were stocked for shooting and angling and the law excluded the landless poor. This is important to note because these activities are almost certainly the first ones to be referred to as 'sport' and, indeed, are still called 'field sports'.

'Field sports' generally involve the killing of animals and from the early eighteenth century this attracted controversy. The Utilitarian philosopher Jeremy Bentham, for example, stated: 'The question is not Can they reason? Nor Can they talk? But Can they suffer?' (Holt, 1992: 32). Other writers suggested that arguments over animal sports were often about something else: public order, perhaps, or the promotion of the Protestant work ethic: as I observed elsewhere in this book, bear-baiting, according to the historian Thomas Babington Macaulay, was banned, not for the pain it brought to the bear, but for the pleasure it brought to the audience.

Interestingly, by the time foxhunting came to be banned by act of the British parliament in 2004 ecology had become part of the argument, with the pro-hunting lobby arguing that fox hunting eliminated vermin.

THE COUNTRYSIDE AND MODERN SPORT

Modern debates are often framed by historical notions derived from the pre-industrial era and central to these notions are ideas of: town versus country, rich versus poor and landowner versus urban worker. In the early industrial era there was a marked decrease in leisure. In 1761 there were 47 Bank Holidays; by 1834 there were only 4. The growth of railways in the 1840s gave urban dwellers access to rural England – for race meetings, perhaps, or simply to admire the scenery. Jealous lovers of the countryside such as Wordsworth opposed bringing railway lines to places of natural beauty such as Windermere in the Lake District (Allison, 1993: 218). But many leading thinkers in Victorian England linked *access* to *conservation* and the marriage of such concerns led to the establishment of the National Trust (in 1895) and the Council for the Protection of Rural England (in 1926). For most people, though, sport generally took place in built-up areas.

POST-INDUSTRIAL SPORT

Working hours did decline greatly in the late twentieth century. The average working week for a manual worker was 44 hours in 1989, two less than 1961 (Allison, 1993: 220). More people are taking two, perhaps three holidays and more money is spent on leisure. Crucially, in the final third of the twentieth century, there was a growth in sport and leisure activities that will ordinarily involve access to the countryside, such as walking, cycling, golf, angling, canoeing, yachting, surfing, water skiing, horse-riding and field sports.

These have clear consequences for the environment, and especially places designated as Areas of Natural Beauty. Thus, access to such areas is now controlled and more consideration given to the ways in which sport and leisure may threaten the environment – through excessive walking, moto-cross, all-terrain biking, jet and water skiing on tranquil lakes, and so on.

But, at the turn of the twenty-first century, seemingly the most pressing issue bridging sport and the politics of ecology was golf.

THE CASE OF GOLF

There are four types of golf course: a course privately owned by members; one that functions as part of a hotel or leisure complex; a pay-as-you-play private course; and a municipal course. All four types thrive in contemporary society. Indeed golf is expanding the world over. In Britain in 1989 the Royal and Ancient Golf Club produced a report called *The Demand for Golf*. This report cited the 'need' for 700 new courses in the UK by 2000. Such a programme would cut huge swathes into the British countryside and, for the most part, designate it for private use – furthermore, in general, for the use of the higher social classes and in the promotion of an elite lifestyle. But golf raises issues not only of the social uses of land but of the well-being of ecosystems. This is especially the case in the Far East where the Global Anti-Golf Movement has been mounting campaigns.

The GAGM was launched in 1993 in Japan with a manifesto that can be viewed at http://www.antigolf.org/english.html. It has a presence in countries throughout the world – in the USA, in Europe, Central and South America – but has been strongest in Asian countries such as Thailand, India, Malaysia and Indonesia. In their manifesto GAGM argue, among things, that:

Golf courses are in fact another form of monoculture, where exotic soil and grass, chemical fertilizers, pesticides, fungicides and weedicides, as well as machinery, are all imported to substitute for natural ecosystems.

These landscaped foreign systems create stress on local water supplies and soil, at the same time being highly vulnerable to disease and pest attacks ... The environmental impacts include water depletion and toxic contamination of the soil, underground water, surface water and the air. This in turn leads to health problems for local communities, populations downstream and even golfers, caddies and chemical sprayers in golf courses. The construction of golf courses in scenic natural sites, such as forest areas and coral islands, also results in the destruction of biodiversity.

Governments, however, are invariably bent on attracting foreign tourists, and thus currency, through the construction of golf courses and in some countries troops have been used to repel protestors. One such country is Vietnam where the same defoliants used by the US Army in the Vietnam War (1961–1975) have more recently been employed in the construction of golf courses. Vietnam is now a favoured destination for golf tourists from the United States, causing some to observe that Vietnam won the war, but lost the peace. In 1996 GAGM staged their fourth 'World No Golf Day'.[1]

Elsewhere, organisations are campaigning for sport to be practised in ways that do the least ecological damage. These organisations include G-ForSE – the Global Forum for Sports and Environment – who back attempts to make, for example, the Olympic Games more conserving of energy resources and biodiversity[2] and Surfers Against Sewage (SAS), formed in 1990, who campaign against the discharge of toxic waste into the sea.[3]

NOTES

1. See http://wwwistp.murdoch.edu.au/publications/e_public/Case%20Studies_Asia/bali_2/csrel1.htm/
2. See http://www.g_forse.com/
3. See http://www.sas.org.uk/

REFERENCES

Allison, Lincoln (1993) 'Sport as an Environmental Issue', in Lincoln Allison (ed.) *The Changing Politics of Sport*. Manchester: Manchester University Press. pp. 207–32.

Holt, Richard (1992) *Sport and the British*. Oxford: Clarendon Press.

McCormick, John (1991) *British Politics and the Environment*. London: Earthscan Publications.

Thomas, Richard (1993) 'Hunting: A Sporting or Political Issue?', in Lincoln Allison (ed.) *The Changing Politics of Sport*. Manchester: Manchester University Press, pp. 174–97.

Thompson, Della (ed.) (1995) *The Concise Oxford Dictionary of Current English* (9th edn). Oxford: The Clarendon Press.

Thompson, E.P. (1985) *Whigs and Hunters: The Origin of the Black Acts*. Harmondsworth: Penguin.

FURTHER READING

Allison, Lincoln (1993) 'Sport as an Environmental Issue' in Lincoln Allison (ed.) *The Changing Politics of Sport*. Manchester: Manchester University Press. pp. 207–32.

The Sociological Imagination

The Sociological Imagination is the title of a book written by the American sociologist and radical C. Wright Mills. First published in New York in 1959 by Oxford University Press, it was put out by Penguin as one of their celebrated Pelican paperbacks a decade later in 1970. It has been in print ever since and continues to be a source of inspiration to the many people who, as writers, teachers, activists or in some combination of those callings, seek to understand human societies.

Mills lived fast and died young. He rode motor bikes, smoked heavily, married three times and was dead at forty-five. His most productive and influential period as a scholar was the 1950s, a time of cultural and political conservatism in the United States and one dominated by anti-communist 'witch hunts' orchestrated by the populist senator Joseph McCarthy and others. This was, in effect, the beginning of the 'Cold War' and people of even mildly leftish opinions (including, of course, many academics) lived in fear of losing their jobs and/or of having their loyalty to the United States called into question. Mills' open scorn for McCarthyism and its appeasers placed him alongside James Dean and

the sociological imagination

245

Marlon Brando in the pantheon of American cultural nonconformity. It also made him many enemies in his own profession of sociology. For example, in a review of *The Sociological Imagination*, the conservative scholar Edward Shils wrote:

> What does this solitary horseman – who is in part prophet, in part a teacher, in part a scholar, and in part a rough-tongued brawler – a sort of Joe McCarthy of Sociology, full of wild accusations and gross inaccuracies, bullying manners, harsh words, and shifting grounds – want of sociology?'[1]

Even some of Mills' intellectual opponents must have winced at the reference to McCarthy – in the sphere of the American academy, Mills, like Arthur Miller in the arts, had been the most unabashed dissenter from McCarthyism. So what had inspired this vituperation?

At a time when most public commentators were calling on Americans simply to feel loyalty to the United States, Mills called on them to think about was happening in the country – about its social structure and, in particular, who ran it. Although his best known book is *The Sociological Imagination* he had by then already published *White Collar* (1951), a study of the new middle classes in America, and *The Power Elite* (1956) which looked at the military-industrial-political complex that appeared to govern the United States.

Mills also wrote critically about the Cold War – in *The Causes of World War Three* (1958) – and in praise of the Cuban Revolution (*Listen, Yankee*, 1960). These were all works of sociology and/or critical political analysis which placed Mills firmly at odds with the American state. But *The Sociological Imagination* is, in part, an indictment of sociology itself and many of the people who practised it in America in the 1950s. In a now-famous passage Mills quotes lengthy and tortuous pieces of writing from *The Social System*, a key text by the leading American social theorist Talcott Parsons. He then declares them to be banalities masquerading, through the extravagant use of technical language, as profundities. Such 'grand theory' and 'cloudy obscurantism', suggested Mills later in the book, 'may be understood as ensuring that we do not learn too much about man and society' (Mills, 1970: see Mills, 1970: 33–59, 86).

In *The Coming Crisis of Western Sociology*, his powerful overview of the profession of 1970, Alvin W. Gouldner (1971) points to the nerve that Mills must have touched in his profession by writing as he did. Gouldner goes on to draw a distinction between sociologists who live *off* sociology and those live *for* it.

This distinction still holds good and is probably more marked than ever. Sociologists in the former category tend to write *about* sociology, dealing largely in theory and in critiques of the arguments of other sociologists.

These sociologists write, in essence, *philosophy* and their best exemplar in British sociology is probably Anthony Giddens, former Professor of Sociology at Cambridge University and later Director of the London School of Economics. Sociologists of the latter category tend to write *through* sociology about various aspects of the life of human societies. In essence, these academics write, or attempt to write, *history* and, in many cases, their intellectual inspiration is Mills.

Mills' sense of sociology's mission – to explain the world and not to hide behind pretentious word-mongering – is set out on the *The Sociological Imagination's* first page:

> Nowadays men often feel that their lives are a series of traps. They sense that within their everyday worlds, they cannot overcome their troubles, and in this feeling they are often quite correct: what ordinary men are directly aware of and what they try to do are bounded by the private orbits in which they live; their visions and their powers are limited to the close-up scenes of job, family, neighbourhood; in other milieux, they move vicariously and remain spectators. (Mills, 1970: 9)

He adds: 'No social study that does not come back to the problems of biography, of history, and of their intersections within a society has completed its intellectual journey' (Mills, 1970: 12).

This deceptively simple sentence has clarified the mission of generations of sociologists – including, of course, many who have sought to explain sport as a social phenomenon. This mission was to bridge history and biography, between private troubles and public issues. Sport, like all social phenomena and more, perhaps, than some, cries out for this kind of analysis. At first sight, sport seems like a galaxy of famous, and not so famous, biographies. Newspapers, TV screens and magazines devoted to sports celebrity are full of information about David Beckham, Tiger Woods, Michael Jordan, Roger Federer, Jose Mourinho, Muhammad Ali, Serena Williams... And, beyond them are the legions of swimmers, cross-country runners, Saturday afternoon cricketers, Sunday morning footballers, squash players, wind surfers and the rest who go to make up sport culture. Remember, though, that sport is not spontaneous. It is an organised, ritualised, rule-bound and historically entrenched activity. It doesn't just 'happen' and it is more than the sum of myriad sporting lives. Following Mills, sociologists can ask what makes the lives of individual sportspeople intelligible on a broader social canvas. What part has it played/does it play in the life of particular societies and groups (women, black people, public schoolboys...).

How, more specifically, might this be done. Take an example, first of all, from my own research. As is the case throughout society, in the football world – now, surely, one of the most researched of all social and professional environments – there are private troubles and public issues. If, for example, one football manager gets the sack it is a private issue – for him, for his family and so on. If a lot of football managers get the sack, year on year (as, of course, they do) then it becomes a public issue. Football management then appears an interesting topic for study. In the subsequent quest to link the biographies of football managers to some sociological history of the game, it seemed useful to pose other questions. For example, football managers used to be little known outside their own localities. Now most people could name some famous football managers. Why is this? Football managers used to wear suits and seldom see their players during the week. Now they wear track suits and train with the players. Why the change? Footballers used to be restricted to a maximum wage. Now they earn as much as they can. Again, why the change? To answer these questions requires viewing football managers and players as figures in a social and political landscape which is changing for complex reasons which we must determine. Such a task requires the sociological imagination and there are of course myriad such tasks in the social study of sport.

As so many students and other readers have found, when sociologists do sociology, the result can often, as Mills suggested, be needlessly mystifying and dispiriting; when they do history, it can be illuminating. The social study of sport is replete with examples of how writers, in effect, took up Mills' challenge to construct bridges between the biography of sporting individuals, celebrities and others, and the history of their societies. Sometimes this task is undertaken in a literal way. Two excellent examples of this are Walter LaFeber's book *Michael Jordan and the New Global Capitalism* (2000) and *Redemption* Song by Mike Marqusee (1999). The title alone of LeFaber's book illustrates Mills' dictum and sociology's mission – to provide a social context in which a leading sportsperson's life becomes more meaningful. *Redemption Song*, Marqusee's book on Muhammad Ali, accomplishes the same task for, arguably, the world's first global sporting hero.

Similarly, Jennifer Hargreaves' *Sporting Females* (1994) and subsequent *Heroines of Sport* (2000) provided a context, where practically none previously existed, in which the relationship of women to sport might be understood. And so on. The sociology and history of sport now have a rich literature, much of it written, as Mills might have wished, out of the sociological imagination. Indeed, as two leading sport historians remarked a few years ago, to paraphrase John Major's memorable remark about commentary on young offenders, maybe writers had 'tried to understand too much'. 'The history of sport', wrote Richard Holt and J.A. Mangan,

> has been keen to establish its historical credentials by considering the social, cultural and political *context* of performance, rather than the performers themselves ... the historian's task has been to explore the social conditions that gave rise to modern sport, the ideological meanings it acquired and the cultural purposes it served. This new (and thriving) approach has mostly focused on types of sport, social classes and entire nations. The individual has been rather overlooked. (Holt and Mangan, 1996: 5)

(See also **History**.)

NOTE

1. This review appeared in *Encounter* 14: 77–80 (1960) and is quoted in Eldridge (1983: 109). Encounter was later found to have been funded by the CIA – see Saunders (2000).

REFERENCES

Eldridge, John (1983) *C. Wright Mills*. Chichester/London: Ellis Horwood/Tavistock.
Gouldner, Alvin W. (1971) *The Coming Crisis of Western Sociology*. London: Heinemann.
Hargreaves, Jennifer (1994) *Sporting Females*. London: Routledge.
Hargreaves, Jennifer (2000) *Heroines of Sport: The Politics of Identity and Difference*. London Routledge.
Holt, Richard and Mangan, J.A. (1996) 'Prologue: Heroes of a European Past' in Richard Holt, J.A. Mangan and Pierre Lanfranchi (eds) *European Heroes: Myth, Identity, Sport*. London: Frank Cass. pp. 1–13.
LaFeber, Walter (2000) *Michael Jordan and the New Global Capitalism*. New York: W.W. Norton.
Marqusee, Mike (1999) *Redemption Song: Muhammad Ali and Spirit of the Sixties*. London: Verso Books.
Mills, C. Wright (1915) *White Collar*. New York: Oxford University Press.
Mills, C. Wright (1956) *The Power Elite*. New York: Oxford University Press.

Mills, C. Wright (1958) *The Causes of World War Three*. New York: Ballantine Books.
Mills, C. Wright (1960) *Listen, Yankee: The Revolution in Cuba*. New York: Ballantine Books.
Mills, C. Wright (1970) *The Sociological Imagination*. Harmondsworth: Pelican.
Saunders, Frances Stonor (2000) *Who Paid the Piper: The CIA and the Cultural Cold War*. London: Granta Books.

FURTHER READING

For more about Mills, see Irving Louis Horowitz (1983) C. *Wright Mills: An American Utopian* (London: Collier Macmillan) and Kathryn Mills with Pamela Mills (eds) (2000) C. *Wright Mills: Letters and Autobiographical Writings*. (Berkeley, CA: University of California Press).

WEBSITES

There are also two websites: http://www.cwrightmills.org/ and C. Wright Mills' home page, http://www.faculty.rsu.edu/~felwell/Theorists/Mills/

Index

index

257